HELLRAISERS, HEROINES, and HOLY WOMEN

Women's Most Remarkable
Contributions to History

JEAN F. BLASHFIELD

ST. MARTIN'S PRESS
NEW YORK

To the longest lasting
hellraisers and heroines
in my life—
my sisters
Carol Frey and Elizabeth Graf

Acknowledgments

We also wish to thank the following persons for their help in assembling the book: Timothy Augello, Barbara Dziorney, Theresa Dziorney, Anne Charles, Jody Sheff, Nick Powell, Dian Smith.

Library of Congress Cataloging in Publication Data

Blashfield, Jean F
  Hellraisers, heroines, and holy women.

  1. Women-Miscellanea. I. Title.
HQ1233.B57   305.4   80-27889
ISBN 0-312-36736-8
ISBN 0-312-36737-6 (pbk.)

Design by Elaine Golt Gongora
10 9 8 7 6 5 4 3 2 1
First Edition

CONTENTS

Author's Note

Neither a Foreword, nor an Introduction, nor a Preface; not even an Apologia. Just a few thoughts on where this book came from, and perhaps where women are going.

Most of my working life has involved the creation of encyclopedias and other reference books. The first encyclopedia I did was a children's science set. In developing the entry list for it, the question came to my mind: Where are the women? Oh, Madame Curie stood out in radium lights, and somewhere within the articles Lise Meitner and the few Nobel Prize winners received brief mention. But that was about it. Women seem to have feared Nietzsche's dictum: "When a woman becomes a scholar, there is usually something wrong with her sexual organs."

The second encyclopedia I worked on was about aviation and space, and (sigh of relief) women were flying there along with the men: Amelia Earhart, Amy Mollison, Jackie Cochran, Jerrie Cobb, Sheila Scott, and even Marianne Montgolfier—without whose fine sewing the first balloon would not have got off the ground. All these women were aviators, however, the exploration of space was, except for a brief visit by Valentina Tereshkova, clearly a male domain (and is still, though the Space Shuttle may change all that).

Somewhere in the years of developing these and other reference materials, I developed a mind-set that latched onto any sign of a woman being involved in events. At first my little acquisitions served as items for my trivia collection, proudly displayed at cocktail parties or thrust at random into embarrassed silences in conversation. The tidbits generally drew a mild, "Oh, I didn't know that."

But the time came when my collection was no longer trivial—people, both men and women, wanted to know about female accomplishments, to build support for feminine pride. All our lives we'd heard legends of women doing their thing while tucked away behind great men; now those women could step forward and be counted on their own.

We needed to know about the women who, through struggles and achievement (or even diabolical accident), changed conditions and possibilities for all women and for all people. Anthropologist Raphael Patai has written: " . . . the emancipation of women directly and immediately affects the lives of all, of the women, their husbands, their parents, and their children. Not since Prometheus brought down fire from heaven to enrich the life of man, has there been an innovation which has thus transformed the lives of all men."

That's pretty strong stuff. However, when one-half the world's population makes a move in one direction, the world does tilt.

My grand compendium of tilt-makers is still in progress, as is the tilting process itself. I offer in the interim a collection of hellraisers, heroines, and holy women, with perhaps a few hard-hearted whores thrown in. They are all women who, by being themselves, by being truly one-of-a-kind, have left their mark on history, albeit the merest smidgen of a mark, sometimes as slight as a joke.

Perhaps the singularity—the mostness, onlyness, whateverness—of these women would not always find mention in a serious record book.

Perhaps some earnest women will be offended by the humorous and occasionally trivial nature of many items.

Perhaps some men will use these hellraisers as weapons in their male superiority arsenal.

Perhaps others will be disturbed to find important firsts mixed with relatively irrelevant onlies, thinking I'm giving them all the same degree of importance.

If so, women can stand a little teasing these days. We've learned our own strengths. And any movement that is all seriousness is doomed to drag its feet from the weight of its own pomposity.

The funny, outrageous, and bizarre in human behavior have never been sex-linked characteristics. A book of male eccentricities could be just as readily created (actually, such a book would be much more easily developed because the doings of men have always been more often noted in print than those of women).

In conclusion, I make no apologies for the subjective nature of many of the so-called records. Each reader is entitled to make his or her own categorizations. In fact, please, dear reader, feel free to send them along to me care of Superlative House, Inc., P.O. Box 888, F.D.R. Station, New York, N.Y. 10150. There will be no discrimination as to sex of the contributor in evaluating the contributions.

Jean F. Blashfield

Calamity Jane (shown here at Wild Bill Hickok's grave):
a figment of the Eastern imagination

1

HOMEBODIES

Most Willing to Give the Girls a Chance
QUEEN MARGARET OF SCOTLAND

❦ In 1288, Queen Margaret took this honor when, by unverifiable tradition, she decreed that any man must marry the woman who proposed to him during leap year unless he could prove he was already betrothed. If he didn't and couldn't, he was fined 100 pounds—a sum which must have guaranteed lots of marriages. France and several Italian cities followed the Queen's lead and enacted similar laws.

NB: The truth must be told: the generous Queen Margaret was only five years old when the decree was made. Although she was already betrothed to the future Edward II of England, it seems unlikely that she personally was concerned about marriage proposals. Perhaps one of her regents had an unmarried daughter of uncertain age.

Grubbiest Way to Encourage One's Husband
in an Enterprise
ISABELLA, THE INFANTA

❦ When her husband, Archduke Albert, was having trouble with Ostend, which had been taken over by heretics, pious Isabella, the daughter of Philip II of Spain, confidently vowed not to change her clothes until the city was retaken by the forces of right. She gave no explanation for the relationship she saw between clean linen and lifting a siege. As it turned out, her enthusiasm was misguided. Three years passed before the city was taken, during which time her clothing took on a peculiar beige hue, perhaps similar to ancient wallpaper, a hue which the local folk called Isabella color. Perhaps in the fury of battle her husband never noticed, but, of course, he might not have smelled so great himself.

Women Most Likely to Regret Their Bargain
147 "MAIDS FOR WIVES" TAKEN TO
JAMESTOWN IN 1620 AND 1621

❦ Sir Edwin Sandys suggested that a number of "maids young and uncorrupt" be sent to Virginia to become wives for tenant farmers. The Virginia Company would pay transport and, when the men married, the company would be repaid with the currency of the times, best leaf tobacco (the going rate some years later was 120 pounds of tobacco for one wife). In a letter from the company to the council at Jamestown, it was noted:

> there hath been especial care had in the choice of them; for there hath not been any one of them receaved but upon good Commendation . . . though we are desirous that the mariadge be free according to the law of nature, yett would we not have those maids deceived and married to survants, but only to such freemen or tenants as have means to maintain them . . . we would have their condition so much bettered as multitudes may be allured thereby to come unto you. . . .

So much for betterment: The population rolls of 1625 listed only a few of the 147 maids not yet succumbed to disease or Indians.

First Woman in America to Be Sued for
Breach of Promise
CICILY JORDAN

❦ In the early days of the Virginia Colonies, widows were expected to remarry promptly because of the shortage of women in the colony. When the Reverend Grevell Pooley proposed to widow Cicily Jordan, she told the reverend gentleman she wasn't ready to marry again immediately. He took this as a promise that, in time, she would marry him—and proceeded to announce the fact in public. Angered, she quickly announced her engagement to another. Reverend Pooley sued her for breach of promise—and lost.

Only Woman to Give Birth to Rabbits
MRS. JOSHUA TUFTS

❦ According to Bergen Evans in *The Natural History of Nonsense*, Mrs. Tufts of Guildford, England, claimed in 1726 that she had been frightened by a rabbit in a field and soon thereafter gave birth to a litter of fifteen of the creatures. The local midwife enlarged on the story, and even so illustrious a personage as the "Surgeon and Anatomist to His Majesty" claimed he had personally delivered some of the bunnies. At least nine pamphlets and books were written about the amazing episode. One of the books was bound in rabbit skin.

Longest Residence of a
White Woman with Indians
MARY JEMISON

❦ Fourteen-year-old Irish-born Mary Jemison was taken captive by Indians in a French and Shawnee raid in 1758. She had the good fortune to be adopted by two Seneca women who didn't treat her as a slave. After marriage to a Delaware Indian, the birth of two children, and the death of her husband, her Seneca family took her to the Genesee Valley in New York. There she remained, gaining renown as "The White Woman of the Genesee," for the next seventy years. She married again and bore several more children. After the American Revolution, she was asked to return to the white community, but she knew her children would not be accepted. In 1824, a visitor interviewed her for long hours and produced *A Narrative of the Life of Mrs. Mary Jemison.* Despite the many years of war and barbarism, she regarded her life as an Indian as a happy one. Only in the last months of her life, remembering her childhood, did she reconfirm herself as a Christian.

Most Prominent American Common-Law Wife
DEBORAH READ

❦ Deborah Read knew and loved Benjamin Franklin when they were both very young, but before they could marry he was sent to England for several years. Loving but busy, he proved a less than satisfactory correspondent, and Deborah's mother persuaded her to accept another offer of marriage. She gave in . . . and it proved a disastrous match. She soon left her husband, who took off for the West Indies, from whence came uncertain reports of his death. When Ben finally returned to Philadelphia, they soon saw that not only was there no chance for divorce, but they couldn't get her husband declared dead, and bigamy was too dangerous. So for forty-four years they lived happily together, and just as often apart, without benefit of matrimony. They had two children of their own and raised William, Franklin's son by another woman. Deborah died while Ben was away—again—in England trying to get the Crown to heed its upstart colonies.

Only Duchess to Be Tried for Bigamy
ELIZABETH CHUDLEIGH, COUNTESS OF
BRISTOL

❦ A lady-in-waiting to Augusta, the Princess of Wales, Elizabeth was an outrageous flirt and willing conquest at court. In the late eighteenth century, she secretly married Augustus Hervey, a son of the Earl of Bristol, and kept the marriage secret even after the arrival of a son—no easy matter. Turning to party-giving, she welcomed all and sundry but preferred royalty and their paramours. She fell in love with one swain, the Duke of Kingston, and wanted to marry him. Husband Number One appears to have stayed safely in Bristol, but Elizabeth apparently felt her marriage to Kingston should be quick and quiet—so quick that she didn't have time to mention her first husband. Elizabeth and Kingston spent four happy years together, and on his death he left her his abundant real and personal estate. That's what caused his nephew to charge Elizabeth Chudleigh with bigamy in 1775. As was due her position, a full regalia trial was held in Westminster, where the prosecution amply proved her bigamy by producing her first husband from Bristol. The penalty for her crime was branding, but she pleaded the privilege of rank and escaped unscathed to the Continent with a yacht and sufficient funds to live in the style to which she thoroughly enjoyed being accustomed.

Only First Lady to Have Been a Bigamist
RACHEL JACKSON

❦ Rachel's first marriage in 1785 to Lewis Robards was beset by jealousies, separations, and reconciliations. Finally in 1790, Robards got state government permission to sue for divorce. The long-infatuated Andrew Jackson, who had been a tenant in Rachel's mother's boarding-house, was a lawyer who didn't know his divorce law. He took that permission to be an actual divorce and married Rachel. They had the shock, two years later, of receiving notification that divorce proceedings had just been started, now on the thoroughly adequate grounds of adultery and desertion. In January 1794, the Jacksons were finally married legally. When, thirty years later, Jackson became a Presidential contender, the scandal of his marriage became campaign fodder. He believed that the dreadful things said about "the adulteress" hastened her death in 1828, just after he was elected President for a second term.

Woman to Most Thoroughly Set a Man on the
Road to Sexual Excess
MAY GRAY

❦ Nurse to the child George Gordon Byron, May Gray was probably mother to the sexual being he was to become. From hints made later it seems likely that the half-Calvinist half-promiscuous woman seduced the boy when he was only nine years old, about 1797. Certainly something opened the floodgates of sex for him, gates that remained wide open the rest of his short life. A few examples:

★ as a Cambridge University student of seventeen he spent far beyond his income, mostly on women;

★ at twenty-one, on a trip to Malta, he had an affair with a married woman, which led to a duel;

★ he had a passionate affair with Lady Caroline Lamb, who described him as "mad, bad, and dangerous to know," after which she tried to kill herself;

★ he had a life-long incestuous passion for his half-sister, Augusta Leigh;

★ during a brief period in Italy he enjoyed, by count, more than two hundred whores;

★ he fathered a child by Claire Clairmont, seventeen-year-old stepsister of writer Mary Shelley;

. . . all of which led to the British refusal to bury the scandalous man, dead by the time he was thirty-six, in Westminster Abbey.

First Woman to Fight for Married
Women's Rights
CAROLINE SHERIDAN NORTON

❦ Poet and novelist Caroline Norton had a brief and very unhappy married life. When she could stand it no longer, she left her husband. He retaliated by charging her and Lord Melbourne with "criminal conversation." In one of the most celebrated of adultery trials, Caroline and Melbourne were acquitted, and Caroline was granted one of the very few divorces given to women in those days. But her husband automatically got custody of the children because women were regarded as incapable of rearing children alone. She began the agitation that gradually led to the passage of the Infant's Custody Act of 1839. This act gave judges, for the first time, the option of granting to the wife the custody of all children under seven plus visiting rights to older children. If adultery were proved against her, however, she could not retain any custody rights.

Caroline Norton's legal tribulations did not end there, however. In 1855, her ex-husband, ever the ne'er-do-well, demanded all the earnings from her writings. He defended his action publicly by writing to the *Times;* she responded by privately publishing a small, thoughtful pamphlet, *English Laws for Women in the Nineteenth Century.* In addition, she wrote to Queen Victoria describing her thoughts. All these actions joined to ease the passage of the Marriage and Divorce Act of 1857, by which women were able to gain at least some divorces themselves and a few other inequalities were abolished. Caroline Norton, never intentionally the feminist, could still write, "I believe in the natural superiority of the man as I do in the existence of God. The natural position of woman is inferiority to a man, that is a thing of God's appointing, not of man's devising."

Last to Know That Joseph Smith Had Decided
That Plural Marriage Should Be Official
Policy of the Mormons
MRS. JOSEPH SMITH

❦ In about 1842, while in Illinois, Joseph Smith began secretly collecting extra wives without telling Emma, his wife of fifteen years. In July 1843, he officially announced that since God had revealed to him that no virgin could enter Mormon heaven, it was the responsibility of every man to ensure the heavenly reward of virgins by accepting them in plural marriage. Mrs. Smith did not cotton to the idea. She made him get rid of all but two wives. He complied but, again in secrecy, began rebuilding his supply until his murder in 1844 by an anti-Mormon mob. When the rest of the Mormons went on to Utah, Emma stayed behind and married a non-Mormon, later proclaiming in public that Joseph had had no revelation about plural marriage. One of the first extra wives, Eliza Snow, went on to Utah, married Brigham Young, and eventually came to be regarded as the "mother of Mormonism."

Most Unusual Marriage of Sisters to Twins
ADELAIDE AND SALLIE YATES

❧ Soon after Chang and Eng, the Siamese twins who were a principal P.T. Barnum attraction, bought land in North Carolina and took out papers to become American citizens, they met the Yates sisters. Chang and Eng had already been on the Gee Whiz circuit for many years and were ready to settle down (though the men would later return to the exhibition halls when they were short of money). When the men and women were introduced at a wedding, Chang was enchanted by Adelaide, who said during a flirtatious discussion of weddings, "What a pity that you who love ladies so dearly can't marry, and that two young ladies can't have such lovely husbands as you would have been." Eng was convinced that any young woman of modesty would refuse to go to bed with a man who was permanently attached to another man. But as he became more charmed by Sallie Yates, it became clear that the brothers had found sisters who were willing to take a chance. The four were married in 1843. In *The Two* by Irving Wallace and Amy Wallace, the authors speculate on the sexual techniques employed by the Siamese twins. The Bunkers (as Chang and Eng were collectively known) left behind no record, or even rumors, on what they actually did in bed, but the Wallaces propose that a sort of off-balance missionary position was probably required, with the nonparticipating male partly leaning on the woman since the abdominal band connecting the men was only five inches long. It's unlikely that a properly trained Victorian woman would have chosen the top position. The two men spent their lives alternating three-day periods with first one in total control of their lives and then the other. Probably the tagalong male could dissociate his mind completely from the emotions of his attached, in-control brother. However they arranged their sex lives, the two couples obviously more than managed. Adelaide and Sallie, between them, produced twenty-one children. After living together for nine years the two couples finally built separate homes, with the twins spending alternating three-day periods in each home. Because they adhered to that routine very strictly, they were at Eng's home when Chang died. A doctor who had promised to quickly separate the men in such an event was unable to reach them before Eng, who had been perfectly healthy, died, too.

Most Persistent Husband Hunter
LADY JANE FRANKLIN

❦ When her husband disappeared during an 1845 Arctic expedition endeavoring to locate the Northwest Passage, Lady Franklin refused to believe him dead. She waited patiently for two years and then encouraged the English government to send help. They sent three expeditions to search for the first, all with no luck. The Admiralty offered a reward and Lady Franklin followed suit, both certain that help could still reach the missing men before they starved to death. She pleaded with American whalers to help, and even President Taylor assisted in publicizing the rewards. An American expedition was launched in 1850 with her funds; it, too, was unsuccessful, although they did find some traces of an old encampment. Lady Franklin then funded another expedition, the British government two more, she another, and Hudson's Bay Company yet another. Finally, in 1857, twelve years after her husband had sailed into the unknown, Lady Jane Franklin made her last effort. Members of that expedition, in the ship *Fox*, disappeared for two full years and then returned with a notebook found in a cairn in the Arctic ice. It related the tale of Sir John Franklin dying, the original ships being abandoned, and the gradual deaths of the remainder of the men through cold and hunger. All these journeys to locate one man, initiated by the persistence of one woman, led to the first mapping of the Arctic. The Royal Geographical Society recognized Lady Jane Franklin in 1860 with its Patron's Medal. However, that all-male organization refused to invite her, a woman, to receive the medal in person.

First Married Feminist to Retain
Her Maiden Name
LUCY STONE

❦ Lucy Stone was an independent spirit from the time she decided she wanted to go to college. She used her savings of ten years to attend Oberlin College, from which she graduated in 1847. During the years that followed, she became a well-known public speaker in the cause of abolition and was unexcelled in the art of talking down hecklers. One of the men who annoyed her most, however, was Henry Blackwell, who spent seven years proposing to her regularly and just as regularly receiving in reply her antagonistic discourse on the inferior position of women in marriage and the curse of perpetual childbearing. In 1855, Lucy finally gave in . . . on her conditions. She and Henry drew up a marriage contract by which she could keep her own name. "My name is the symbol of my identity," she said, "and must not be lost." In addition, the contract read, in part,

> . . . we deem it a duty to declare that this act on our part implies no sanction of, nor promise of voluntary obedience to, such of the present laws of marriage as refuse to recognize the wife as an independent, rational being while they confer upon the husband an injurious and unnatural superiority, investing him with legal powers which no honorable man would exercise and no man should possess.

Actually, Lucy Stone hedged the issue a bit during the first months of her marriage, often using the name Mrs. Blackwell. Gradually, however, she firmed up her stand and became only Lucy Stone. Women who keep their maiden names after marriage are now often called "Lucy Stoners." A number of states have upheld a woman's right to continue using her original name after marriage.

NB: In reality, Dr. Mary Walker (see more on her on page 90) was married a few weeks before Lucy and never used her husband's name at all. But Dr. Walker made no public statement on the matter and she divorced her husband in just a few years.

Most Influential Nineteenth-Century Arbiter
of Family Behavior
MRS. SARAH ELLIS

❦ Mrs. Sarah Ellis wrote for the middle-class English housewife in the 1830s, forties, and fifties. Her books, *Women of England, Wives of England, Daughters of England,* and *Mothers of England*—effectively covering just about every female in the kingdom—told women how to behave in their proper spheres, which certainly did not include any independence or education with any aim save wifehood. In one chapter on how to behave toward husbands, for example, Mrs. Ellis offered this advice: "In the case of a highly-gifted woman, nothing can be more injudicious than an exhibition of the least disposition to presume upon such gifts. Let a husband once be subjected to a feeling of jealousy of her importance, and her peace of mind and her free agency are alike destroyed for the rest of her life; or at any rate until she can convince him afresh, by a long continuance of the most scrupulous conduct, that the injury committed against him was purely accidental and foreign alike to her feelings and inclinations." The only creditable use of intelligence in a woman was to relieve the tedium of family life by keeping conversation scintillating.

Mrs. Ellis, wife of a missionary, patterned all her views on the family behavior of Queen Victoria, which defined women in an inferior relationship to men (though there is no evidence that Victoria ever suggested to Albert that he run the kingdom). Just about every home owned a copy of at least one of Mrs. Ellis's books, which served as the final arbiter in any discussion of decorum.

Only Wife of Brigham Young to Divorce Him
ANN ELIZA WEBB YOUNG

❦ Having grown up in a Mormon family where her father took several wives even before the church officially approved polygamy, Ann developed early on a hatred of the practice. Brigham became interested in her when she was only sixteen, but she refused to become one of his many wives. At eighteen, she married a plasterer, divorcing him two years later. After various shenanigans including a threat to bankrupt her brother, Brigham Young finally "won" Ann. Depending on who's counting, she became either the sixty-eight-year-old's nineteenth "real" wife—as opposed to his fifty or more "spiritual" wives—or the twenty-seventh (if nineteenth, what must have been the status of the wives between nineteen and twenty-seven?). She felt herself ignored among the crowd, and after four years, encouraged by a non-Mormon reporter, she sued for divorce in 1873. The reporter set her up as a lecturer on the always fascinating subject of what it's like to live in a polygamous marriage. Audiences in Washington heeded her on the evils of the practice and started legislation against it. Soon after, the courts in Utah finally judged against Young's claim that Ann was only a "celestial" wife and gave her a real divorce. Continued struggles to get him to pay alimony, however, ultimately led to a court deciding that the marriage had never been legal in the first place. Ann married again, this time to a man who managed to divorce his other wife first. But that marriage, too, eventually broke up. Ann Young told her own story in *Wife No. 19* (later revised as *Life in Mormon Bondage*). In recent years it has been retold in Irving Wallace's *The Twenty-seventh Wife*.

Woman to Do the Most for Masochism
as a Way of Life
COUNTESS ZENOBIA, AUNT OF LEOPOLD
VON SACHER-MASOCH

❦ The basic story of Countess Zenobia, which Leopold von Sacher-Masoch later enjoyed embellishing for the edification of his female friends, went that prepubescent Leopold fell madly in adoration with his beautiful aunt. On one early occasion he helped her fasten a shoe and boldly kissed her foot. She reacted by kicking his face and creating a pain that he regarded as exquisite, coming as it did from the object of his juvenile rapture. Again, he hid in a clothes closet, watched as she brought a lover to her room, made a noise in his excitement and was caught. The pain of punishment exacted by

Zenobia, according to James Cleugh's *The Marquis and The Chevalier*, set "Leopold's feverish imagination aglow, before the age of puberty, with a fire that was never to leave the depth of his mind." When Leopold was in his twenties, about 1860, he became involved with Anna von Kottowitz, wife of a doctor (neither she nor the doctor had any great regard for fidelity), and found a willing partner in the creation of pain for sexual pleasure. Their fights, often about money, ended in the greater pleasure for blood being drawn and blows felt. Soon, however, Leopold began subtly to encourage Anna to have an affair with another man so that they could experience the pleasures of her punishment, which was likely to be severe. But the plan backfired when the new lover gave Anna syphilis. Leopold quickly dropped her. It was from reading of the affair between Anna and Leopold von Sacher-Masoch that Dr. Krafft-Ebing, German neuro-psychiatrist, coined the word "masochist."

Smallest Woman Ever to Marry an Even Smaller Man
LAVINIA WARREN

❦ The happy couple were Lavinia Warren, thirty-two inches tall and weighing about thirty pounds, and Charles Stratton, better known as General Tom Thumb. The groom was smaller than the bride: twenty-five inches short and only fifteen pounds (midgets, however, often continue to grow through adulthood and by his death he measured a whopping forty inches and seventy pounds). The couple were married on February 10, 1863, at Grace Church in New York City in a "quiet" P. T. Barnum-type ceremony with two thousand guests. Lavinia's maid of honor was her sister Minnie, who was a few inches shorter. The best man was the loser in the quest for Lavinia's hand, Commodore George Washington Morrison Nutt, a twenty-nine-inch, twenty-four-pound fellow Barnumite. During the reception at the Metropolitan Hotel, the tiny receiving line stood on a grand piano in order to shake hands with their guests. And at eighty pounds, the wedding cake weighed more than the bridal couple together. The diminutive pair never were able to have children, so showman Barnum borrowed a baby for publicity purposes. The real mother would stand in the background pretending to be the wet nurse. Most of the public would have sworn that the popular midgets had their own normal-sized child.

Lavinia married again two years after General Tom Thumb's death in 1883. Her new husband was an Italian dwarf, Count Primo Magri, whose title, conferred by the Pope, was more legitimate than the ones Barnum invented for his performers. The count, however, was ever after known as Mrs. Tom Thumb's husband. Lavinia kept a picture of Tom in a locket around her neck, leaving Magri in little doubt about where he stood in her matrimonial hierarchy.

Largest Group of Women to Take Part in an Experiment in Human Eugenics
THE WOMEN OF THE ONEIDA COMMUNITY

❦ John Humphrey Noyes founded the Oneida Community in upstate New York in the 1870s. Noyes believed that "in a holy community, there is no more reason why sexual intercourse should be restrained by law, than why eating and drinking should be—and there is as little occasion for shame in the one as in the other." He also believed, however, that women should not have to pay the price for male sexual license. Thus in building his perfectionist society, any man or woman was free to ask a person of the opposite sex for a "private visit" but the visit had to be approved by a committee of elders. The older women were to train the younger men in sexual pleasure that did not lead to orgasm, and the older men trained the young girls. Noyes called the relationships thus developed "complex marriage." But after some years he realized that Oneida was self-destructing: no completed sexual intercourse, no children to carry on the community. So Noyes initiated a program for breeding a great race of Oneidans, which he called "stirpiculture" (Victoria Woodhull later advocated stirpiculture in her campaign for the Presidency).

Fifty-three women signed the following agreement:

> 1. That we do not belong to ourselves in any respect, but that we do belong to *God*, and second to Mr. Noyes as God's true representative.
> 2. That we have no rights or personal feelings in regard to childbearing which shall in the last degree oppose or embarrass him in his choice of scientific combinations.
> 3. That we will put aside all envy, childishness and self-seeking, and rejoice with those who are chosen candidates; that we will, if necessary, become martyrs to science, and cheerfully resign all desire to become mothers, if for any reason Mr. Noyes deem us unfit material for propagation. Above all, we offer ourselves "living sacrifices" to God and true Communism.

Thirty-eight young men also agreed to "offer ourselves to be used in forming any combinations that may seem to you desirable. We claim no rights. We ask no privileges. We desire to be servants of the truth. With a prayer that the grace of God will help us in this resolution, we are your true soldiers."

Eighty-one people became parents (Noyes himself fathered nine children, a fact which some rejected men did not take with quite the humble martyrdom they were expected to feel). Fifty-eight children were raised in the Children's House, where the selfishness of motherly love could be avoided. But the system itself collapsed when neighbors of the community, seeing what was apparently free love, drove Noyes away. Those couples who could marry did so to make their children legitimate. The children that Noyes had fathered were, of course, left fatherless. And eventually the community, under the leadership of one of Noyes's stirpiculture sons, became a manufacturing-oriented gathering of conventional families, now renowned for its sterling tableware. But the children produced by the experiment were known to have been, in fact, brighter, healthier, and longer-lived than the average.

First Female Birth Control Criminal
MRS. ANNIE WOOD BESANT

❧ Working in London in 1877 with Charles Bradlaugh, publisher of the weekly *National Reformer*, Mrs. Besant printed and distributed a cheap edition of *The Fruits of Philosophy, or The Private Companion of Young Married People,* by Charles Knowlton, a contraception pamphlet that had been quietly circulating for over forty years. They were arrested for reprinting the "dirty, filthy book" and tried in June 1877. The jury's decision was indecisive: "We are unanimously of the opinion that the book in question is calculated to deprave public morals, but at the same time we entirely exonerate the defendants from any corrupt motive in publishing it." The judge held that the verdict meant they were guilty, but Bradlaugh won them an appeal on a technicality. The publicity the case was given achieved the effect desired by Besant and Bradlaugh: a full discussion of the various methods of contraception and the airing of a subject that had been only whispered about for many years. Sales of *The Fruits of Philosophy* multiplied by the thousands during the trial. And Annie Besant published her own book, *The Law of Population*, which also sold widely. As a result of the trial, though, Annie Besant lost custody of her daughter because the court decided she was a bad influence on a growing girl.

Most Confirmed Promotherhood Feminist
ELLEN KEY

❧ Swedish-American reformer and writer Ellen Key was opposed to the suffrage movement and any other movement that would take women away from childrearing. Her concept of motherhood, however, held no place for men except as regrettably necessary donors of sperm—an activity that did not require the institution of marriage. About 1890, she argued for government support of mothers. This innovative woman would have been pleased to see Sweden's modern-day support programs for unwed mothers and all children regardless of the economic status of the parents.

Most Obedient Widow
ELIZABETH DOE ("BABY DOE") TABOR

❦ Baby Doe was the second wife (through an infamous scandal) of Horace
Tabor, one of the wealthiest mine-owners in Denver. For years there was
no counting the money when Baby Doe and Horace wanted something. But
it didn't last. The bottom fell out of the silver market, and before Horace
died in 1899 he instructed her to "hang on to the Matchless," convinced that
that particular mine would someday be productive again. She and her
daughter moved into a shack at the head of the Matchless in Leadville.
There they lived in penury, with Baby Doe making occasional forays into
Denver to "borrow" money on the strength of the Matchless's potential.
She froze to death at the head of the Matchless in 1935. Her story has been
told in an opera, *The Ballad of Baby Doe*, by John Latouche and Douglas
Moore.

Only Woman to Have a Memorial
to Her Constructed Just Because
Her Sons Loved Her
MRS. KENEY

❦ Keney Memorial Tower, a "monument to mother," was built in 1898 in
Hartford, Connecticut. It stands in Keney Park, which was donated to the
city by the Keney sons in her memory.

Most Polite Woman
COUNTESS OF ROUEN

❦ During the last century, when form was perhaps more important than
content, the Countess was widely known for the exquisiteness of her
manners. She delighted in visitors and the whole panoply of ritual that
went with having guests. One day, however, when visitors arrived at her
Paris home she sent her servant to say, "The Countess of Rouen sends her
compliments but begs to be excused. She is engaged in dying."

Woman With the Most Urgent Need
to Get a Divorce
ANNA GOULD

❦ The American heiress Anna Gould married a Frenchman, Count
Boniface de Castellane. Gould himseif was no piker when it came to
spending, but he taught his daughter Anna to pay attention to where the
money went. Plain Anna bought handsome Boni with a dowry of $15
million, which he fully intended to spend in enjoyable fashion. For example,
he invited three thousand guests to one party; purchased ten *miles* of
carpet to prevent guests at an outdoor party from wetting their feet in

dew; built a pink marble palace that included a private five-hundred-seat theater; bought a yacht with a crew of one hundred; as well as not one, but two châteaux outside Paris. In addition Boni indulged in quite flagrant—and expensive—infidelity, figuring that the privilege of being married to him was quite sufficient recompense for the use of her fortune.

Anna, tired of asking Daddy for more money and realizing that she would soon be broke, divorced Boni in 1906. Eighteen months later she married Boni's cousin. When Boni ran into his cousin, he clubbed the newlywed with his walking stick. Failing to achieve results by that tactic, he reluctantly began what was to be his career during the rest of his life—selling antiques.

Most Faith of a Mother in a Son's Ability
MRS. C. DIXON

❦ In Columbus, Ohio, around 1907, Mrs. Dixon's bright son constructed a homemade dirigible. The dirigible included a small gasoline engine and a very large gas bag, which had been sewn and varnished by hand. Mrs. Dixon encouraged and helped her fatherless fourteen-year-old, even to the extent of test flying the fragile airship herself in the skies over Columbus. She had, as she noted, no fear because she had complete confidence that he could not build a vehicle that would crash.

Biggest Fan of Mothers
ANNA M. JARVIS

❦ In 1907, in commemoration of the death of her own mother, Anna Jarvis arranged for her church in Philadelphia to hold a special service in which children would honor their mothers. She then started the Mother's Day International Association, which spread the good word in pamphlets distributed around the world. One noted this interesting fact: "The common possession of the living world is a mother. Everyone has—or has had—a mother." In 1914, the United States Congress officially dedicated the second Sunday in May to mothers. Other nations celebrate the event on different days. Miss Jarvis, who never married and was never a mother, spent her later years fighting the blatant commercialism that became associated with Mother's Day.

Fathers followed closely behind mothers in recognition. In 1910, Mrs. John Bruce Dodd, working with the clergy of Spokane, Washington, started Father's Day.

Guess who came last! The first Mother-in-Law Day was held on March 4, 1934, in Amarillo, Texas. A local newspaperman, Gene Howe, liked his mother-in-law, Mrs. W. F. Donald, and wanted to recognize her. Not surprisingly, the idea has not caught on across the nation.

Mothers also have a tree they can call their own: the white birch, designated Mother's Tree by the American Forestry Association.

The Loneliest Woman
MARTHA MARTIN

❦ The wife of a prospector in Alaska in the 1920s, pregnant Mrs. Martin was left at their camp while her husband went to run an errand to a neighboring island. While he was gone, a series of disasters struck. An avalanche on the mountainside pinned her unconscious under a rock for several days with a broken arm and leg. A storm prevented her husband's return and supplies were gone because they had been on the verge of closing the camp for the winter. Stranded, injured, and alone, she knew her baby would soon be born, with no help in sight. She quickly learned to be self-sufficient—killing animals for food and using their fur to make coverings for the coming baby, splinting her own leg, making a cast for her arm. Bit by bit, she burned the cabin for heat. She hadn't even seen a child being born when she went into two days of labor. But she kept her head and helped herself when her daughter finally arrived. She baptized the infant Dannas. Weeks later, some Indians appeared and she finally had help until her husband, who had been caught on the other island, arrived. The diary Mrs. Martin kept, *O Rugged Land of Gold*, was published years later.

The Youngest Mother
LINDA MEDINA

❦ This five-year-old, part-Indian from the Andean foothills of Peru gave birth by Caesarian section to a six-pound baby boy on May 14, 1939. The senior Medinas felt that perhaps the whole extraordinary event occurred because the child wandered into the "Pool of Birth" near their village: The Indians believed that if a virgin entered the pool she would have a child. At least no other fatherhood explanation was ever offered, nor did the doctors know if Linda had a menstrual history prior to her pregnancy. Linda's mother had a birth certificate showing that the child was four years and eight months old when her son was born, but some doctors believe that the girl must have been a tiny nine-year-old. Linda called her son "the crying doll the doctors gave me," and he was reared as her little brother.

Most Generous Woman in the Development of
Contraceptive Techniques
KATHARINE DEXTER McCORMICK

❦ A biologist in her own right (the second woman ever to graduate from the Massachusetts Institute of Technology), Katharine Dexter married the youngest son of Cyrus McCormick (see Nettie Fowler McCormick on page

24). When he died after years of schizophrenia, this woman, who was often herself regarded as eccentric, controlled a major fortune, much of which she used to further biological projects of interest to her. She had come to know Margaret Sanger, the birth control heroine, quite early and followed her work with interest. Together Kate and Margaret went in 1951 to Dr. Gregory Pincus, founder of the Worcester Foundation for Experimental Biology in Shrewsbury, Massachusetts, and asked him to find a pharmaceutical means of contraception. He remembered reading that the hormone progesterone had been used to prevent ovulation in rabbits (progesterone was already being used in humans to treat difficult menstrual periods). This was a long way from an easy-to-use pill that would effectively and safely prevent conception, but he agreed to try. Initial research funds came from the Planned Parenthood Federation, and over the next few years almost $4.5 million of Mrs. McCormick's money went into the project. In 1956, "the pill" was ready for major field tests. In San Juan, Puerto Rico, thirteen hundred women volunteered to be guinea pigs. A year later, not one single pregnancy among those women could be attributed to the failure of this method of contraception, only to the forgetfulness of those tested. The tests were broadened, and in 1960, Enovid, the first contraceptive pill, was approved by the Food and Drug Administration. Today, in spite of some problems that have arisen with the pill, millions of women all over the world have found their lives eased through its use. Hudson Hoagland, a Worcester Foundation director, wrote of the early days, "The government would give us nothing for work on antifertility compounds nor would philanthropic foundations, both for the same political reason—fear of the Catholics. . . . Had not Mrs. McCormick come to our rescue financially, 'the pill' would not have been developed. It was a direct growth of her financial aid." When Kate McCormick died in 1967 she left $5 million to Planned Parenthood as well as another million to the Worcester Foundation.

Only Known American Woman to Be Struck by a Meteorite
MRS. HEWLITT HODGES

❦ One day in 1954 Mrs. Hodges was napping on the couch of her Sylacauga, Alabama, home. She woke abruptly when a ten-pound chunk of extraterrestrial stone plunged through her ceiling. It hit her a glancing blow on the head and thigh and ended at rest on her living room floor after hitting a radio. There have been numerous other reports from all over the world but this is the only case that is thoroughly documented.

Only First Lady of a Modern Nation to Marry
Her Husband Sight Unseen
FATHIA NKRUMAH

❦ Kwame Nkrumah, Prime Minister of the new nation of Ghana, had been told by a soothsayer that the savior of Africa would be the son of an Egyptian woman and a black African man. His urge to found a messianic dynasty got the better of his deeply ingrained fear of marriage and the knowledge that the black women of his nation would not look kindly on a white wife from the north. He commissioned a friend to find him an Egyptian wife. A Coptic girl was preferred because of the Copts' pure Egyptian lineage. Fathia Ritzk, seemingly cast aside at the age of twenty-six, was chosen and willing to accept the honor, and they married in December, 1957. During the first months of her marriage, she was confronted with learning to cope with an alien tongue and culture in a hostile country whose only interest in her appeared to be whether or not she lost weight, with a promiscuous husband who held her, except briefly, at arm's length. In 1959, she gave birth to a first son, Gamal. Seven years later, however, Nkrumah was deposed, his messianic dreams ended. Fathia Nkrumah took her children and returned to Egypt.

Only Grandmother to Give Birth to
Quintuplets
INES MARIA CUERVO DE PRIETO

❦ When she gave birth on September 8, 1963, thirty-four-year-old Ines of Venezuela was already mother of five, including a seventeen-year-old daughter who had made her a grandmother, and stepmother of eight. The birth of five seven-month boys prompted the Venezuelan government to offer assistance with their housing and education. Offer gratefully accepted.

Only Woman to Spend a Lifetime Searching
for Her Father's Penis
MARIA RASPUTIN

❦ Gregory Rasputin, the Russian monk, became a great power at the Russian court not long before the Revolution by seemingly being the only person who could ease the hemophilia suffering of the Grand Duke Alexis, heir to the throne. This gave him such power over the empress that, although politically ignorant, the monk became the final authority in things political. Maria, Rasputin's eldest daughter, said years later, "I was never in doubt for a single instant that my father had supernatural powers." It certainly must have seemed so on December 16, 1916, when a small group of men, led by Prince Yussupov, conspired to kill the "mad monk." First they gave him poisoned cakes and madeira. Then Yussupov shot Rasputin, who fell to the ground. But soon he rose, enraged, and ran out into the courtyard, where he was shot again, failed to die, and was beaten and knifed by the incredulous conspirators. Sometime in the bloody mêlée Rasputin may have been castrated, though Yussupov's own book on the conspiracy says nothing about it. The hard-to-kill man was finally thrown into the icy Neva River where he drowned. Fifty-four years later, Maria put the emphasis on the probably accidental castration. She told Charles Higham in *Celebrity Circus* that Yussupov, perhaps himself a homosexual, thought Rasputin's power over the empress was sexual. "I believe," Maria said, "that Yussupov and his fellow officers did not originally intend to kill, but when they began to castrate my father, they panicked at the blood and had to get rid of him." She had sought her father's missing penis ever since. She traveled the world with Ringling Brothers and Barnum & Bailey Circus, first with a pony act and then as a lion tamer, billed as "The Daughter of the Famous Mad Monk Whose Feats in Russia Astonished the World." When Higham interviewed her in 1970, he was shown what Maria thought might be her father's penis. It looked, he said, like nothing so much as a dried banana.

Only Woman to Have a Baby Shower Given
Her by the U.S. Senate
NANCY MOORE THURMOND

❦ Nancy Thurmond, the twenty-five-year-old second wife of sixty-nine-year-old Senator Strom Thurmond, was so feted by the Senate in 1971. Since then the pair has produced four children who have been called into action to barnstorm the state of South Carolina campaigning for the Senator's reelection.

Only Woman to Have a Baby
While Serving in Congress
YVONNE BRATHWAITE BURKE

❦ A Democratic congressperson from California, Yvonne Burke was married during her campaign for election in 1972. The following November, in 1973, she gave birth to a daughter, Autumn Roxanne.

Most Public Breakup of a Marriage
PAT AND WILLIAM LOUD

❦ The daily events—or lack thereof—of the Loud family of Santa Barbara, California, were filmed for seven months in 1971, and later aired in 1973 as a Public Television series called "An American Family." The Louds accepted the request to film an average, attractive American family at home just as all attempts to save their marriage from infidelity had reached an end. Before the filming was finished, divorce proceedings had started and the film showed all the bitterness and recriminations leading to the split. Mrs. Loud later wrote about the marriage and its televised breakup in *Pat Loud: A Woman's Story*. She used the proceeds from the book to move to New York, leaving Bill in Santa Barbara where he remarried in 1976.

Most Forgiving Bride
LINDA RISS PUGACH

❦ In 1959, Linda Riss of New York split up with her boyfriend and became engaged to another man. The boyfriend she had tossed over had someone throw lye in her face, completely blinding Linda in one eye and legally blinding her in the other. The attacker went to prison for fifteen years, and the ex-boyfriend became an ex-lawyer and served fourteen years. In 1974, Linda married Burt Pugach, the man who had ordered her disfigurement by lye. They told the story of their strange relationship in *A Very Different Love Story*. That's putting it mildly!

Biggest Help for Housewives
Who Want to Stay at Home
JINX MELIA

❦ According to the Bible, while Martha was in the kitchen busily getting dinner ready for visitors, her sister Mary was in the other room listening to Jesus. Martha finally went to Jesus and said, "Sir, doesn't it seem unfair to you that my sister just sits here while I do all the work? Tell her to come and help me." Jesus didn't; he just told Martha not to fret so about the details. But a lot of women like the details of living and don't want to be made to feel guilty for not getting out into the world more. However, they also want to feel less isolated while remaining in their homes. It was for these women that Jinx Melia of Virginia founded the Martha Movement in 1976. The Martha Movement, headquartered in Burke, Virginia, publishes a newsletter, *Martha Matters*, has a speakers' bureau, and is working to develop agencies for providing free professional counseling for alcoholism, depression, and the other severe problems that may affect homemakers. Of prime importance is the continuing task of giving women who work at home a more positive image, both of themselves and from the world at large.

Jinx Melia herself stayed at home only three years after her children were born. She returned to the outside world to run her own career-training service for women.

2

CAREER GIRLS

Most Famous Governess to Marry Her Boss
MADAME DE MAINTENON

❦ Perhaps Jane Eyre might be considered the most famous fictional governess to marry her boss, but in real life the most famous was Madame de Maintenon, keeper of Louis XIV's children by his mistress, Mme de Montespan. Françoise Scarron, a young widow, was given charge of Montespan's first child, born in 1669, at a house in Vaugirard. As more children were born, the governess's income increased until, in 1674, she was able to purchase an estate at Maintenon, and started calling herself Mme de Maintenon. Soon thereafter, the king decided to legitimatize the children and have them live with him. Mme de Maintenon accompanied them to their new home and the king became fonder and fonder of her equable temper in the face of the increasing tantrums exhibited by Mme de Montespan. He made the Maintenon estate a marquisate, made Mme de Maintenon a marquise, and made Montespan furious. She behaved so badly that the king sent her away.

And where was Louis's wife all this time? Marie Thérèse of Austria had been queen consort since 1660 by virtue of a treaty granting her Louis as a husband on condition that she yield all claim to the Spanish throne. Some deal! He ignored her, except for fathering six children by her, until not long before her death in 1683 when Maintenon herself got the two on speaking terms again. Finally, two or three years later, Mme de Maintenon succeeded to the position of queen by secretly marrying the king, though she was never publicly acknowledged as queen consort in the thirty years they were together. Even so, her influence on him behind the scenes was great. Mme de Maintenon remained a governess in spirit at least by establishing St. Cyr, among the first and most famous schools for girls in France.

Lady-in-Waiting with the Most
Interesting Job Assignment
COUNTESS PRASKOVYA BRUCE

❦ A Russian married in the late 1700s to a soldier of Scottish ancestry, the countess was Empress Catherine II's close friend and confidante—so close, in fact, that she became known as *L'Eprouveuse*, the tester. She has been described by Catherine's biographer Joan Haslip as "gay, witty, totally amoral, and at the same time amazingly discreet." A fortunate thing because it was her job to try out the sexual skill of the men who caught Catherine's eye as potential Royal Favorites. The men were all young because, as Catherine observed, "if they were older, people would say they governed me." Catherine was generous with those who achieved the rank of favorite, so competition must have kept the countess busy . . . perhaps so busy, however, that she forgot the basic rule of testing only *before* Catherine selected a lover. The countess became particularly fond of one young man who kept returning to her couch, on her invitation, even after he started occupying Catherine's. The countess promptly lost her job and Catherine made sure that her replacement was considerably less attractive than Countess Bruce.

First Woman to Hold an Official Government
Position in Aviation
MARIE BLANCHARD

In 1804, Napoleon named Mme Blanchard, the wife of a pioneering aeronaut, his Chief of Air Services after peremptorily firing her male predecessor. Although he believed in the military possibilities of balloons, Napoleon probably limited Mme Blanchard's function to the purely cere-monial one of piloting beautifully decorated balloons into the skies to astound the crowds at festivals. For years after Waterloo, Mme Blanchard drew great crowds as an entertainer. During one spectacular night ascension in a hydrogen-filled balloon, the colorful fireworks she was carrying ignited the bag, and she plunged through the night sky to her death—the first woman to die in an aviation accident.

Only Female Mail-Stage Driver
COCKEYED CHARLEY PARKHURST

The friends who bragged about Charley's daring driving on the run from San Jose, California, never knew that the tough, mean-looking, one-eyed driver was a woman. And no one thought to question it when Charley Parkhurst voted in the town of Soquel in 1868. But thirteen years later, Charley died at age seventy-three and was found to be a woman. She was later identified as Charlotte Parkhurst, originally of New Hampshire, an orphan who had probably escaped from an orphanage dressed in boys' clothing.

Most Successful Female Financial Wizard of
the Nineteenth Century
HETTY ROBINSON GREEN

Often called "the Witch of Wall Street," Hetty Robinson was born to a small fortune that she increased to over $100 million during her lifetime.

She wrote to newspaperwoman Dorothy Dix, "I was forced into business. I was the only child of two rich families and I was taught from the time I was six years old that I would have to look after my property." Hetty took her Quaker training of thrift to heart, marrying in 1867 the wealthy Henry Green only when convinced that he was not a spendthrift, and contesting in a long-drawn-out legal battle her aunt's will, which gave her an additional income of $70,000 a year (the case was finally dropped when relatives accused Hetty of forging her aunt's signature to a holographic will). She ran a close race with the moths for possession of an aged woolen cape, and carried her personal thrift to the point of denying her injured son medical attention so that eventually he lost his leg, and even left her husband after he made some bad investments against her advice.

Relying only on her own business sense, she made investments all over America and often traveled to see the properties on which she held mortgages. Her instinct was always sound, a fact which made many dislike her. At one time she said, "I am in earnest; therefore they picture me as heartless. I go my own way. I take no partner, risk nobody else's fortunes, therefore I am Madame Ishmael, set against every man." Despite the fact that she was one of the richest women on earth, made so by her own achievements, Hetty Green opposed woman suffrage: "I am willing to leave politics to the man, although I wish women had more rights in business and elsewhere than they now have. I could have succeeded much easier in my career had I been a man."

Woman with the Strangest Combination of Accomplishments
ISABEL C. BARROWS

❦ When her husband, who was a phonographer for Secretary of State William Seward, became ill in August 1868, Isabel Barrows served in his place, becoming the first woman to hold the position. Seward found Mrs. Barrows's stenographic work acceptable and was not disturbed by her presence as a woman. Three years later Mrs. Barrows became the first female stenographic reporter for Congressional committees. Curiously enough, in between these two firsts, Mrs. Barrows found the time to chalk up another, vastly different in nature. In 1869, she and Dr. Mary Safford, a friend from the Woman's Medical College of the New York Infirmary for Women and Children, where Mrs. Barrows entered training in 1868, went to Austria and became the first women admitted to the prestigious University of Vienna. "They were so dazed at the idea of two young women wanting to matriculate" she wrote, "that before they fully recovered consciousness after the stunning effect of our unheard-of demand, we had signed the papers, paid the insignificant fee, and were students." Back home in Washington, Isabel Barrows combined her activities as stenographer, eye surgeon, and medical lecturer at Howard University.

First Women to Run a Brokerage House
VICTORIA CLAFLIN WOODHULL AND
TENNESSEE CLAFLIN

❦ The house of Woodhull, Claflin and Company in Wall Street was established in 1869 because Victoria Woodhull felt that only custom, not law, prevented women from entering the business world. It was only women's lack of backbone that kept them out. Not long before, Victoria and her sister Tennessee, new to New York and pretending to be miracle healers, had met Commodore Cornelius Vanderbilt. Seances held by Victoria, magic magnetic treatments, and Tennessee in his bed made the Commodore quite receptive when Victoria suggested that he might like to back them in their new enterprise. Their firm immediately prospered, clearing a profit of two-thirds of a million dollars in the first three years. Reporters and cartoonists delighted in picturing them running roughshod over other financiers. Soon, however, Vanderbilt's new wife reclaimed her strayed husband and the sisters' interest turned elsewhere, particularly to women's rights and Presidential politics (see page 49).

Biggest Female Seller of
Nonprescription Medicines
LYDIA ESTES PINKHAM

❦ In 1873, when her husband's dreams of making a fortune had brought her and her family near destitution, Lydia Pinkham's sons suggested she sell the herbal remedies that she had been giving to neighbors in Massachusetts. The prize recipe was for a medicine that appeared to be useful for "female complaints," to be used when a woman was reluctant to go to a male doctor. Mrs. Pinkham mixed a large supply, added a goodly proportion of alcohol, and started to sell it as Lydia E. Pinkham's Vegetable Compound. Her sons became the salesmen of the small bottles that bore her dignified picture and the modest claim, "The Greatest Medical Discovery Since the Dawn of History." In writing advertising copy, she acquired skill in telling the women of America all the things they should and shouldn't do to be healthy, both physically and mentally. She invited the public to send in questions, eventually answering them with a booklet called *Guide to Health and Etiquette*. Among the people who helped promote the vegetable compound were leading figures in the Woman's Christian Temperance Union. Ironically, long after Lydia Pinkham's death and after a well-publicized campaign at the turn of the century to expose such patent medicines for being mostly alcohol, Lydia E. Pinkham's Vegetable Compound reached its sales peak during Prohibition.

Most Popular American Female
Lighthouse Keeper
IDA LEWIS

❦ Ida Lewis became keeper of Lime Rock Lighthouse in Newport, Rhode Island, at age fifteen when her father was paralyzed by a stroke. But it was not for another twenty-two years, seven years after her father died, that she was officially designated Keeper of the Light in 1879, probably the first American woman to keep a lighthouse. During her years of service, she personally saved at least twenty-two persons from foundering boats, and each time the newspapers delighted in building up the story of the lady on the rock. She became so popular a figure that her rowboat, *Rescuer*, which had been presented to her by the people of Newport, was exhibited at the 1893 Columbian Exposition in Chicago.

Most Celebrated Prostitute
CALAMITY JANE
(a.k.a. Martha Canary Burk . . . or Hickok
. . . or Washburn . . . or White . . .)

❦ Most of the deeds attributed to Calamity Jane came from her own pen and those of Eastern writers, but there is no evidence to prove they actually happened. Even her marriage to Burk, the name under which she was buried, goes unrecorded. Orphaned at age fourteen, Martha probably latched on to a railway construction gang and then drifted into a brothel in Wyoming. For much of her life, brothels remained "resthomes" to be visited when she was broke or weary. For the most part, she lived with individual men, calling each, in turn, husband. Between men, she may well have worked as a bullwhacker, guiding oxen-powered freight trains. Working generally as a woman in the age-old profession, Calamity lived like a man, engaging in riotous drunken sprees, gambling, and following the gold rushes or at least the men attached to them. Long before her death in 1903, she was a popular figure to Eastern city folk yearning to believe there were heroines in them thar western hills.

Largest Firm Created by a Woman
INTERNATIONAL HARVESTER

❦ When Cyrus Hall McCormick, inventor of the mechanical reaper, prepared to abandon his firm after the plant was destroyed in the 1871 Chicago Fire, his wife, Nettie Fowler McCormick, took the reins, in reality if not in title, during its rebuilding and expansion. After his death in 1884, she led the drive to amalgamate a number of farm machinery firms into an organization that later became the giant International Harvester. After 1902 when Cyrus, Jr., took over, she was able to devote her time to personally selecting the beneficiaries of over $8 million in profits that she herself had generated.

Largest Farming Enterprise Run by a Woman
THE KING RANCH

☙ In 1885, Henrietta Chamberlain King inherited a debt-ridden spread of five hundred thousand acres in Texas from her visionary but impractical husband. She ran the huge place with her son-in-law, developing some of the earliest scientific techniques for beef production. The development of hardy but meaty Santa Gertrudis cattle, for which King Ranch is now renowned, started under her direction. When she died at age ninety-two in 1925, the King Ranch consisted of well over one million acres. She had cleared all debts and left an estate of over $5 million. Today, the King Ranch is the largest "farm" in the world, with holdings in Brazil, Argentina, Venezuela, and Australia, as well as Kingsville, Texas.

First International Cosmetics Tycoon
HARRIET HUBBARD AYER

☙ At age fifteen, Harriet Hubbard married a wealthy man who proceeded to make her into a well-known clotheshorse. Although she lived and dressed with elegance, her husband found more and more reason to stay away, and eventually Harriet left him and moved from Chicago to New York with her children. When her ex-husband lost his fortune she lost her alimony and was forced to earn a living—not an easy thing in the 1880s for a woman who was used to the good and comfortable things in life. She found work, however, selling antiques and soon became a buyer. On a business trip to Paris, she bought some face cream, liked it, and, on an impulse, purchased the formula from the chemist who claimed his grandfather had made it long before for the Napoleonic beauty, Madame Récamier. Back in New York, Harriet found a backer and went into business making the cream. She gambled that the public of 1886 was ready for tinted creams and a little facial magic. In the first major cosmetics advertising campaign, she told the public that Madame Récamier had used the very cream they could now buy, a cream with great healing and youth-keeping powers. The public eagerly bought the new product and even the Princess of Wales allowed her name to be used on an endorsement of the products of Récamier Preparations. Mrs. Ayer's profits, however, were eaten up in a series of lawsuits, including one brought by a Frenchwoman who claimed the Récamier cream recipe belonged to her.

In 1893, Mrs. Ayer's ex-husband and daughter had her committed to a private mental asylum on the grounds that her depression, stemming from the death of a child in the Chicago Fire twenty-two years before, made her unfit to handle her business. During the fourteen months it took for friends to get her released, Récamier Preparations foundered. Ultimately, Harriet Hubbard Ayer returned to the beauty business by writing newspaper columns on beauty. It was another company, however, that in the twentieth century, after her death, used her famous name on a line of cosmetics.

Only Woman to Race Phileas Fogg
Around the World
NELLIE BLY

❦ Inspired by Jules Verne's *Around the World in 80 Days*, published in 1872, Nellie Bly (the pen name of Elizabeth Cochrane) decided to challenge his record by traveling around the world in less than eighty days. She took her idea to the *New York World*, for which she worked as a reporter. Her managing editor wasn't enchanted, but the owner, Joseph Pulitzer, was taken with the idea, though he allowed that he would rather have had a man do the stunt. Armed with a twenty-four-hour watch, lots of money, a small satchel, and a totally unconfirmed itinerary, Nellie left New York on the *Augusta Victoria*. The publicity started next day and followed her around the world—London, France (where she met Jules Verne), Brindisi, Port Said, Ceylon, Penang, Singapore, Hong Kong, Tokyo, San Francisco, Chicago, and home. Seventy-two days, six hours, and eleven minutes! A headline screamed: "Even imagination's record pales before the performance of the World's Globe Circler." If they'd had them, there would surely have been Nellie Bly T-shirts. Forgotten were her years of serious investigative reporting, when she worked in a sweatshop to be able to tell about it, when her sensational activities had had a purpose. Nellie had beaten Phileas Fogg's time around the world!

First Black American Female Millionaire
Businesswoman
MME C. J. WALKER

❦ Working in her washtubs, which were more usually filled with other people's clothes, Mme Walker (actually Sarah Breedlove Walker) created around 1905—from a dream, she said—a formula for removing stubborn kinks in black women's hair. It was used with a special procedure of brushing and heat treatments that soon required her to train "hair culturists" who set up franchised businesses in "the Walker System" across America. She later developed a whole line of cosmetics and creams that were sold house to house by a staff of three thousand women.

Most Philanthropic Woman
MARGARET SLOCUM SAGE

❦ Before her husband's death in 1906, Margaret Sage had managed, at his request, the huge grocery business that had created the fortune. But she never gave away any of the huge profits because he frowned on do-gooderism: What was his was his, and he intended to keep it. After his death, perhaps in reaction to an obituary noting her husband's lack of philanthropy, Mrs. Sage began her beneficence by giving $10 million to establish the Russell Sage Foundation, dedicated to social improvement. The name must have made him turn in his grave, but she felt it would be entirely inappropriate for a lady to have her name on a public organization. After the foundation was established, she gave smaller amounts to whatever caught her fancy and stood up as worthy after careful scrutiny. Universities, museums, YMCAs, missionary societies, and so on all felt her interested and generous touch. By the time of her death in 1918, she had given away nearly $80 million.

Most Famous Store Started by a Woman
NEIMAN-MARCUS

❦ Mrs. Carrie Marcus Neiman, her husband, and her nephew, Herbert Marcus, founded Neiman-Marcus in 1907 with the objective of dressing the newly wealthy women of the West in style. Legends of the store, its customers, its other-worldly Christmas catalog, abound. Suffice it to quote society-watcher Lucius Beebe: "If Jordan Marsh in Boston or even Marshall Field in Chicago should disappear utterly and not be replaced, the loss, while massive, would not be fatal. Dallas, for all its oil companies, banks, insurance, Sheraton hotels, and a minor university wouldn't exist without Neiman-Marcus. It would be Waco or Wichita, which is to say: nothing."

First Sob Sisters
"ANNIE LAURIE" AND FRIENDS

❦ The first "sob sisters" were a group of four female reporters who sat front row center at the 1907 trial of Harry K. Thaw for murdering architect-philanderer Stanford White. His wife, Evelyn Nesbit Thaw, was the star witness—perhaps performer is a better word—as she related how White had debauched her, which in turn had prompted Thaw to murder him. The four female reporters, all well known in their own right, were Winifred Black, who wrote under the name "Annie Laurie," Dorothy Dix, Ada Patterson, and Nixola Greeley-Smith. A male colleague watching them, finding as much story in the reporters' behavior as in the trial, noted their frenzied notetaking at the jerk of a tear on the part of Evelyn Nesbit.

And in an article of his own, he called the women "sob sisters." The rank of Chief Sob Sister, the one remembered best for vivid, lump-in-the-throat writing, was Winifred Black (Bonfils). William Randolph Hearst's answer to Nellie Bly, Winifred went wherever the action was: Galveston's flood that took seven thousand lives (she entered the town disguised as a boy and stayed to direct the *San Francisco Examiner*'s well-publicized relief effort), the San Francisco earthquake, the St. Louis cyclone. The adept writer could switch at the drop of a pencil from society editor, to drama critic, to political commentator, to war correspondent, to city editor.

Youngest Strike Organizer
BESSIE ABRAMOWITZ

❦ After emigrating from Russia to Chicago in 1910, Bessie was hired at age fifteen to sew on buttons at the Hart, Schaffner & Marx plant. Soon after she started, the piece-work rate at which she labored was lowered. She led seven fellow seamstresses out on strike and soon more than twenty thousand sympathizers were out, too, for five full months. The strike finally ended with no increase in wages, but Bessie was chosen to represent her fellow workers on an arbitration committee, one of the first in American labor history, to sign a collective-bargaining agreement. Later, she and her husband organized the Amalgamated Clothing Workers of America.

Most Effective Threat in the American
Struggle for Recognition of Working Women
THE 1917 PROPOSAL OF A ONE-DAY STRIKE

❦ This proposal suggested that all women should stay home for one day— in response to the widely held tenet that "A woman's place is in the home." It was never planned that the strike would actually take place. Instead, letters detailing the strike scheme were sent to women's clubs across the United States and copies "just happened" to make their way into the hands of newspaper editors. When the idea was written up in the papers, the protest was immediate and loud. Stores, hospitals, telegraph and telephone companies, schools—every place of employment that relied mainly on women—bewailed the losses that would result from the absence of women for even one day. The women who had proposed the strike were denounced in editorials. And they, of course, couldn't have been more pleased: the importance of women to the smooth running of business was thereby being recognized.

In 1975, the National Organization of Women attempted a real work boycott, designating October 29 as Alice Doesn't Day and anticipating that women all over America would demonstrate their value to the economy by staying away from work. But Alice Did (go to work, that is)—and the day had a spectacular lack of impact.

Creator of the Most Famous Perfume
COCO (GABRIELLE) CHANEL

❦ In 1922, fashion designer Coco Chanel created a new perfume, calling it Chanel #5. The #5 was her lucky number, not the fifth try at getting it right. Chanel #5 has always been sold in very simple bottles; the elegance is inside, not in the dressing. As a designer, Coco Chanel shortened skirts, introduced artificial fabrics, extracted women from tight corsets and put them into casual, loose-fitting clothes, and—in short—revolutionized women's clothing. Jean Cocteau, in *Harper's Bazaar*, wrote of her, "She has, by a kind of miracle, worked in fashion according to rules that would seem to have value only for painters, musicians, poets." Yves St. Laurent calls her "the godmother of us all."

Only Woman Crossword Puzzle Creator
Widely Known to Puzzle Fans
MARGARET FARRAR

❦ In 1919 at the *New York World*, Margaret Farrar took on the laborious task of preparing the puzzle each week for the Sunday edition. Five years later, she published the first book of crossword puzzles and puzzles became a national fad. Every newspaper had to publish one regularly to be successful. The last major bastion of puzzlelessness, the prestigious *New York Times*, held out until 1942, then hired Mrs. Farrar. She spent the next thirty-two years at the *Times*, turning their crossword puzzle into an elitist cult, with standing in the cult indicated by whether one filled in the puzzle with ballpoint pen or erasable pencil.

In 1934, when variations on the crossword puzzle theme had been sprouting for some time but dying on the vine, Elizabeth Kingsley presented the *Saturday Review of Literature* with a highly literate form called the Double Crostic. It still appears inside the back cover of each issue.

Oldest Female Labor Organizer
"MOTHER" MARY HARRIS JONES

❦ In 1871, when she was in her forties, Mary Jones went to a Knights of Labor hall after losing her dress-making establishment in the Chicago Fire. For the next sixty years, until her death at almost a hundred, she appeared in the thick of any organizing and strike activity. Coal miners from Virginia to Arizona, Pennsylvania to Alabama, found fierce, fighting Mother Jones a staunch ally when on strike, a goad when resting on their laurels. Nor were the miners alone: she also took on child labor in cotton mills, railways, steel, John D. Rockefeller, and, just before her death in 1930, John L. Lewis. She ignored women's suffrage, thinking it was a diversionary tactic of the plutocrats: "You don't need a vote to raise hell!"

Worst Deal Made by a Woman
MRS. MORTON PLANT

❦ In 1929, Mrs. Morton Plant exchanged her house at the corner of Fifth Avenue and Fifty-second Street in New York City for a pearl necklace she saw in Cartier's. The necklace was valued at just under a million dollars and Cartier was happy to make the exchange. Pearls have since largely lost their value because of commercial culturing: the property now has a value as large as anyone cares to calculate.

Second only to this deal was the one made in 1978 by an unidentified Chinese woman who found a one-hundred-fifty-carat diamond in a field. She promptly turned it in to her superiors and was rewarded with two thousand dollars, a tractor of her very own, and the official title of "Worker."

Greatest Inspiration to Handicapped People
HELEN KELLER

❦ "Never bend your head. Always hold it high. Look the world straight in the face." So said blind and deaf Helen Keller to a blind child. And so she said to the world . . . after she learned to speak. Left blind, deaf, and mute by a childhood disease, she was out of touch with the world, and increasingly uncontrollable, until her parents heard of the example of Laura Bridgman (see page 162). Through the Perkins Institution, where Laura had studied years before, they found Helen a teacher, Annie Sullivan. Helen Keller later called the day the teacher arrived at her Alabama home the most important in her life. Weeks of effort brought comprehension that letters being spelled into her hand meant something. "I knew then that 'w-a-t-e-r' meant the wonderful cool something that was flowing over my hand. That living word awakened my soul, gave it light, hope, joy, set it free!" Helen Keller went on to school at the Perkins Institution in Boston, then to the Horace Mann School for the Deaf where pioneering educator Sarah Fuller taught her to speak and to read lips with her fingers. In 1900, Helen Keller did the seemingly impossible by entering Radcliffe College. She graduated *cum laude*, with honors in German, the first of five languages she was to master though she never heard one of them spoken. She became a writer and lecturer, with Annie Sullivan (Macy) interpreting her unclear speech, and gradually became involved in social issues as a prominent Socialist. In the 1920s, to the dismay of friends, Helen and Annie went on tour as a vaudeville act that drew plaudits from cynical crowds. Throughout her life, Helen Keller raised funds for the American Foundation for the Blind, which in her later life helped support her. Throughout the many activities that made her known to the world, she served as a priceless example to all handicapped people of the way that trials can be conquered. Several years before Helen Keller's death in 1968, John F. Kennedy said to her, "You are one of that select company of men and women whose achievements have become legendary in their own time."

First Stewardess to Be Involved
in an In-Flight Drama
ELLEN CHURCH

❦ On May 15, 1930, Ellen Church, a trained pilot and nurse, taking the first flight in an experiment she had persuaded Boeing Air Transport to conduct, shepherded twelve passengers during the twelve-hundred-mile, five-stop, fifteen-hour flight from Oakland, California, to Cheyenne, Wyoming. Her nurse's training proved invaluable when she recognized the symptoms of appendicitis in one passenger, asked the pilot to make an unscheduled stop, and had the man rushed to a hospital. Pilots soon liked the idea of being freed to just fly the plane. Passengers began to ask for flights served by the new female flight attendants, and the idea quickly became a fact of flight instead of just an experiment.

First Publicly Recognized Sex Shop Owner
BEATE UHSE

❦ Doctor of medicine and test pilot of Messerschmitt aircraft for the Luftwaffe, this versatile woman's career as a sexologist began in Germany after World War II when friends kept asking her about birth control. She wrote a small booklet, then a book, then another. When she soon found herself with a bestseller on her hands with the mind-boggling title of *The Book of a Thousand Positions*, she became more and more involved in the distribution of her books. To her, the logical answer was dealing directly with the buying public. So, about 1950, she opened the first sex shop, called, simply, Beate Uhse. It carried her books as well as sex-related merchandise. Her shops are now found all over Germany and she runs a million-dollar business. Her second husband sued for divorce on the grounds of infidelity (she is a nudist even when photographers are around), and she talks about it all on numerous TV talk shows.

Greatest Friend to Typists
BETTE CLAIR NESMITH (GRAHAM)

❦ In 1956, working in her kitchen in Dallas, Texas, Bette Nesmith developed a white, quick-drying liquid to use in painting out typing errors. She and her son's friends used the family garage to package the new product, which they called Mistake Out. In the 1960s, the name was changed to Liquid Paper and sales expanded fantastically as typists discovered the ease with which their mistakes could be covered up.

Only Woman to Take and Pass the Original
Astronaut Tests with Flying Colors
JERRIE COBB

❦ A pilot since her teens, Jerrie Cobb bought her first plane with money earned by playing semiprofessional softball. She started making a name for herself in 1957 with record-breaking flights. Attracting the attention of the National Aeronautics and Space Administration, she was urged to take the stringent physical and psychological tests given to select the astronauts of the Mercury program. For eight days she went through a battery of eighty-seven tests, and came through with "exceptional" ratings in all of them. The exciting word went out: NASA had found its first woman astronaut. About the possibility of going into space, Jerrie Cobb said, "I'd want to do it even if I didn't come back." But then NASA decided against using women astronauts, ostensibly because of the cost of redesigning equipment. Jerrie Cobb, made a "consultant" to NASA, noted, "Millions for chimps but not one cent for women."

Twelve other women went through the astronaut tests at the same time, though none with Jerrie Cobb's spectacular success. Among them was Jane Hart, wife of Michigan senator Philip Hart, mother of eight and a helicopter pilot. In the 1970s, the requirements for selecting women astronauts to work aboard the coming Space Shuttle were not nearly so stringent as the original astronaut selection process. All the women chosen have been designated Mission Specialist instead of Pilot-Astronaut.

Most Successful Doll
BARBIE

❦ Somewhere in Barbie Heaven are the approximately 115 million tall, slim-hipped, high-breasted dolls called Barbie (or her friends Francie, Skipper, Ken, etc.) that have been sold since she was developed in the late 1950s by Ruth Handler of Mattel Toy Company. Barbie was named for Handler's daughter, who yearned for a doll she could play "grown up" with—meaning one with breasts, which dolls at that time just didn't have. So Mrs. Handler had the toy firm that she, her husband, and a friend had started in 1945 create one. And they've been creating ever since—there's even been a "Growing Up Skipper" doll whose breasts developed before your eyes when the arm was turned: instant puberty. It was removed from the market within two years because of opposition by feminists.

In 1974, Ruth Handler sold her firm, Mattel Toy Co., which is the largest in the world based on Barbie's success, but she didn't get out of the breast business. Following her own mastectomy, she founded a hugely successful company that makes "Nearly Me," carefully designed and fitted prosthetic breasts.

Most Male-Oriented Firm to
Be Run by a Woman
ALFRED DUNHILL LTD.

❦ From 1961 to 1975, the chairman of this world-famous firm of British pipe-makers and tobacconists was Mary Dunhill, daughter of the founder.

She had joined the company at age seventeen and worked her way up. Along the way she learned to hand-roll the occasional cigar she smokes. While she was chairman, Dunhill profits rose from $1 to $14 million.

Most Famous Weight Control Organization
Founded by a Woman
WEIGHT WATCHERS

❦ In 1963, Jean Nidetch founded Weight Watchers International. The idea for the company grew out of her own loss of weight (she had been overweight since childhood) by working with a group of friends who encouraged each other in their efforts to stick to a medically recommended diet. After losing seventy-two pounds herself, Mrs. Nidetch kept working with other informal groups until she and her husband decided to make it a business, with franchized organizations that help people lose weight through a program of group encouragement developed by Jean Nidetch. In addition, the firm sells special frozen meals and other low-calorie foods that fit into the Weight Watchers plan, and it even runs summer camps for overweight children.

Greatest Career Switch Made by a
Congressional Wife
BETTY SHINGLER TALMADGE

❦ The wife of Georgia Governor and U.S. Senator Herman E. Talmadge paid her dues in the political wives' hostess association for many years in Atlanta and Washington, D.C. Then Betty and Herman were divorced. Betty returned to Georgia and went into the ham business, turning a tiny, one-woman, many-pig concern into a thriving business with international sales. In 1977, "America's Greatest Pig Woman," as her staff call her, published a very knowledgeable cookbook, *How to Cook a Pig and Other Back-to-the-Farm Recipes.*

Only Woman to Take a Superstition to Court
JANET BONNEMA

❦ It's long been believed—by men, of course—that it is bad luck for a woman to enter a mine or a tunnel. Disaster is sure to follow. Ms. Bonnema, an engineering technician on the huge Straight Creek Tunnel being dug through the Rocky Mountains, felt, however, that to do her job properly she needed to go into the tunnel itself, as her male counterparts did. The project manager didn't claim he kept her out because of superstition, although he did say, "Some years ago I took my wife into a tunnel we were working in Climax. The next day we had a man get killed. So you really don't know." It looked as if the court would know, though, and when she brought suit in 1972, the Colorado Highway Department settled with Janet Bonnema out of court.

First Unwed, Pregnant Teacher to Fight
Publicly to Retain Her Job
HARRIET WARDLAW

❦ Late in 1974, when high school teacher Harriet Wardlaw let it be known that she was pregnant, the school administrator moved her to work in the library of a special pregnant students' section. She took the school board to court, claiming that it was sex discrimination, pointing out that an unwed father wasn't removed from *his* job. The District Court judge denied her reinstatement and denied that she was a victim of sex discrimination. The high school had enough problems keeping its students unpregnant without having an unwed example constantly before them.

Youngest Woman to Head a Huge
International Company
CHRISTINA ONASSIS

❦ When her father, Aristotle Onassis, died in 1975, twenty-four-year-old Christina was willed the fun things: a getaway island, a super yacht, plenty of money. And she was also willed 47.5 percent of the multifaceted Onassis business empire. (The other 52.5 percent of stock is owned by the foundation Onassis established in 1974 in memory of his son Alexander, killed in a plane crash, who had been heir to the business.) Christina was expected to look for fun and ignore the business, leaving the circle of men who control the foundation stock to run things. But she soon announced that she would herself run Olympic Maritime and the Onassis holdings, which include a controlling interest in over seventy firms and are worth an amount variously estimated at between $500 million and $1 billion. The shipping segment alone is made up of fifteen supertankers, twenty-six tankers, ten cargo vessels, and a provisioning firm. It was soon clear that Christina had a great deal of the shrewdness of her father. As the vicissitudes of oil shipping have gone up and down, somehow Olympic Maritime has ended up ahead of the game. In addition, she had the wisdom to hire away from Exxon a general manager to run the day-to-day business of the Monte Carlo-based parent company. A *Redbook* study of her concluded, "Christina has proved herself Greek enough to take charge of a proud family clan, American enough to stake out a career and mature enough to realize that today's woman can succeed—even in a business where males have stood alone at the helm."

However, Christina's shrewdness appears to be lacking when it comes to marital affairs. At twenty, she married a forty-seven-year-old real estate broker, to her father's dismay. Four months after her father's death, she married again, to another shipping heir, but that merger didn't take either. Then, in 1978, in the strangest marriage yet, she wed a Russian "shipping agent," who apparently did little but may have been, as many relatives suspect, in the pay of the Soviet KGB. That marriage ended in 1980, with his demanding $100 million of Christina's assets as alimony. The final settlement was described publicly only as "multimillion dollar."

Most Innovative Business Started by a Woman
NATURAL LAWN TRIMMING

❦ In 1975 Anette van Dorp of Bonn, West Germany, founded an "all natural" company, an environmentally safe lawn-trimming enterprise. She rented sheep to home-owners who preferred not to mow their lawns with power equipment and yet had too much pride just to let the grass grow. Sheep were rented for the summer grass-growing season at very reasonable rates; the actual profit to Fraulein van Dorp came in autumn when the customer-fattened livestock were butchered or sold for breeding.

Woman Responsible for the First Court
Decision That a Woman Need Not Put Up with
Sexual Harassment from Her Boss
DIANE WILLIAMS

❦ In 1972, Diane Williams had been fired from her job as a public information aide at the Department of Justice in Washington. She filed suit on the basis of sex discrimination, alleging that she had been fired because she had rejected her boss's sexual advances and that men did not have to face such on-the-job nuisances. When ruling on the case in 1976, U.S. District Court Judge Richey observed that "the conduct of the plaintiff's supervisor created an artificial barrier to employment which was placed before one gender and not the other." He also noted that probably the only employer who would be free to harass his or her employees would be one who was bisexual and made equal demands on all employees.

Best Example of Counting on Your Friends in
a Labor Dispute
TEAMSTERS UNION

❦ An unidentified toll booth attendant on the Pennsylvania Turnpike was fired from her job "for conduct unbecoming an employee," a very generalized euphemism for using her toll booth to offer sexual services to a trucker or two when they happened by. Eventually the woman was reinstated because of pressure exerted by—you guessed it—the Teamsters Union.

3

GIRL SCOUTS AND PIE THROWERS

Most Naked Political Activist
LADY GODIVA

❦ How much of the story of Lady Godiva is history and how much legend is uncertain. Supposedly this good lady of the eleventh century thought her husband, Leofric, should do something to remove the tax burden of the people of Coventry, England. He agreed on condition that she ride naked through the streets of the city. Spreading the word that the townspeople were not to look, and adjusting her long hair strategically over her body, she made the ride at high noon. The one foolish man who watched her—a tailor named Tom—was mysteriously struck blind and became forever after a warning to other Peeping Toms. The taxes were lowered, and Lady Godiva rode into history—or legend, as the case may be.

In the New World, in early Salem, Massachusetts, Mrs. Lydia Wardwell, a woman of good repute, used the same attention-getting technique when she walked naked into a Sunday church meeting to protest against wicked "priests and rulers." However, the response of the town was less favorable: Town officials tied her to a tavern post and whipped her, though probably more for her opinions than for her actions.

First Woman to Demand the Right to Vote
MARGARET BRENT

❦ When Margaret Brent arrived in the Maryland colony in 1639 with a group from Gloucester, England, she claimed that since she had brought other colonists with her, she was entitled to a land grant like her brothers had received. Cecilius Calvert, Lord Baltimore, the proprietor of the colony, agreed, and Margaret became the first female freeholder in Maryland, taking land at St. Mary's City, the capital. She signed the papers "Margaret Brent, Gentleman." She had a strong but unidentified relationship with Governor Leonard Calvert—she may have been his lover and he may have married one of her sisters. But it is certain that Margaret assisted him in putting down a Protestant revolt. When Calvert the proprietor died, Margaret Brent found herself the executor of his estate. As both a freeholder and his "sole executrix" and "Maryland attorney for Lord Baltimore," she appeared before the Maryland Assembly on or about

January 21, 1648 (other dates are sometimes given) and demanded two votes. She was refused, after which she protested all proceedings of the Assembly as illegal. Quarrels between her and new Lord Baltimore on the handling of his business matters grew until, about 1651, she and her sister Mary left—or were forced to leave—Maryland for Virginia where they settled on an estate called "Peace."

Only Known Female Mason
ELIZABETH ST. LEGER

❦ Be a Mason or die. Some choice! That's what Elizabeth St. Leger of Ireland was told when, in 1693, the young woman was caught eavesdropping on a masonic ceremony being held in her father's house. The gathering turned into a kangaroo court that condemned the girl to death for hearing secrets no non-Mason must ever know. One man less ready than the others to defend masonic secrets to somebody else's death persuaded them of another way to prevent Elizabeth's telling. And so the woman was initiated into the first and second degrees of masonry, thus effectively sealing her lips. There is some evidence that even after marriage she remained an active Mason and may even have been Master of her Lodge.

Nosiest Queen
MARIA THERESA OF AUSTRIA

❦ In 1747, perhaps in offended reaction to her husband's philandering ways, Maria Theresa formed the Chastity Commission to oversee the morals of the empire. This was no high-powered, high-minded committee that laid down guidelines for moral behavior. On the contrary, this was a nasty little group of men who spied on anyone they felt deserved it. No one was safe. Any man seen with an opera singer or dancer was automatically assumed to be involved in an illicit affair and was quickly arrested. Even the most high-born lady was in trouble if she accidentally chanced to display her ankle. And woe betide her if she were caught with a man not her husband: She would be banished from the empire or confined to a convent. All mail could be opened to prevent pornography from entering the country. Even the famous Casanova became victim of the anti-sex regime and was forced to send away his Viennese mistress, whom he publicly called his sister, to live elsewhere. Gradually, stunned reaction turned to incredulity and then to anger. The Emperor, Francis I, or perhaps someone else of influence, stepped in and persuaded Maria Theresa to abandon her sexual interloping, and the Chastity Commission was abolished. However, official voyeurism must have been ingrained: twenty years later, when the atmosphere within the Austro-Hungarian Empire became even more Inquisition-like, many former Chastity Commissioners became paid police informers.

First Group Political Action by Women
THE EDENTON TEA PARTY

❦ A group of fifty-one women in the North Carolina town of Edenton met on October 25, 1774, and signed a declaration that they would forgo the joys of tea-drinking until the tax Britain had placed on tea was removed. An Englishman wrote to his brother in America saying that the episode had caused a hullabaloo in London. He asked, "Is there a female Congress at Edenton too? I hope not, for we Englishmen are afraid of the Male Congress, but if the ladies should attack us, the most fatal consequence is to be dreaded."

Only Woman to Have a National Anthem
Created about a Flag She Made
MARY YOUNG PICKERSGILL

❦ Mary Pickersgill, a fine needle woman, put her needle skills to work making a flag to fly over nearby Fort McHenry. In September 1814, the fort was attacked by the British, but it was valiantly defended. Offshore, a young lawyer named Francis Scott Key waited out the battle in a boat; he felt so relieved to see the flag still waving when the smoke of battle cleared that he quickly composed a poem to the "star-spangled banner." Mrs. Pickersgill's tattered flag can still be seen in the Smithsonian Institution.

Best Female Example of the Adage
"The Best Laid Plans . . ."
FRANCES WRIGHT

❦ In the early nineteenth century, Frances Wright, a Scottish-born heiress, was attracted to America, a free land peopled by free men and women. A stay at New Harmony, Robert Owen's experiment in communal living in Indiana, convinced her that a cooperative community might be a solution to the pressing problem of slavery. In 1826, on land she purchased in Tennessee, she started a community called Nashoba where she hoped to turn a muddy clearing in the woods into a model of equality. Black slaves would go to school side by side with whites and earn their freedom, thus serving as an example to Southern planters. Marriage would not be necessary because free and equal men and women could not be bound by old-fashioned legal ties. Eventually the races would all meld into one, and everyone would be happy. But the slaves didn't understand what Fanny Wright was getting at. The neighbors shunned the community because of its scandalous free love advocacy. Everyone came down with malaria from the nearby swamps. And Fanny herself was usually away, leaving her sister Camilla to get increasingly restless and disenchanted with running the place. Fanny Wright was forced to close down Nashoba and resettle the slaves in the West Indies. She then returned to New Harmony, where she started a new career as a lecturer, giving her first speech on the Fourth of

July (probably the nation's first female Independence Day speaker). She spoke on education for women, birth control, married women's property rights, unions, the clergy, and any other subject that interested her, to what were probably the first mixed audiences held in thrall by a female speaker.

First Influential Woman to Enter Saloons in the Name of Temperance
DELECTA BARBOUR LEWIS

❦ Temperance was a man's movement until about 1846. Then Mrs. Lewis, wife of a habitual drunk, organized the women of Clarkesville, New York, to hold prayer meetings in saloons. While not a terribly effective technique at the time, she did pass her antagonism to liquor on to her son Dio. About 1870 Dio Lewis became a famous temperance lecturer, often reminding women of his mother's ventures into saloons to fight the evil spirits. The result of his speaking at meetings in Fredonia, New York, and Hillsboro, Ohio, was the formation of the Woman's Christian Temperance Union.

Woman Who Had the Most Negative Effect on the Issue of Slavery
IRENE SANFORD EMERSON

❦ Mrs. Emerson's husband, an Army surgeon, took a slave named Dred Scott with him when he was transferred to Illinois, a free state, and then to Minnesota, a territory declared free by the Missouri Compromise. On Dr. Emerson's death, Scott claimed to be free on the basis of his residence in free territory. Mrs. Emerson fought the claim, and won in the first trial. Scott won in a retrial. She in turn won in the state supreme court, where the case was called (and would be thereafter) *Scott* v. *Sanford* (or Sandford) because she had remarried and thus had no authority over her first husband's estate: Her brother took over as defendant. The basic question became whether Dred Scott was a citizen and therefore entitled to bring suit in court. Eventually, in 1857, the infamous Dred Scott Decision was made by Chief Justice Roger Taney and his cohorts: that no Negro was a citizen because slaves had not been citizens at the time of the adoption of the Constitution (the same circular argument would be used against women in years to come) and that the Missouri Compromise was unconstitutional because Congress had no power to regulate slavery in the states. It took a war to reverse that decision and Mrs. Emerson's effect.

Most Successful Early Effort Uniting Women
THE UNITED STATES SANITARY COMMISSION

❦ Though ostensibly headed by a board of men, this organization, through the efforts of thousands of women, managed the welfare of Union soldiers during the American Civil War. The women ran hospitals, supplied food, made clothing, raised money at local gatherings, and contacted families of soldiers. More than seven thousand local societies raised a total of at least $50 million (a similar, earlier effort during the American Revolution had netted about $7000). At the Battle of Antietam, the only supplies the Union soldiers had were those brought them by members of the Sanitary Commission because the Army couldn't get through. An account written soon after the war found it a cause for marvel that women were efficient and organized enough to maintain correspondence files, keep inventories of materials, balance books, organize meetings from local to national level, and, somehow, direct all their efforts to easing the problems of the individual fighting man. Several hundred women rose to the top of the busy work caldron, and their names are enshrined in local and regional history. More importantly, however, women got a taste for politicking and organizing themselves to achieve a goal.

Only Woman to Form an Important Club
Because She Couldn't Meet Charles Dickens
JANE CROLY

❦ Take one visit to the New York Press Club by the illustrious author Charles Dickens, a group of male journalists who refused to admit women to the great event, a female journalist who wrote women's news under the pseudonym Jennie June and who wanted very badly to meet Mr. Dickens, *et voilà*, you have a new movement for women. As a result of those events, Jane Croly formed Sorosis, the first professional women's club, on March 21, 1868, in New York. The first president—albeit a reluctant one—was writer Alice Cary. Before her term of office was up a similar club was started in neighboring Brooklyn. Twenty years later, at an anniversary function of Sorosis, the many professional women's clubs of America were united in the General Federation of Women's Clubs.

A footnote to the Dickens episode: The New York Press Club, belatedly ashamed of itself, invited the Sorosis women to a dinner, but didn't ask a single woman to speak. A few weeks later, Sorosis graciously invited the Press Club to tea . . . and didn't allow a single man to speak. The Press Club got the point, and held another banquet with both men and women on the program—perhaps the first such mixed dinner ever held in America. (See also page 48.)

Most Famous Temperance Worker
CARRY NATION

❦ Described in *Notable American Women* as a "direct-action temperance reformer," Carry Nation's direct action consisted of breaking up saloons with a hatchet. She was led, she claimed, by divine will. Her first experience with saloons was in hunting for her alcoholic husband within weeks of her 1867 marriage. Forced to work after his death, she taught school until dismissed in a contretemps over the pronunciation of the letter "a." Her marriage to David Nation, a combination lawyer-editor-minister, was not as alcoholic as her first and it lasted longer but was really no more successful as she moved with him through Missouri, Texas, and Kansas. It was in Medicine Lodge, Kansas, that she first saw herself as defender of public morals. At first, her technique consisted of singing hymns in saloons until shamefaced barkeeps closed the doors. Then she improved her method by punctuating the conclusion of each hymn by swinging wildly about her with a hatchet, smashing everything in sight. About this time, her husband divorced her for desertion. This left Carry Nation free to take on the rest of the nation, occasionally using her method of "hatchetation," as she called it, but more usually writing and speaking in public, even on the vaudeville circuit. At one point, a judge, sentencing her to ninety days for disturbing the peace, acknowledged her great lack of popularity: "God forgive me for not strangling her with my bare hands." Mrs. Nation used her trusty hatchet for the last time in 1910 in Montana when the saloonkeeper confronted her and beat her up. The saloonkeeper was a woman.

It is now generally conceded that though she was undoubtedly crazy (her mother, who thought she was Queen Victoria, had died of syphilis), Carry Nation brought attention—and thus success—to the temperance movement that it might otherwise not have had.

Only Women Actively to Seek Loss
of Voting Rights

❦ About two hundred fifty thousand women signed a petition about 1886 urging Congress to pass the Edmunds-Tucker Bill which would disenfranchise the women of Utah Territory who had been voting for seventeen years. The petition was the work of the "Mormon Division" of the Woman's Christian Temperance Union; these women felt that multiple Mormon wives were voting as their husbands demanded, thus keeping polygamy a territorial policy. If women couldn't vote, some of the more reasonable men might eliminate polygamy. The Edmunds-Tucker Act, which passed in 1887, was one in a series of Congressional acts leading Utah's religious authorities finally to have "revelations" forsaking polygamy, thus making Utah eligible to join the United States.

Most Influential Female to
Oppose Woman's Suffrage
QUEEN VICTORIA

❦ When the votes-for-women movement became known to Queen Victoria, she had one of her spokesmen declare: "The Queen is most anxious to enlist every one who can speak or write to join in checking this mad, wicked folly of 'women's rights,' with all its attendant horrors, on which her poor female sex is bent, forgetting every sense of womanly feeling and propriety . . . It is a subject which makes the Queen so furious that she cannot contain herself."

First Woman Deliberately to Force Her Own
Arrest for Being a Woman
SUSAN BROWNELL ANTHONY

In November 1872, Susan B. Anthony led fifty other women in registering to vote in Rochester, New York. The men at the registration center, a barber shop, didn't have the courage to refuse them in the face of Susan B.'s recitation of the recently ratified Fourteenth Amendment, which does *not* state that only men can vote. Four days later, fourteen of the women gathered the courage actually to vote for state representative; two weeks after that Ms. Anthony was obligingly arrested on the federal charge of voting illegally. She spent the time before her trial talking to everyone in town, realizing that they were all prospective jurors. In response, the court moved the trial to the Federal Court House in Canandaigua, New York.

Ms. Anthony's attorney observed at the opening of the trial, "I believe this is the first instance in which a woman has been arraigned in a criminal court merely on account of her sex." Using the Fourteenth Amendment as her defense, Ms. Anthony declared that "citizen" meant "person." A woman was a "person" (although it wasn't until 1971 that the Supreme Court decided a woman was, in fact, a "person"). In charging the jury, the judge pulled out a written opinion that he had obviously drawn up before the long hours of testimony had even begun. Ms. Anthony was convicted, fined, and sentenced to six months in jail, with the stipulation that the fine was to be paid first. She never did pay the fine, so she never went to jail.

At her sentencing, ignoring the judge's attempts to keep her quiet, Ms. Anthony pointed out that there was no way she could legally be sentenced under the Constitution because "of all my prosecutors, from the corner grocery politician who entered the complaint, to the United States marshal, commissioner, district-attorney, district-judge, your honor on the bench—not one is my peer, but each and all are my political sovereigns; and had your honor submitted my case to the jury, as was clearly your duty, even then I should have had just cause to protest, for not one of those men was my peer; but, native or foreign born, white or black, rich or poor, educated or ignorant, sober or drunk, each and every man of them was my political superior; hence, in no sense, my peer."

Woman to Do the Most to Bring Peace to the
Last Years of British Horses
ANNA LINDO

❦ Anna Lindo succumbed to the late-Victorian mania for do-gooder organizations by starting a Home of Rest for Horses. By 1898 at least six hundred animals had found comfort at her rest home. Especially aided were the work animals of the city poor who could not afford to keep the animals once their useful years were over. Barbara Corrado Pope, writing as a contributor to *Becoming Visible: Women in European History*, noted that in this period of do-goodism "the line between charity, silliness, and self-gratification could be very thin."

First Female Hunger Striker
MARION WALKER

❦ In 1909, Marion Walker was jailed in Holloway Prison in Britain for painting a slogan on a wall of the House of Commons. After fasting for ninety-one hours, she was released, and women discovered they had a new weapon in their attention-getting arsenal. At first, prisons released the starving women when they became weak. When most of the women were promptly rearrested for new "misdeeds," however, the prison wardens, under orders from Home Secretary Winston Churchill, started force-feeding the women. This usually consisted of forcing a tube down their throats and pouring liquid nourishment into their stomachs. The public reaction to this procedure brought about, in 1913, the Prisoner's Temporary Discharge Act. This nasty little piece of legislation provided for hunger strikers to be released when they became weak and then immediately returned to prison after they had regained their health. Appropriately enough, it was called the Cat and Mouse Act. Some women were in and out of jail as if through a revolving door. Parliament had unwittingly given the suffragettes an irreplaceable way of bringing public sympathy over to their cause.

Only Suffragists to Write and Produce an
Opera for the Cause
ALVA VANDERBILT BELMONT
AND ELSA MAXWELL

❦ Called *Melinda and Her Sisters*, its sole performance in 1916 netted $8000 for the cause of the Congressional Union for Woman's Suffrage.

Women Most Inspired by Lord Baden-Powell
GIRL SCOUT COOKIES

❦ In 1908, a young girl, Allison Cargill, got some British friends to join her in forming a troop imitating the new and very popular Boy Scouts. By

1909, Lord Baden-Powell, the biggest Boy Scout of them all, saw that enough girls' troops had sprung up to require some organization. At his request, his sister Agnes took on the task and formed the Girl Guides. It was Olave, the new Lady Baden-Powell, however, who soon became Chief Girl Guide of the World.

Juliette ("Daisy") Gordon Low met Lord Baden-Powell in 1911. Spurred by what she learned of the Boy Scouts and Girl Guides, she formed a Girl Guide troop near her vacation lodge in Scotland. When she returned to her home in Savannah, Georgia, she set out to give America's girls the same kind of character- and body-building program. On March 12, 1912, eight girls gathered at her home and enthusiastically formed the first American troop. It soon became Girl Scouts rather than Girl Guides because Mrs. Low felt "scout" had connotations of American heritage. Within one year the movement had grown enough to have national headquarters in Washington, D.C.

Most Ardent American Woman Antisuffragist
JOSEPHINE JEWELL DODGE

❦ Although concerned with women's activities to the extent of supporting day nurseries for children of working mothers and even founding the National Federation (later Association) of Day Nurseries, Josephine Dodge of New York did not, as other such concerned women did, develop from her work an appreciation of the need for greater rights for women. Instead, she felt that all progress in civil rights for women had come from male-run state legislatures and would continue to do so. Believing that women would inevitably upset the apple cart, she decided they should not be given the vote. She supported her view by speaking in state legislatures against woman's suffrage and by founding, in 1911, the National Association Opposed to Woman Suffrage. Her organizing work done, the association moved to Washington, D.C., under the leadership of more politically wise women. The first national meeting was held in 1917 "to protect America from the enemies within her borders." When the antisuffragists' cause was lost, they never recognized that the fact they could organize and act at all was due largely to the work of earlier suffragists.

Only White Woman to Become a Blood
Brother of Australian Aborigines
DAISY BATES

❦ An Irish girl who went to the Antipodes for her health about 1884, Daisy Bates married a drover, left him, returned to London for some years, and then, in 1889, was drawn back to Australia. This time she ventured to see what the Outback was all about. Traveling alone, she investigated an almost extinct tribe for the state government and found the cause that would occupy her until her death in 1951. During a camel trip across the Great Australian Bight, she began to gather around her the halt and lame who were cast out of their own tribes, finally creating a permanent camp on the edge of the Nullarbor Plain. In time, she spoke 188 dialects, leading one visiting journalist to say she had even "learned to think 'black.'" Called "the Preserver," Daisy Bates once said, "There is no hope for tomorrow, but I can help each one of them for today." Her masterful book, *The Passing of the Aborigine*, was published in 1938.

Only Woman to Deliberately Martyr Herself for Woman's Suffrage
EMILY WILDING DAVISON

❦ Feeling that "the cause has need of a tragedy," Emily Davison threw herself in front of the galloping horses on Derby Day in 1913 at Epsom Downs. The horse that did the fatal damage just happened to belong to George V. The self-made martyr died four days later of internal injuries. Thousands of suffragists accompanied her coffin across London in one of the largest women's marches of that demonstrative era.

Only Woman to Start a Major Revolution in Race Relations by Taking the Bus
MRS. ROSA PARKS

❦ On December 1, 1955, Mrs. Parks, a seamstress in Montgomery, Alabama, boarded a bus. A seemingly unimportant move, but when a white man asked for her seat she made it important by refusing to move to the back of the bus, where Negroes were supposed to sit. Her subsequent arrest precipitated a bus boycott by blacks that brought a young minister, Rev. Martin Luther King, Jr., to prominence. In 1976, the main street through the area of the 1967 race riot in Detroit, where she had moved not long after her arrest, was renamed Rosa Parks Boulevard, and in 1980, she became the first woman to receive the Martin Luther King, Jr., Award.

Nine years before the Rosa Parks episode, segregation had been outlawed on interstate buses after Irene Morgan of Virginia had refused to move to the rear of a Greyhound bus. The National Association for the Advancement of Colored People took her case to the Supreme Court. The Court ruled, however, not that segregation was unconstitutional but that it placed an unnecessary burden on interstate commerce. It took the Montgomery case to have segregation on buses declared unconstitutional.

Only Mother of a Governor to Be Arrested in a Civil Rights Demonstration
MRS. MALCOLM PEABODY

❦ Mother of Governor Endicott Peabody of Massachusetts, Mrs. Peabody was arrested on March 31, 1964, in St. Augustine, Florida. Feeling that some older people were needed to balance the multitude of young ones active in racial demonstrations, the seventy-two-year-old grandmother had gone to Florida where the current action was. The wife of an Episcopal bishop, she and two other ministerial wives had only wanted to try to get the church to recognize the rightness of what the demonstrators were doing. But she quickly found herself an activist in deed when she joined a sit-in at a segregated motel restaurant. The police asked Mrs. Peabody to move on. She refused and was arrested . . . after informing her governor son by telephone. Jailed, she was held on three charges: conspiracy, trespassing after a warning, and behaving as an undesirable guest. Her bail was set at $450. She refused to leave jail, however, when the sheriff said he would accept only cash bonds from the other two hundred demonstrators arrested during the weekend. The publicity she received forced the sheriff to accept bonds from bail bondsmen for everyone. Mrs. Peabody went home, much to the relief of her captors.

Only Titled Spanish Female Activist
LUISA ISABEL ALVAREZ DE TOLEDO, THE
DUCHESS OF MEDINA-SIDONIA

❦ Fairly conventional until her 1955 marriage except for her habit of wearing blue jeans, the duchess then began working with rural peasants and talking and writing about the rights of the poor. This led, in 1964, to her first arrest for provoking a demonstration. For her part in one protest she served eight months in prison, embarrassing officials by agitating for prison reform during her stay. As she has noted, "If I go to prison . . . it is the Duchess who goes to prison . . . I find the prison deputies who think I should get some *extra* punishment because I am a Duchess." The duchess gained world recognition when she led a protest over the inadequate compensation paid by the United States after radioactivity was released over Palomares farmland in the crash of a B-52 carrying unarmed nuclear bombs. The duchess left Spain in 1970 when, in a case involving a controversial book she wrote about government suppression of strikes, the court found her guilty on appeal by the prosecution. At that time, she also lost custody of her children when the courts declared her an unfit mother and was not allowed back into Spain until after the death of Generalissimo Franco.

Oldest Person to Start an
Activist Rights Organization
MAGGIE KUHN

❦ A retired church official, Maggie Kuhn and some friends came to feel that old, retired people were given short shrift in America. In 1970, at the age of sixty-four, she started the Gray Panthers to try and improve the lot of the elderly. The Gray Panthers is a true activist group, and has taken on the American Medical Association, mass transit, banks, Congress, and TV's portrayal of laughable old people. In 1973, the Gray Panthers merged with Ralph Nader's action group on aging. Ms. Kuhn said that old people are burdened with an image of being past it and useless. "I am proud of my gray hair, wrinkles and arthritis. I intend to use these credentials for change," she told a *TV Guide* interviewer.

Woman to Devise the Cleverest Method to
Fight Availability of Hand Guns
SUSAN SULLIVAN

❧ Seemingly blocked by the constitutional rights of citizens to own guns, Susan Sullivan of Winnetka, Illinois, and her Committee for Hand Gun Control sought instead to limit availability of bullets for those guns. In 1975 she petitioned the Consumer Product Safety Commission to limit the sale of bullets to police, security guards, licensed pistol clubs, and, of course, the military. As she said, "How can they talk about bicycles and medicine cabinets and pins being dangerous, but not bullets?"

Woman to Make the Biggest Protest
by the Littlest Gesture
MRS. RHODA CLARKE

❧ Mrs. Clarke of Brixham, England, refused to shell out one pound (about $2.80 at that time) for a dog license as a protest against "H-bomb tests, German rearmament, the flouting of the Magna Carta and the Declaration of Human Rights, and British Government policy."

4

POLITICOES

Only Women to Be Given the Vote and Then
Have It Taken Away
WELL-TO-DO WOMEN OF NEW JERSEY

❧ When New Jersey was admitted to the new United States, suffrage was granted to anyone with property worth fifty pounds. Laws passed in 1790 and 1797 specified that women were included in the right to vote. However, charges of fraudulent voting abounded when subsequent elections didn't turn out quite as some men wanted, and the state legislature was "forced" to reconsider their gift to women. In 1807 they cancelled woman's suffrage on the grounds that it was necessary to the "safety, quiet, good order, and dignity of the state."

Woman to Give the Best Reason for Women
Being Involved in Politics
MME DE CONDORCET

❧ Wife of French philosopher and equal rights proponent Marquis de Condorcet, Mme de Condorcet reportedly replied to Napoleon's statement that women should not dabble in politics by saying, "You are right, General. But in a country where their heads are cut off, it is natural they should wish to know the reason why."

Only Woman to Gain Votes for Women by
Inviting Men to Tea
ESTHER MORRIS

❧ Esther Morris was a forceful figure in the gold rush town of South Pass City, Wyoming, and when she talked, the male candidates for the territorial legislature listened. One day in 1869, she invited William Bright and his opponent H.G. Nickerson to tea and extracted from them a promise that whichever one won the election would introduce in the legislature a bill giving votes to women. Fortunately, William Bright, who had already been primed for woman's suffrage by his wife—and was thus unable to ignore his promise—won the election. He did introduce the bill, and the legislature, wanting to attract women to the territory where men outnumbered women seven-to-one, passed the bill on December 10, 1869.

Only Presidential Candidate to
Be in Jail on Election Day
VICTORIA WOODHULL

❦ Victoria Woodhull might be called the first woman to run for the Presidency, but there is no strong evidence that anyone but her friends voted for her in 1872. This free-love and eugenics advocate, spiritualist, and stockbroker had to form her own party in order to be nominated, and the man she selected as her running mate, Frederick Douglass, wasn't the least bit interested in the honor. Her campaign split the woman's suffrage movement, with Elizabeth Cady Stanton and Susan B. Anthony keeping most of the real leaders with them, while Victoria went off and formed her own group. To top matters off, the candidate was in jail on election day for sending obscene matter through the mails: a special issue of her newspaper *Weekly* telling in rather lurid detail the story of minister Henry Ward Beecher's affair with Mrs. Theodore Tilton (she got the information from *Mr.* Theodore Tilton, who was one of her numerous lovers). Tilton publicly charged Beecher with adultery; he was acquitted but only after the jury deliberations went to fifty-two ballots. Woodhull and her sister Tennessee Claflin were also acquitted, but Victoria's political endeavors were finished. So much for free love.

Oh, in case you're wondering, Woodhull lost the election to Ulysses S. Grant.

Victoria and her sister took off for England, in effect forced out of the country by the heirs of Commodore Vanderbilt (see page 23) who were trying to contest his will on the basis of Vanderbilt's interest in spiritualism (an interest fanned by Victoria and Tennessee). In England, Victoria married a banker, much to the dismay of the banker's family. But she did manage to quiet down her life somewhat, only occasionally returning to America to take up cudgels again. On one of those sojourns Victoria Woodhull Martin again entered her name in the Presidential lists of 1892 with little hoopla and no success.

First Woman to Become an Indian Chief
HARRIET MAXWELL CONVERSE
(Chief Ya-ie-wa-noh)

❦ When the State of New York tried to separate Indian tribal land into individual allotments in 1891, Harriet Converse, an investigator of Indian lore, became involved in defending Indian rights. Knowing that this would be fatal to tribal life, she fought the bill and succeeded in stopping its enactment. The Senecas at the Tonawanda Reservation, long her friends, accepted her into the tribal council, giving her the name Ya-ie-wa-noh (sometimes written Ga-is-wa-noh), after the wife of a famous chief. The next year, Ya-ie-wa-noh was raised to the status of sachem, or chief. When Harriet Converse died in 1903, she was buried only after both the rites of the Episcopal Church and the Indian ritual had been performed.

Only American Queen to Be Deposed
LILIOUKALANI, QUEEN OF HAWAII

☙ After she became queen of the Hawaiian Islands (the only queen America ever had) on the death of her brother in 1891, Lilioukalani made a determined effort to rid Hawaii of American influence. She quickly developed a new constitution that would have removed power from the hands of the Americans and others who had never been naturalized but felt that the tropical islands were theirs to run. A landing by U.S. Marines convinced Queen Lil that she hadn't a hope, and a "Committee of Safety" run by the missionaries' sons forcibly removed her from office in 1893. The next year she had to sign an oath of allegiance to the newly formed Hawaiian republic. That republic, too, was short-lived—Hawaii was annexed as a Territory of the United States in 1898.

First Female Bureaucratic Thief
COUNTESS PANINA OF RUSSIA

☙ The Countess, a supporter of the Russian Revolution, was named a deputy minister working with social welfare by the Kerenski Provisional Government in 1917. After the Bolsheviks' October Revolution, her position was filled by Alexandra Kollantai, who had the full rank of cabinet minister (see below). One of her first tasks was to locate the welfare funds that had disappeared when Countess Panina left office.

First Woman to Hold the Full Rank
of Cabinet Minister
ALEXANDRA KOLLANTAI

☙ Appointed by Lenin as People's Commissar of Social Welfare in November 1917, Alexandra was the first woman ever to hold the full rank of cabinet minister. Most of the men in the Soviet bureau objected, however, and went on strike when she was named. Though she held the post only six months, it was a critical period during which most of the basic Soviet policies, such as women's emancipation, were laid down. When over a hundred thousand soldiers' wives marched demanding more rations, she was the only leader with the courage to see them. She promptly organized the women into a union that happily performed the tedious job of overseeing the welfare program that was developed by Lenin. Mme Kollantai later resigned because of basic policy disagreements with Lenin. Some years after, she became the first woman ambassador in the world (see page 57).

Woman to Cast Most Consistent Anti-War
Votes in the U.S. Congress
JEANNETTE RANKIN

❦ A Republican from Montana and the first woman to be elected to a national legislature, Jeannette Rankin cast the first vote ever by a female in Congress on April 5, 1917. She voted against entering the First World War. Forty-nine male colleagues also voted no, but she was the only one condemned for it. Twenty-five years later when she was again in Congress (as the first woman to serve two terms), an identical issue arose on December 8, 1941. Again she voted no but this time she was the lone dissenter. She has said, "America has the war habit. It is a habit we must break before we are broken by it." In the late 1960s, then in her eighties, she formed the Jeannette Rankin Brigade to protest the war in Vietnam.

First Woman to Be Elected to the British
House of Commons
COUNTESS CONSTANCE DE MARKIEVICZ

❦ In spite of her fancy foreign-sounding name (Constance Gore-Booth had married a Polish widower during a sojourn as art student in London), she was the only woman, out of seventeen female candidates, who was elected to Parliament in that first election with women having a vote. Elected from the St. Patrick division of Dublin, on December 14, 1918, she unseated a man who had been incumbent for twenty-six years, in spite of the fact that she was in prison during the campaign. Christabel Pankhurst by the way, won the most votes of the sixteen losers. The countess never took her seat at Westminster, however, because she and the other seventy-three Irish of the Sinn Fein who were elected decided to boycott Parliament and form their own Irish Parliament, the Dail Eireann, which they declared to be the legal government of Ireland. Thirty-six of the seventy-three were in prison at the time for acts against the British, and Constance de Markievicz soon rejoined them after making a "seditious" speech. (This was only one of numerous spells of incarceration for her, starting with a year in prison for her role in the Easter Rebellion of 1916 during which she was one of only two women officers. The countess was staff lieutenant in charge of trenches and barricades.) This woman, whom the *New York Tribune* called "quixotic and shrewd, mystical and wayward," was named Ireland's Minister of Labour by Eamon de Valera.

The British Empire's first female cabinet minister spent most of her first months in office in prison. Released, she found the Dail had been suppressed by the British and gone underground. It continued to function, however, by meeting at seemingly random places, with the more adventurous like the countess going to the rendezvous in disguise. She spent the next two years in and out of prison until, in July 1921, the United Kingdom reached a truce with Ireland, leading to formation of a republic within the British Commonwealth. Although she objected to Ireland's remaining in the Commonwealth, she found the situation "too funny, suddenly to be a Government and supposed to be respectable!" She was forced to resign from her cabinet position, however, when she continued to talk against the terms of Ireland's new respectability. Her Dublin constituency kept electing her to the Dail even though she couldn't take her seat because she refused to swear an oath of allegiance to the King.

Only Woman to Be the President's Right
(and Left) Hand
EDITH BOLLING WILSON

❦ Edith Bolling married President Woodrow Wilson on December 18, 1915, sixteen months after his first wife's death, little dreaming that four years later she would be required to act, in many ways, as the President. Exhausted from the Paris Peace Conference leading to the Treaty of Versailles, topped off by an eight-thousand-mile train journey across America seeking support for U.S. membership in the League of Nations, Woodrow Wilson suffered a stroke on October 2, 1919. The next eight weeks made up the period that Mrs. Wilson came to call her "stewardship." The public was not told how critically ill the President was, and her main job was to make decisions and report them as if they were the considered decisions of a man who only needed rest. The doctors declared that the President must not be disturbed the least bit, and she took it on herself to make certain of it. And there could be no question of his resigning: the doctors said that such an act, virtually guaranteeing the end of all chance for League of Nations ratification, would kill him. So Mrs. Wilson took over, not arrogantly but certainly not timidly either: There was a job to be done. The only thing that made the deception possible was that she probably knew more of what Wilson did and thought than any previous First Lady had known of her Presidential husband. Mrs. Wilson had all papers and documents brought to her, discussed them with the officials concerned and, when she could not maneuver the officials into making final decisions for themselves, would save up questions for the few minutes a day Wilson could spend on business. She later claimed in her memoirs, "I, myself, never made a single decision regarding the disposition of public affairs. The only decision that was mine was what was important and what was not; and the very important decision of when to present matters to my husband." There is no one really to question that statement. No one but Mrs. Wilson and the doctors saw the President during that period. But, of course, even her selection of what was "important" has been called into question time and again. Within two weeks the President was at least able to sign documents. In December, after he sent a long message to Congress that he had dictated to his wife, Edith Bolling Wilson's stewardship was over. No other woman has come so close to the full power of the Presidency.

First Woman to Take Her Seat
in the House of Commons
LADY NANCY LANGHORNE ASTOR

❦ American-born Lady Astor, with no experience other than that of watching her husband at work in his Plymouth constituency, contested and won her husband's seat in 1919 when he was elevated to the House of Lords. For twenty-five years she kept Commons lively with her repartee and wit. She once said, "My vigor, vitality and cheek repell me—I am the kind of woman I would run from." Although never sticking with any particular trend in her Parliamentary interests, she did show a fairly consistent concern for child labor and women's interests—even to the point of advocating birth control. On a visit to the United States in 1923, she observed, "I can conceive of nothing worse than a man-governed world except a woman-governed world. I feel men have a greater sense of justice, and we of mercy. They must borrow our mercy and we must use their justice. We realize that no one sex can govern alone." In 1945, when Lady Astor finally lost her seat in Commons, it was to another woman, Socialist Lucy Middleton.

Lamest Duck Senator
REBECCA LATIMER FELTON

❦ More symbol than senator, all Rebecca Felton did during her term as Democratic senator from Georgia was be sworn in. When Thomas Watson, the senator whose election she had worked for, died two years into his term, eighty-eight-year-old journalist and suffrage leader Rebecca Felton was appointed in 1922 to serve until a new senator could be elected, probably as a sop to women since the governor had voted against the Nineteenth Amendment. But Congress wasn't in session and wasn't about to be, despite the urging by women's groups to get President Warren G. Harding to call a special session; they knew that a permanent senator would have been elected by the time a regular session came around. Mrs. Felton and others persuaded Walter George, the senator who was duly elected, to delay presenting his own credentials at a special Third Session of the 67th Congress (called on an entirely different matter), so that she could at least be sworn in. He agreed on condition that it didn't cause any recriminations in the Senate. On November 21, 1922, Senator Walsh of Montana spoke long and eloquently of the reasons why Rebecca Felton should be not seated. The women in the Visitors' Gallery sighed . . . then he added, but, no senators dissenting, she should be sworn in. None did.

She was sworn in as a U.S. Senator, and even the male senators joined the applause. The next day she made her only speech, pledging to the Senate that "you will get ability" when women finally join that august group. Senator George then presented his credentials and the women's limelight was turned off in the Senate for another ten years.

Only Woman Governor to Regain
Her Apron Strings
MA FERGUSON

❦ The colorful Miriam ("Ma") Ferguson of Texas was elected the same day in 1924 as Nellie Tayloe Ross of Wyoming. But Ross gets the credit for being the first woman governor because she was sworn in two weeks before Mrs. Ferguson, one of the vicissitudes of state laws. Ma Ferguson ran for the office after her husband and predecessor was impeached, kind of just to keep the job in the family. The suspicion that her husband would actually be running the state (the same not-unfounded suspicion that faced Lurleen Wallace of Alabama forty years later) wasn't stilled by her campaign slogan, "Me for Ma. And I Ain't Got a Dern Thing Against Pa." In her term from 1925 to 1927, however, "Pa" did such a bad job of running the state through her that she, too, almost got impeached. And she wasn't nominated for another term. However, in 1932 when Ma Ferguson ran again, she publicly fired "Pa," and was elected for another term as governor, becoming the first woman to serve two terms.

First Woman to Break the Parliamentary
Ruling That Female MPs Should Have Their
Heads Covered When Speaking
SUSAN LAWRENCE

❦ When Susan Lawrence became Labour Member for the Poplar district of London in 1930, she already had a reputation for eccentricity. When first starting in politics she wore a monocle and attended meetings driving a dogcart. Her refusal to cover her head while speaking in Parliament was thus hardly surprising. The ruling, of course, rapidly fell into disuse.

Only Senator to Achieve Office Through Being
Declared a "Person"
CAIRINE WILSON

❦ After all Canadian women received the vote in 1921, the woman most frequently mentioned as the best choice for first woman senator was Emily Murphy, prominent writer (under the name Janey Canuck), women's rights leader, and first woman police magistrate in the British Empire. But the authorities decided that there must be a judicial decision on whether women were qualified to sit in the Senate. The Canadian Supreme Court

decided that they were not because the British North American Act
creating the Dominion of Canada did not specifically state that women were
"persons." Emily Murphy and her supporters went in 1929 to appeal
directly to the Privy Council in London. On October 18, 1929, the Judicial
Committee of the council reversed the Canadian Supreme Court decision.
Canadian females thus became "persons." Two prime ministers, however,
found themselves unable to support Emily Murphy. When one, Mackenzie
King, was willing to appoint a woman, he was of the wrong party. He was a
Liberal and Emily Murphy a Conservative. Therefore, in 1931, the honor of
being first went to Liberal Cairine Wilson.

Senators in Canada are appointed for life (working until age seventy-five
and then pensioned) by the Governor-General on advice of the Prime
Minister; though theoretically the upper house (comparable to the House of
Lords), the Senate does not have the power of the House of Commons.
Thus appointments tend to be honorary in nature. Mrs. Wilson, a Liberal,
had been prominent in women's organizations.

Most Effective Use of Women's Potential
Power in Party Politics
MOLLY DEWSON

❦ In 1933 Molly Dewson became director of the Women's Division of the
National Democratic Party. Her influence with Roosevelt got a number of
women appointed to top government positions. Within the party itself,
however, not much happened until Ms. Dewson managed to get a woman
alternate appointed to every position on the Platform Committee of the
1936 Democratic National Convention. Because each woman alternate was
ready to be at each meeting, the men, for the first time, had to attend
strictly to business or face a platform written by the women. *The New York
Times* called it "the biggest coup in years."

Longest Serving American
Woman Cabinet Officer
FRANCES PERKINS

❦ A New York public official for many years, Frances Perkins was
appointed Secretary of Labor—the first female Cabinet member—in 1933
by President Franklin D. Roosevelt. She remained in the job until his
death in 1945. The initial reaction to the appointment of Miss Perkins by
both labor and management, according to New York Parks Commissioner
Robert Moses, was "like that of habitués of a water-front saloon toward a
visiting lady slummer—grim, polite and unimpressed." Unemployment was
so high in 1933 that men were demanding that all married women be fired.
Although Frances Perkins did not have full control of labor policy in
government because of Roosevelt's propensity for creating boards, she was

able to put through a variety of schemes to give the American worker more security than he or she had ever had before. These included both Unemployment Insurance and Social Security. In most day-to-day work, however, her "welfare-worker" approach tended to antagonize both sides.

Most Record-Breaking Woman
in the U.S. Congress
MARGARET CHASE SMITH

❦ On the death of her Congressman husband in the spring of 1940, Margaret Chase Smith was elected to his seat as a Republican from Maine, and then was elected to her own term the following fall and each term until 1948 when she ran for the Senate. She won and became the only woman ever to serve in both the House of Representatives and the Senate. She remained in the Senate until 1972, longer than any other woman. In all those years of public service, Margaret Chase Smith racked up quite a number of other records:

★ First female senator to be elected without previously having been appointed.

★ First to win over another woman in the race for a Senate seat (Lucia Maria Cormier ran against her in 1960).

★ First elected public official to speak out against Senator Joseph McCarthy's activities (in her first important address to the Senate in 1950, she made a "Declaration of Conscience" signed by herself and six other Republican senators).

★ First woman to sail on a Navy destroyer in wartime (she was on a commission investigating production of destroyers for World War II).

★ Winner of the highest majority in the history of Maine politics (in her 1948 run for the Senate and repeated with an even higher majority in 1960).

★ Holder of the record for the highest number of consecutive roll call votes in the history of Congress (2941 straight votes with never an absence. Each day almost one-fourth of all male senators fail to appear).

★ First woman senator elected to a position of leadership (chairperson of the Senate Republican Conference in 1967).

★ And, hardly least, first woman to seek the Presidential nomination of a major political party.

U.S. News and World Report quoted Margaret Chase Smith in 1964 as saying that there are two main reasons women haven't been more successful in politics: "These reasons are (1) men, and (2) women—men because they vigorously oppose women's holding office—and women because they haven't stood together and exercised their majority voting power."

Only Female Diplomat to
Rescue a Royal Family
DAISY (FLORENCE J.H.) HARRIMAN

❦ A leading Democrat, Daisy Harriman had been appointed in 1937 Envoy Extraordinary and Minister Plenipotentiary to Norway, to the initial dismay of the Norwegian government which had never known a female diplomat. But when, in 1939, she dissuaded a German diplomat from holding an American—and thus supposedly neutral—freighter, they knew they had a fighter among them. In April 1940, she revealed to the world by radio that the Nazi invasion of Norway had taken place and then proceeded to help the Norwegian leaders make their way through air raids to safety. She took Crown Princess Martha and her children in her own car and escaped with them to Sweden. Mrs. Harriman remained in Sweden for several months helping other Americans escape from occupied Norway, then accompanied the Royal Family to the United States.

Only Woman to Precede Her Husband
in the U.S. Congress
EMILY TAFT DOUGLAS

❦ In 1942, Mrs. Douglas's economics-professor husband, Paul, ran for the Senate from Illinois and lost. Even though fifty years old, he then enlisted in the Marine Corps. While he was serving in the South Pacific, Mrs. Douglas was asked in 1944 to run on the Democratic ticket as Representative-at-Large. Since she had to campaign over the entire populous state, she literally did run . . . and won. In 1946, she lost reelection to a returned veteran, and two years later her own returned veteran won his second bid for the Senate.

Most Highly Rewarded "Sexually
Emancipated Communist Woman"
ALEXANDRA MIKHAILOVNA KOLLANTAI

❦ In 1943, Mme Kollantai became the first woman ambassador in the world. Having served as Soviet minister in Sweden since 1930, her duties were unchanged by her promotion: the Soviet Union had only a legation in Sweden, not an embassy. The title was a reward for her long service, begun in 1908 when czarist leaders exiled her from Russia for attempting to organize women laborers. During her exile, any group of workers, from Italy to Belgium, to Sweden and even the United States, were targets for her urge to unionize. She also worked as a novelist and writer on women's rights, though she did not consider herself a suffragist because she felt women suffrage leaders were only interested in voting, not in freeing women. The year 1917, of course, found her welcomed back in the new

USSR. At least she was welcome after Kerenski, who jailed her, had been ousted. Mme Kollantai was immediately appointed to the Bolshevik Party's Central Committee. The next few years were spent at home, alternately in the good graces of the leaders—during which she became the world's first female cabinet minister—and in serious trouble—as when only the intervention of Lenin himself prevented her execution for neglect of duty during a stormy love affair with a seaman. Soon after that she began her official travels as a representative of the Soviet Union. There is strong indication that, in addition to being painfully outspoken, her tendency to practice what she preached about free love (seemingly no male official was exempt and they must have got tired of her) may have been influential in getting her sent out of the country . . . and kept out. She spent six years as minister to Norway, broken by a stint in Mexico, and fifteen years in Sweden, the last two as ambassador. She later revealed all in *The Autobiography of a Sexually Emancipated Communist Woman.*

Only Woman to Serve in Parliament at the Same Time as Her Husband
JENNIE LEE

❦ Jennie Lee met Aneurin Bevan at Parliament in 1929 when they were both Labour MPs, both from Depression-ridden coal mining country, she from the Scottish constituency of North Lanark, he from Welsh Ebbw Vale. She was twenty-four; he was thirty-two; she lost the next election; he didn't. In 1934 they were wed, and Jennie Lee turned journalist with an occasional stab at a new election; he just kept getting elected and criticizing Churchill. In 1945, they got together in Parliament again when Jennie Lee was elected from Cannock. A fighting Labourite in Parliament and journalism, she wrote in her autobiography, "I had taken it for granted in all my growing years that my special job in life was to fight coalowners and all they stand for. I loved that particular fight. . . . It was unanswerably, triumphantly worthwhile."

Most Important Female Diplomat
MME VIJAYA LAKSHMI PANDIT

❦ Sister to Jawaharlal Nehru and aunt to Indira Gandhi, Mme Pandit served as an ambassador from India to three major powers and three minor nations and was president of the United Nations—all within a fifteen-year period. Probably no other diplomat, male or female, has held so many key posts.

When, in 1935, Britain granted the Indian National Congress the right to participate in general elections, both Mme Pandit and her husband were elected to the National Assembly. The next summer she was elected

Minister of Local Self-Government and Public Health for the United Provinces. Indian-British cooperation ended in 1939 when the British government declared India at war without consulting the Indians; internal strife began anew. Mme Pandit spent much of the next five years in prison and lost her husband to an illness that developed while he, too, was in prison. America and a long lecture tour provided her a platform to carry India's views to the world. She made India's presence felt at the founding of the United Nations, challenging the British colonialist (official Indian) delegation every step of the way . . . and got a great deal more publicity. A year and a half later, however, at the insistence of the British, she led the Indian delegation to the United Nations.

In 1947, with India soon to be independent of Britain, Mme Pandit was appointed ambassador to the Soviet Union, the first woman ambassador to serve in Moscow. She also continued to represent India at the United Nations. Two years later, she left Moscow for Washington (serving as ambassador to Mexico at the same time). In Washington also, she was the first female ambassador that town had seen. Years later in a BBC interview she recalled that in Moscow she was given all the recognition due any ambassador; in Washington, she was expected to retire with the wives after dinner. "With the Russians my sex made no difference. The Americans never could accept me as anything but a woman."

In 1951, Mme Pandit was replaced in Washington at her own request; she wanted to return to Indian politics. Within months, however, she was again in New York at the UN, struggling to ease tensions between the Soviet Union and the United States over Korea. Her success brought her, on September 17, 1953, election as president of the United Nations General Assembly, the first woman to hold that position. Within the year of her term, the number of female delegates to the UN doubled. 1954 saw Mme Pandit begin a seven-year period as India's High Commissioner—as the ambassador sent from one Commonwealth nation to another is called—in Great Britain. She also served as ambassador to Ireland and Spain, becoming the first person ever to hold three ambassadorial posts simultaneously. In 1961, she relinquished all of them to return to the India she had not really seen for fifteen years.

After only a brief rest, Mme Pandit accepted appointment as governor of Maharashtra, the largest Indian state, during which she served on one more delegation to the United Nations. When, in May 1964, her brother Nehru died, Vijaya Lakshmi Pandit returned to India again, gave up the governorship, and ran for election to the National Assembly, determined to promote her brother's goals for India.

Only Ambassador to Be Featured
in a Musical Comedy
PERLE MESTA

❦ Perle Mesta was appointed U.S. minister to the Grand Duchy of Luxembourg in 1949 because she had been an early Truman backer. Best known as a Washington party-giver where covert politicking could go on—hence her title of the "hostess with the mostest" in *Call Me Madame*—she was active in the 1940s in the lobby for an Equal Rights Amendment. As envoy to Luxembourg she was the first U.S. minister to that small nation; prior to Mrs. Mesta's arrival on the scene, diplomatic duties there had been carried out by the ambassador to Belgium. A Republican until 1940, she returned to the GOP in 1960, for which she was often called "Two-Party" Perle.

Most Versatile Woman Ambassador
CLARE BOOTH LUCE

❦ A truly Renaissance woman, before being named by President Dwight D. Eisenhower to serve as ambassador to Italy in 1953, Mrs. Luce had been an actress (starting as understudy to Mary Pickford), publicist for the National Woman's Party, magazine editor, close friend of F. D. Roosevelt turned Republican, playwright (*The Women*, *Kiss the Boys Good-bye*, and *Margin for Error* were all successes in the 1930s and are still highly regarded), congresswoman from Connecticut from 1943 to 1947, seriously involved in foreign affairs, wife to one of the great communications powers in the nation, and Roman Catholic convert, who wrote intelligently about her conversion. While serving in Italy, she successfully mediated a years-long territorial dispute between Italy and Yugoslavia. Mrs. Luce resigned in 1957 because of ill health but two years later was offered the ambassadorship to Brazil. She was filibustered out of the position by a senator who had been attacked by Mrs. Luce's husband's *Time* magazine.

Only Known Congresswoman to Lose Her
Seat Because of a Conspiracy
CORA KNUTSON

❦ In 1958, Mrs. Knutson had already served four years in the House as Democrat from Minnesota and was up for reelection when her alcoholic husband wrote a letter to newspapers in which he blamed her continued absence for the breakup of their marriage and accused her of playing around with her male administrative assistant. She lost the election. A hearing was held later at which her husband admitted writing the letter at the behest of rivals for Mrs. Knutson's seat. A columnist noted, "Women are held to a far higher standard of accountability in politics than men are."

Only Woman to Chair the Communist
Party of the United States
ELIZABETH GURLEY FLYNN

❦ When Elizabeth Flynn was elected on March 13, 1961, the U.S. Communist Party's membership was down to less than ten thousand from the eighty thousand it had been ten years before. An activist from childhood, she had been, while only a teenager, an organizer for the Industrial Workers of the World, or Wobblies, and was arrested for the first time at sixteen. During the next years, wherever there was a workers' strike, Ms. Flynn was there and was often arrested. She said of her arrests in her autobiography, "in every instance the denial of the Bill of Rights has been involved." Her experiences made her a logical founding member in 1920 of the American Civil Liberties Union, an organization that, ironically enough, expelled her in 1940 for joining (after long years of association with it) the Communist Party of the United States. In the 1950s, at age sixty-five, she was tried for advocating the overthrow of the government and sentenced to three years in prison. She served twenty-eight months. As chairman of the Communist Party, she failed in her effort to get the Supreme Court to rule that advocacy of violent overthrow is not a crime; she did, however, manage to get that body to grant passports to Communists. Thus at age seventy-four, Elizabeth Gurley Flynn made her first trip to her spiritual homeland, the Soviet Union. There she died and was given a full state funeral.

Most Public Political Visit to America of a
Woman with No Official Standing
MME NGO DINH NHU

❦ Mme Nhu, the sister-in-law (and acting First Lady) of the widowed President Ngo Dinh Diem of South Vietnam, visited America in 1963. People-watchers and pressmen followed the movements of "the Dragon Lady of Vietnam" across the nation in her effort to learn "why we can't get along better." Her own parents, Mr. and Mrs. Tran Van Chuong, did not even see her; they had recently resigned as Vietnamese ambassador to Washington and UN Observer respectively, because they could not support the repressive measures of Diem against the Buddhists. Mme Nhu, on the other hand, chided newsmen for even paying attention when a Buddhist priest immolated himself. Her father publicly repudiated her and called her power hungry. Her intransigence against those she regarded as Vietnam's enemies kept even Vietnamese officials on tenterhooks: Sometime before her trip to the U.S. she had been forcibly incarcerated in a convent to prevent her from sabotaging some delicate negotiations. Just before the beautiful and fascinating Mme Nhu was scheduled to leave the United

States, her brother-in-law's government was overthrown; he and her husband were assassinated. She accused the Kennedy administration of backing the Communist takeover attempt and left America for exile in Paris and then Italy. Through the months of Mme Nhu's travels in the United States, the appeal of an attractive woman seemingly at odds with the whole world made daily front-page headlines.

Only Woman to Administer the
Oath of Office to a President
SARAH T. HUGHES

❦ Sarah Hughes of Texas had been appointed to a Federal judgeship by John F. Kennedy at the urging of Vice President Lyndon B. Johnson and Sam Rayburn, even though she was already in her sixties and the American Bar Association opposed her appointment. When President Kennedy was assassinated in Dallas, Texas, on November 22, 1963, Johnson's advisors said he should be sworn in before leaving Dallas. He remembered Dallas' Sarah Hughes. She was rushed to Love Field where the ceremony took place in *Air Force One*. In the middle of the chaos of that day, she started administering the oath of office only to have to stop while a Bible was found.

Only Unmarried MP to Bear
a Child While in Office
BERNADETTE DEVLIN

❦ Elected to Parliament in 1969 at age twenty-one, Bernadette Devlin was the youngest MP ever. A leader of the Ulster civil rights movement, she was elected as a Socialist from Northern Ireland. Shattering tradition, she made her maiden speech on her first day in Parliament instead of politely waiting her turn and she bitterly attacked the British for participation in the struggle in Northern Ireland. During the remainder of her term in Parliament, she spent several short stays in jail, generally for involvement in riots, gave birth to a child, and then got married. She lost her seat in February 1974 to a male civil rights activist. Devlin later told her story in an autobiography, *The Price of My Soul*.

Only Ex-Dancer to Become a President
ISABEL PERON

❦ Isabel Peron became president of Argentina on the death of her husband, Juan, on July 1, 1974. Though born in Argentina, she was performing as a dancer in Panama when she met Juan Peron in 1955 or 1956 (legend and official pronouncement vary as to year and type of dancing she was doing). She became his secretary and followed him into exile in Madrid where they were married in 1961. She served as emissary to Peronist followers in Argentina and played a role in getting the military government of the late sixties and early seventies to allow Peron to return—a not-too-difficult task in that the government needed the support of the Peronists to survive. In November 1972, Peron was allowed to return to Argentina. Women had long been the main support of the Peronist movement because of the feminine appeal that Eva Peron, Juan's first wife, had had. The Peronists, having seen Isabel in action, knew enough to take her seriously when she ran for vice-president to Peron's presidential bid in September 1973, with Isabel claiming to be purely a Peron "disciple." During the following months she was reported to be working earnestly to understand the ins and outs of government, and winning the respect of the people. When Peron died of heart failure following bronchitis, Isabel took over the presidency, faced with harsh economic problems. Within five months, she removed the constitutional rights of the people in response to riots and violence. The nation that earlier had refused to accept Eva Peron as vice-president because it was an affront to masculinity found itself in the hands of a woman.

In July 1975, President Isabel Peron lost considerable authority by giving in to labor strikers on the matter of a 150 percent increase in wages, compounding her economic, and thus political difficulties. Things didn't get any better. The military became more and more involved in controlling riots, and gradually, gained control of the country. She was shunted into the position of puppet of the military. Violence spread, the peso collapsed, and the citizens began to plead for the military to take over completely. On March 24, 1976, the generals obliged. Mrs. Peron's presidency was over.

Only Former Child Star to Be an Ambassador
SHIRLEY TEMPLE BLACK

❦ Shirley Temple Black, formerly the child star Shirley Temple, was approved by the Senate as ambassador to Ghana on September 12, 1974. The public reaction was an odd mixture of "mop-top goes from good ship lollipop to ship of state," and scathing denunciations of a film actress daring to see herself as qualified to represent the United States. She was, however, qualified, having spent thirteen years in government and diplomatic work, including a hefty stint as a U.S. delegate to the United Nations after her success at raising a million dollars for the Republican Party. She just smiled and went on learning about the nation she would be serving in. In June 1976, Mrs. Black was brought home to become the first female Chief of Protocol.

Only Known Madam to Run
for Legislative Office
BEVERLY HARRELL

❦ Campaigning on the slogan, "I'll show them how to run an orderly house," Beverly Harrell of Lida Junction, Nevada, ran for state assembly in 1974. It all started when columnist Jack Anderson, with his inimitable talent for noting incongruities, observed that the United States government, largest landowner in Nevada, was owner of the land housing Ms. Harrell's Cottontail Ranch bordello. The government quickly canceled her lease. She moved her girls to a house on private land and promptly began her campaign for the state assembly as a form of retribution. She lost to a grandfatherly conservative . . . but not by much more than the hairs on the end of a cottontail. In 1975 she wrote *An Orderly House* about her Cottontail Ranch.

Only Female Foreign Minister to Be Fired in
an International Scandal
ELIZABETH BAGAYA, PRINCESS OF TORO

❦ In 1974, the Princess of Toro was named foreign minister of Uganda by Idi Amin. The dictator removed her from the post before the end of the year because, he declared publicly, the princess "made love to an unknown European in a toilet" in Paris. The princess sued one London paper for printing that accusation as fact, another for asserting that she was pregnant with Idi Amin's child, and a third for using her name erroneously in the caption under a nude photo. She won all three suits.

The First Admitted Lesbian
Elected to Public Office
ELAINE NOBLE

❦ Democrat Elaine Noble ran for the Massachusetts state legislature in 1974. She came out in the open about her sexual preferences because, as *Time* reported, "I thought people in my district might at least respect me for having the guts to stand up and say who I am." She lost her job in an advertising firm because of her frankness but won the election.

Only Mayor to Have Been a Madam
SALLY STANFORD

❦ Elected mayor of Sausalito, California, in March 1976 at age seventy-two, Sally Stanford had been madam of a luxurious brothel in San Francisco in the 1940s. She had later moved to Sausalito, opened a restaurant, and changed her name. Four failures in trying to get on the city council finally prompted her to return to her better known name of Sally

Stanford; she won the council election of 1972, and became mayor of Sausalito.

Only Major Film Actress to Be Elected to Her National Legislature
MELINA MERCOURI

❦ Ms. Mercouri's father had been a deputy much of his life and her grandfather had long been mayor of Athens, so politics wasn't new to the actress. When a military junta took over Greece in 1967, she joined the resistance, but her publicity value made the colonels revoke her citizenship and seize her property. Melina was sent into exile where she kept up sniper fire against them for the seven years the military was in power. More people around the world knew of her and of her opposition to the government in Greece than could name the colonels governing Greece. When the civilians regained control in 1974 and democracy was once more at work, the actress immediately began to run for parliament. She lost the first time by only a few votes but won three years later in 1977, with a higher percentage of her working-class district's vote than was gained by any other deputy. She currently arranges her filming commitments so they don't conflict with her legislative duties. She told a *Chicago Tribune* interviewer, "I think it's right to mix art and politics. Artists are more sensitive than others to what is happening in the world; they have very much rapport with people."

NB: Helen Gahagan Douglas, a U.S. congresswoman in the 1940s, had been in live theater for many years but appeared in only one film before she went into politics—and was later ousted from office by Richard M. Nixon.

5

COPS AND
ROBBERS

Most Murderous Woman
ERSZEBET BATHORY OF HUNGARY

❦ For many years during the sixteenth century, this countess had girls
from the neighborhood brought to her castle at Csejthe in the Carpathian
Mountains. There they died after being tortured in every kind of gruesome
device her fertile mind could invent. She would use their warm blood to
bathe in, believing that it kept her young. Gradually, the noblemen of
nearby castles, who seem to have been singularly obtuse, took alarm,
especially when she started taking girls of noble families, not just peasant
girls, into her net. They brought the countess to trial in 1611, using as
primary evidence the countess's own records of the sadistic deaths of six
hundred and ten women and girls. The court found her guilty and
sentenced her to be walled up in a small room of the castle where she lived,
insane and alone, for three more years.

In a kind of reverse situation, almost five hundred women were once held
responsible for one murder. In 1939, in a South African village, all the
womenfolk participated in eliminating one voracious, male moneylender by
stoning him to death. The punishment was parceled out, with each woman
receiving a sentence of three to six months in jail.

First Woman to Be Tried
by a Jury of Her Peers
JUDITH CATCHPOLE

❦ In 1656, Judith Catchpole was tried for the murder of her child in
Patuxent, Maryland. The jury of both married and single women used its
own method to determine the truth in the case: they inspected the
defendant's body and decided that she had never even borne a child and
thus could not have murdered it. She was acquitted.

In 1679, an all-woman jury in Accomac, Virginia, used a different
method. An unmarried woman was accused of murdering her newborn
infant. The jury had the body of the baby disinterred and had all the
suspects touch it. The woman's stepfather gave himself away and was
found guilty. The stepfather's relationship to the unwanted infant is not
recorded.

Best Way to Infiltrate the Ranks
ANNE BONNY

❦ Irish-born daughter of a South Carolina attorney, Anne Bonny was reared as a boy—he told friends she was his apprentice clerk. She eloped with a sailor to the Bahamas, where she abandoned him for Jack Rackam, a privateer. Dressed as a man, she joined him in stealing a ship from the harbor, and they gathered a pirate crew, one of whom was another woman, Mary Read. Mary, too, had been reared as a boy because her mother refused to admit that her son had died. The pirates plundered towns and ships along the island coasts for several years, with Anne taking one break in Cuba to have a baby. In 1720 their ship was captured and the pirates were sent to Jamaica for trial. Two of the crew, to the astonishment of the judges, claimed they should not be executed: "We plead our bellies." A startled doctor examined the two pirates and found Anne Bonny and Mary Read to be pregnant. The remainder of the pirates were hanged. Mary Read died in childbirth. Anne Bonny was later pardoned, perhaps through her father's influence. No one knows what became of her.

Only Husband Murderer to Marry a Member
of the Jury That Acquitted Her
BECKY COTTON

❦ In 1806, Becky Cotton of Edgefield, South Carolina, was brought to trial for the ax murder of her third husband, though found in the same pond with him were the bodies of two earlier husbands—one with a mattress needle run through his heart and the other poisoned. Mason Locke Weems, the moralizing clergyman pamphleteer who invented the tale of George Washington and the cherry tree, happened by about that time and wrote, "as she stood at the bar in tears, with cheeks like rosebuds wet with morning dew and rolling her eyes of living sapphires, pleading for pity, their subtle glamor seized with ravishment the admiring bar—the stern features of justice were all relaxed, and both judge and jury hanging forward from their seats breathless, were heard to explain, 'Heavens! What a charming creature.'" They acquitted Mrs. Cotton and she promptly married the leader of the pro-Becky group. Weems, however, had the satisfaction of recording that God had His revenge: Becky Cotton was later murdered by her own brother.

Only Woman to Gain Immortality
as a Motor Vehicle
MARIA LEE

❦ She was a large, powerful black woman who kept a boarding house for sailors in Boston's North End. Whenever disturbances occurred in her neighborhood, she would step in and intimidate the participants. Soon the watch came to expect help from Black Maria when rioters or criminals needed subduing. Gradually the name was transferred to the carriages, then the trucks, that came to help.

Longest Lasting Court Case
Brought by a Woman
MYRA CLARK GAINES

❦ In 1835, Myra Gaines entered a suit to claim her father's estate. Involved over the next *fifty-six* years were the issues of her legitimacy, maladministration of the trustees, a decision of the U.S. Supreme Court in her favor followed by a quick reversal, an alleged suppressed will (which she "found" by writing it herself and which the Louisiana courts and the Supreme Court actually upheld), a varying number of defendants depending on who happened at any one time to own some of the property originally owned by her father, federal courts, Confederate courts, the City of New Orleans, at least thirty lawyers, some of whom made their whole careers out of the case, and a will of iron on the part of Myra Gaines. In 1891, six years after her own death, Myra Gaines's heirs were awarded more than half a million dollars from her father's estate.

Most Horse-Thieving Female Bandit
of the Wild West
BELLE STARR

❦ Born Myra Belle Shirley in Missouri, Belle Starr's father soon took her to Texas where her older brothers turned the Shirley farm into a hideout for remnants of Quantrill's raiders, the Younger brothers, and the James boys. Her two brothers had both been killed by 1867, but she kept up the family tradition of hospitality on a ranch near Dallas, even to the extent of bearing Cole Younger's child. However, she may have eloped with Jim Reed, a Quantrill type; at least she bore him a child. Though she probably didn't join Reed in his work, she was named accessory in an 1874 stage holdup in which Jim Reed was killed. Legend has it that she refused to identify his body so the deputy who shot him couldn't claim a bounty. The community around Belle's ranch was letting her know that they didn't like what she did to the neighborhood, so Belle moved to Oklahoma. There she proceeded to take care of herself quite well by dealing in stolen horses. Any horse thief who happened by knew where he could find a buyer for his merchandise. In 1880, Belle married Sam Starr, a Cherokee renegade, and their farm in Arkansas, which was on an Indian reservation, became a hideout for Jesse James and others. She did join in on the fun, finding an occasional bout of horse stealing particularly enjoyable. On one horse raid, she was finally caught and jailed for nine months, the only time one of her plentiful indictments actually led to prison. In 1889, Belle was shot in the back, one rumor making the cowardly killer her son, Edward Reed.

Most Successful Female Swindler
THÉRÈSE DAURIGNAC

❦ For twenty-five years, from 1878 to 1902, this French-peasant-born-but-determined-to-do-better girl lived as the heir to the vast but highly contested fortune of Robert Henry Crawford, the late American multi-millionaire—or so it was believed. Poor Mr. Crawford's wishes were just having an awful time being carried out. Seems that every time Thérèse was about to receive her inheritance, two nasty nephews found another court to say that *they* should have the money. And so poor Thérèse would find herself in a temporary bind, needing to borrow funds against her prospective inheritance once again. This went on for twenty-five years to the tune of an estimated $11 million, as well as ten suicides among the people who had loaned her money, when someone finally thought to check into the validity of the Crawford fortune. No such person . . . no money. The French, who seem to admire a good swindle, sentenced Thérèse and her husband to only short terms in prison.

Woman Who Went Farthest on Promises
GOLDBRICK CASSIE

❦ Cassie L. Chadwick, whose real name was Elizabeth Quigley, was a penniless but ingenious Canadian girl. About 1880, she started her fraudulent career by having calling cards engraved that said she was an heiress. Perhaps made numb and dumb by such candor, stores in plenty were happy to grant her credit . . . until she ventured into the United States and was arrested. Undeterred by a short spell in prison, she married a doctor after convincing him she was the illegitimate daughter of Andrew Carnegie. As "proof," she had faked promissory notes totaling $5 million from that industrial giant. They established themselves in Cleveland, Ohio, where all she had to do for several years was to show the notes to banks and officials would fall all over themselves to give her money—to the tune of over a million dollars a year. The first loans were repaid so no one suspected that later ones might not be so easily recovered. Indeed, no one thought to verify the promissory notes until finally one Boston bank did so as a matter of routine. Lo and behold, Andrew Carnegie had never heard of the girl. Word went out and at least one bank, Citizens National Bank of Oberlin, Ohio, folded because of Cassie Chadwick. In 1905, "Goldbrick Cassie" went to prison where she died after only two years.

Oldest Con Woman
ELLEN PECK née NELLIE CROSBY

❦ Nellie Crosby's first fifty years were spent as teacher, wife, mother, suburban matron, but that left her almost another forty to work her cons. Her new career started in 1880, when she stole some negotiable bonds from a millionaire and then got him to hire her to locate the thief. It took several months and several large expense payments from him before she disappeared. Located by the police four years later, she served her first prison term for her first con. Ellen Peck alternated cons with high living, with jail terms, and even with an occasional quiet bout at home with her husband. But she must have retained her charm because even at eighty-four she gained the deeds to several plantations from a Latin American businessman whom she blackmailed over his affair with her. Perhaps her major con, however, was accomplished with her husband as victim. Even after thirty years he never believed her guilty of more than being caught up . . . several times . . . by strange circumstances.

Last Victim of Jack the Ripper
MARY KELLY

❦ Twenty-four years old, pregnant, in debt, and drinking heavily, Mary Kelly returned to soliciting after a live-in man left her. On the night of November 9, 1888, she ignored the fact that four other girls had been mysteriously and gruesomely slain during the previous two months in her area of Whitechapel, London, and she went out to work because she was behind in her rent. A neighbor heard Mary come home in the middle of the night, probably with a man, and later heard some screams that were not too different from those often heard in that area. But the next morning, a messenger sent by her landlord to evict her found Mary Kelly's horribly mutilated body. Police figured that the murderer had spent at least two hours removing her breasts and kidneys. Mary was the only Ripper victim killed inside a room. Many Ripper devotees hold that the murder of Mary Kelly was a culmination of bloody destruction that sent him to suicide or else he became so blatantly insane that his relatives had him committed instantly to an asylum. Others held that Mary was the ultimate target of the killer. A less frequently touted theory calls for "Jack" to have been "Jill," perhaps a female abortionist or midwife.

First Woman to Be Convicted of Murder on
the Basis of Her Fingerprints
FRANCESCA ROJAS OF ARGENTINA

❦ Accused of murdering her two children because her lover wouldn't marry her if they were around, Francesca Rojas was convicted in 1892 on the evidence of her bloody fingerprints found on the door of her house. It was just her hard luck that Juan Vucetich, a police official in Buenos Aires, happened to be developing what became one of the major fingerprint classification systems and was on hand when her prints were found.

In a related case, the murder of a Mrs. Farrow of Deptford, England, was avenged in 1905 through the first European use of fingerprints. She and her husband managed a shop on the High Street. One morning when the shop failed to open on time, an investigating constable found them dead. The only lead of any kind was a blurred finger mark on an empty black metal cash box that should have contained about 13 pounds. Two brothers had been seen near the shop that morning. Scotland Yard, which had been recording prints just for identification purposes since 1902, took the men's prints and found a match. The prosecutor decided to introduce the match in court and see what would happen. Although the judge instructed the jury not to accept the print alone as evidence, the jury thought it sufficient and returned a verdict of guilty.

Most Famous "Murderer" Who Was Never Found Guilty
LIZZIE BORDEN

> Lizzie Borden took an axe
> And gave her mother forty whacks.
> When she saw what she had done
> She gave her father forty-one.

❦ Or so says the poem that has entered American folklore. But the jury acquitted her, probably because of her sex. The facts are these: On August 4, 1892, at 11 A.M., Lizzie called to the maid that she had just found the body of her father, Andrew, a prominent banker in Fall River, Massachusetts. A few minutes later, Lizzie sent the maid upstairs where she discovered the body of Mrs. Abby Borden, Lizzie's stepmother. Both had been murdered with a hatchet (but with only eleven and nineteen blows respectively). One week later, Lizzie was arrested, but only for the murder of her father; the double murder charge didn't develop until December. The prosecution claims at the trial the following year were that Lizzie had decided ahead of time to murder her parents because she hated her stepmother, that she alone had had the opportunity to murder them, that she had lied repeatedly in her initial testimony, and that she had burned a possibly bloodstained dress after the murders. A very effective defense argument and a statement from the judge that subtly implied her innocence led the jury to find her not guilty.

Robert Sullivan, a Massachusetts judge, in reviewing the entire case eighty years later, in *Goodbye Lizzie Borden*, summed up: "Can there seriously be any doubt that Lizzie Borden was guilty, proven so beyond a reasonable doubt? I think not." He attributes her acquittal to reluctance on the part of the jury to impose the mandatory death penalty on a woman.

Last Stagecoach Robber
PEARL HART

❦ In 1899, the imagination of this small-town Arizona girl, a cook in a mining camp, was caught by tales of the not-so-long-dead Wild West. With the assistance of reluctant but drunk Joe Boot, she stopped the Wells Fargo stage and lifted $431 from its passengers. She paid for her fun with two and a half years in Yuma Territorial Prison, where she was the only female prisoner.

Only Woman to Have Printed Invitations Sent Out for Her Execution
ELIZABETH POTTS

❦ Elizabeth and her husband Josiah of Elko, Nevada, were presumably happily married. But evidently Elizabeth liked a little variety, for on a trip to California in 1890 she married again, bigamously. Some months later she left Husband Number 2 and returned to Elko. He, however, followed her and found her living with Josiah, her real husband. The objections he made only got him murdered, mutilated, and buried beneath their house. Elizabeth and Josiah quickly left town, but not quickly enough to evade the law when new tenants in the house found the mutilated body. The town decided to make a showcase of the hanging of the Pottses and sent out printed invitations. The frilly touch turned out to be appropriate: Elizabeth Potts was the only woman in Nevada history to be executed.

Most Successful Murderer to Advertise for Her Victims
MRS. BELLE GUNNESS

❦ A mother of three living in Laporte, Indiana, Mrs. Gunness found that she loved the handyman. And, my, wasn't it nice of her husband to die very conveniently of a severe head wound! The coroner's jury ruled it an accident. Soon afterward she had an idea for advertising in Chicago papers for men interested in marriage. Several men answered her ads, they corresponded, and some even came to see her in Laporte (how they reacted at first sight of the five foot five inch tall, two hundred eighty pound woman is not recorded). But they stayed around long enough to find murder, not marriage. Not just for the fun of it, but for the funds the men were bringing to help the poor widow woman with her mortgage. "Come prepared to stay forever," she wrote one suitor lovingly. On April 28, 1908, the Gunness farmhouse burned. Investigators found not just a woman and three children but, slowly, horrifyingly, the artifacts and remains of perhaps thirteen men. Thirteen bodies which had been beheaded, dismembered, and buried in quicklime (which, Belle didn't know, actually preserves instead of destroying). But strangest of all, the female body found with three children could not have weighed more than one hundred and fifty pounds. The authorities accepted the body as Belle's and looked no further for the estimated $30,000 taken from the victims. But Ray Lamphere, the lover/handyman, died in jail claiming that somewhere far away, Belle

Gunness was living the good life on the $30,000 she was supposed to have shared with him.

Only Mother and Daughter Spies to Be Executed
MATA HARI AND HER DAUGHTER BANDA

🥄 Mata Hari was born Margaretha Geertruida Zelle in the Netherlands. Like her real name, the real facts about her were all rather dull—certainly not living up to the image that Greta Garbo later gave her—except for the indisputable one that she wandered the World War I capitals of Europe, dancing, rather badly, almost naked and was eventually shot as a spy. She did live in the "mysterious East"—in Java with her much older, alcoholic, soldier husband, Campbell MacLeod. And there she learned a bit of the beautiful Balinese temple dancing. She left her husband (who later divorced her) and her daughter and ventured to Paris, arriving transformed into the Indian sacred dancer, Mata Hari, a name she said meant "Eye of the Dawn." Her "sacred" dancing demanded nudity and could be done only before a select few, who paid well for the privilege. Turn-of-the-century Paris found her fascinating . . . at least for a few years. When her lovers began to dwindle in number, she took off for Berlin. It was in Germany that high-up army officers began to remove money from intelligence funds to pay for her favors: What the crown prince could delight in, they could, too. She, in return, agreed to report what scraps of information came her way. She may have gone briefly to espionage school but if so, the lessons didn't take: Little of what she learned in bed had much military value. In 1915, she returned to Paris, but the French had been warned that the exotic dancer was probably a spy. She was watched as she dispatched messages to Germany through the diplomatic pouches of ambassadorial friends. Confronted by the French, "H21," as she was identified by the Germans, chose to work for them rather than be deported. Belgium, Spain, the Netherlands, England—all saw double agent Mata Hari in the next months, presumably working for the French. But it was the Germans themselves who decided enough was enough. She was too costly for the value of information received. In Spain, she was given a check for services rendered that was easily traceable to Germany. She was arrested in Paris before she could spend it. Though various French officials-cum-lovers spoke for her at the trial and it was clear that she had never conveyed information of importance, Mata Hari was condemned to be shot. At dawn, on October 15, 1917, Mata Hari died before a firing squad at Vincennes.

Banda, the daughter Mata Hari had abandoned in Java, grew up to become a renowned hostess, without revealing who her mother was. Her uncle blackmailed her into using her parties to spy for the Japanese who had invaded Indonesia at the beginning of World War II. But she also spied for the Dutch underground against the Japanese. Later she was very influential in gaining independence for her nation from the Dutch. In 1950, this time probably working for the United States, she learned in Korea of the plans for the Communist invasion of the South by the North, though officials didn't believe her in time to act. Caught by the North Koreans, she, like her mother, was shot at dawn, but without benefit of official trial.

(Note: There's a fair chance that Banda was in no way really related to the famous Mata Hari but that saying so gave her an exoticism she enjoyed. Even if that is the case, there's no real evidence as to the identity of the woman who was shot. And why spoil a good story?)

Last Woman Convicted of Cattle Rustling
ANNA RICHEY

❦ A cultured, well-to-do divorcee living in Wyoming, Mrs. Richey changed character when she went to work on her ranch in boots and overalls. Folks thereabouts were used to seeing her working with the cattle and so gave it no thought when one day in 1919 she single-handedly drove thirty-two head of cattle into the railway town of Fossil, loaded them aboard a train, and shipped them to Nebraska. But when neighbors counted their own cattle, they accused her of rustling. A masked man shot Mrs. Richey on the way to her trial. When she recovered, she was found guilty of altering eight brands and was sentenced to six years in prison. She was allowed to return, on bond, to her ranch to settle her affairs. There she died, poisoned, some say, by a mysterious stranger.

Most Successful Female Swindler
NOT to Play the Role of Heiress
MARTHE HANAU

❦ A Parisian who married into a vaguely monied family, Marthe Hanau watched her not-very-clever husband lose both his and her money through stock investments. She noted that what one loses, another gains and decided that from then on she would always be the gainer. In 1925 she opened a small brokerage firm which published a tipster's sheet—a sheet that grew increasingly powerful in a patriotic France charmed by a broker who claimed to buy only French stocks and to return a 40 percent yield. Hundreds of investors began to send their funds to Mrs. Hanau to manage. She soon had almost five hundred employees, sixty thousand investors, and a public endorsement by major governmental figures. Soon, too, however, rumors of bribery among officials (carried out by her ex-husband and close partner, Lazare Bloch), plus the story that the government was going broke—not a terribly uncommon event for the French government— sparked an investigation. Marthe was arrested for swindling. Within minutes of getting their hands on her papers, government investigators discovered that indeed she was a swindler . . . of the first order. New investors had been paid dividends from old investors' capital so that confidence in her firm was maintained and more money flowed in that for some reason didn't pay dividends quite so promptly. The final figure for the bankruptcy court was a deficit of 28 million francs. At least seven investors committed suicide and the government fell.

During the long court proceedings, Marthe Hanau sued everyone who appeared against her, including one judge when some of her papers disappeared from his courtroom. She and her cronies were denied bail, so she retaliated by going on a hunger strike. After twenty-five days of starvation, she still had the strength one night to escape the prison hospital where they had been trying to force-feed her. But all she did was find a taxi that carried her around town for a while and then returned her to the original prison. Two days later she was released on monumental bail. When the five-month trial in which she had served as her own lawyer finally ended, she was found guilty. On appealing the short sentence she received, this amazing woman was let go during the appeal process, free to open a new brokerage house, which advised its clients on the basis of what the gods—according to Hanau—had in store for the market. Her luck was good and investors' capital flowed back. But three years later the slow appeal process finally caught up with her, and the sentence was increased, just because she had appealed (this is one of the peculiarities of the French judicial system). In February 1935, Marthe Hanau was finally sent to prison where, four months later, she committed suicide.

Most Notorious American Female Criminal
"MA" BARKER

☙ Mother of four sons, Ma Barker planned their bank robbing and other criminal activities in the 1920s and thirties. Born Arizona Donnie Clark (often called "Arrie"), her little girl's heart and imagination were drawn toward Jesse James, who was killed when she was ten years old. Marriage to a farm laborer didn't fulfill her fantasies but did produce four boys who quickly learned that stealing could bring some nice things into their drab lives and few reprimands from Ma, as long as they went to church with her each Sunday. The first real arrest came for oldest son Herman at age sixteen. The ruckus Ma raised in the police station prompted the police to release him in order to get rid of her. A few more such episodes and Ma elected to make a fresh start in Tulsa, Oklahoma. There youngest son Freddie spread the word that their home was available as a hideout for men on the run. And from these fugitives the boys learned a great deal. Son Lloyd robbed a post office and spent the next twenty-five years in federal prison at Leavenworth, effectively eliminating him from the family picture. Son Arthur, called Doc, killed a nightwatchman and spent the next thirteen years in prison, getting out just in time for the denouement of the family enterprise. Next Freddie went to prison, leaving only Herman free, but he died in 1927 after a high-speed police chase; he probably turned his own gun on himself, though Ma never believed that. Ma, figuring she might as well be completely alone, left her ineffectual husband, George, and earned her living running a hideout hotel for wanted criminals. In 1931, she was successful in getting Freddie released from prison, which he left with a new friend, Alvin Karpis. Al and Freddie, under Ma's planning, began a series of robberies and rather indiscriminate killings. Along the way, Ma had Arthur Dunlop, a lover of whom she had tired, eliminated by a willing friend—just as a favor, you understand. The group then moved to Minnesota where the Green Lantern Club in St. Paul became the headquarters of a larger gang. There they would return for "R and R" after bank robbing forays around the country. Then, at Ma's suggestion, they took up kidnapping. It was not one of her better ideas since it exposed them to the FBI and their carefully preserved anonymity was destroyed. In 1935, an informer helped agents capture Doc in Chicago; a map in his apartment led them to Florida where Ma and Freddie were hiding. FBI agents surrounded their resort cottage on Lake Weir and fired into the cottage for forty-five minutes. The two bodies were completely riddled. One bullet was found to have gone so directly into Ma's heart that it seems likely she committed suicide. Fourteen years later, son Lloyd (remember him?), released from federal prison, was murdered by his wife. The End.

Most Infamous Female of a Male-Female Pair
of Crooks That Was Not Really a Twosome
BONNIE PARKER

❦ Bonnie Parker, whose husband was doing a ninety-nine-year-term for murder, would freely sleep with just about anyone but not so her friend Clyde: He had learned quite early in jail that he was a homosexual and liked it that way. But sometimes during their two-year spree of murder, bank robbery, and general mayhem, they would share a sexual object . . . as when they kidnapped a young gas station attendant, kept him tied up and both repeatedly raped him. Or so he said when he was caught by the police for participating in a robbery. Another friend, Ray Hamilton, often joined them in their work, keeping Bonnie contented at the same time. Their work, primarily bank robbery, wasn't terribly efficient. In try after try, they never netted more than $1500 at a time and usually managed to kill someone while at it. As big-time crook Dillinger reportedly complained, "They're giving bank robbery a bad name." Movie to the contrary, Bonnie was not a very pleasant person, and she and Clyde were missed by practically no one when, in 1934, near Gibland, Texas, a Texas Ranger and his posse poured almost two hundred bullets into the twosome.

First Woman to Make the FBI's
Ten-Most-Wanted List
RUTH EISEMANN-SCHIER

❦ Ruth Eisemann-Schier and two men were accused in 1968 of kidnapping Barbara Jane Mackle, daughter of a Florida millionaire, and holding her for half a million dollars in ransom. The girl was buried in a box with air holes and provisions. After eighty hours of terror, she was released in a wooded area near Atlanta, Georgia. G. S. Krist, an escaped convict, was quickly caught with most of the money on him. Three weeks later, in Norman, Oklahoma, Ruth Eisemann-Schier was captured. She pleaded guilty and was sent to prison.

Only Woman to Sue a Lover for
Giving Her a Venereal Disease
MARGARET HOUSEN

❦ In 1970, Ms. Housen, a resident of Washington, D.C., had an affair with Angier St. George Biddle Duke, son of an ambassador. He passed a case of gonorrhea on to her and she was told by her physicians that she would most likely be unable to have children. She entered suit against Biddle Duke in his home state of Wyoming and told her story to a fascinated small-town jury. Ms. Housen was awarded $1.3 million in damages.

Only Woman to Be Awarded Damages for
Being Turned into a Nymphomaniac
by an Accident
GLORIA SYKES

❦ Just slightly injured by a San Francisco cable car, Ms. Sykes later sued on a claim that the accident had caused a psychological affliction requiring her to have sex with just about any man who came her way. The court, enchanted, awarded her $50,000 in damages, perhaps so she could continue her therapeutic activity in comfort.

First Woman to Put a Price
on the Pain of Rape
MARY KNIGHT

❦ Taken prisoner by two men on a Washington, D.C., street in 1972, Mary Knight was pushed into a car, taken into Virginia, and raped a number of times. The two men were tried and sentenced to prison but Mrs. Knight found little satisfaction in that. As she told *The National Observer*, she finally decided to sue for damages because "I just wanted to see if society would put a price on what they did to me, the hurt and the pain and the mental anguish." In January 1976, a Montgomery County, Maryland, court found in her favor, awarding her $40,000 in compensatory damages and $350,000 in punitive damages. She had no real hope of ever getting the money, but she was satisfied that her point had been made.

Only All-Woman U.S. Supreme Court

❦ On February 16, 1973, a mock court was held across the street from the Supreme Court Building in Washington, D.C. Nine women from the National Organization for Women dressed in robes and read a script to indicate how silly it would be if laws were made, enforced, and interpreted only by women. The hypothetical case was *Adam and His Brothers against the United States*, the issue being whether men are subject to laws made by women. For example: "In the lower federal court, our worthy sister Justice pointed out that these men, while protesting government process, are using the very system against which they protest, and expecting it to protect them. The attorney for Adam and his brothers instructs the Court to take judicial notice of the fact that they have no other means available to them for their redress of grievances. She also instructs the court to take judicial notice of some of the reasons why these men are not present in greater numbers on the various benches in the U.S.: they are encouraged at a very young age to concentrate heavily on their appearance, keeping flat stomachs and luxuriant hair; they are taught to be pleasing at all times to women, and apparently, many women do not feel that being a judge is one of the things a manly man should do; they are pressured to marry at a young age, to a successful woman, and often this liaison is dominated by a concentration on the wife and her career needs, with moves across the country to improve the wife's professional status, and use of the family resources to aid the wife in her success, with the result being that the man frequently finds, upon reaching his thirties, that he has very few opportunities to strike out on his own, in general, and in specific, to enter such occupations as politics or government."

First American Female Police Officer
Killed in the Line of Duty
GAIL A. COBB

❦ Ms. Cobb, a probationary officer and mother, was walking her beat in the downtown area of Washington, D.C. on September 20, 1974, when a man approached and said he had just seen another man run into an underground garage carrying a gun. Officer Cobb knew that police in the neighborhood were already chasing two men who had been foiled in a savings and loan holdup. She went into the garage and met the gunman as he came out of a washroom. He shot before she could draw her revolver. She fell, and he ran out, only to be forced to surrender a few minutes later. At funeral services for Officer Cobb, the District of Columbia Police

Department chaplain said, "It is now an established fact that a criminal makes no distinction between the sexes."

Only Woman Swindler to
Be a Con Man—Literally
"MRS. G. ELIZABETH CARMICHAEL"

🐛 As president of the Twentieth Century Motor Car Corp., "Mrs. Carmichael" approached the public in 1974 for funds to develop a three-wheeled car that would cost less than $2000 and would get seventy miles to the gallon of gas. Energy- and money-hungry investors came out of the woodwork and invested $30 million. The figure—supplied by Mrs. Carmichael—turned out to be considerably less than a million dollars and Mrs. Carmichael turned out to be less than truthful in another way. "She" was Jerry Dean Michael, a transsexual who claimed to have been through at least part of the sex change surgery to become Geraldine Elizabeth. Allowed to appear in court as a woman, she was convicted on thirty-one charges of theft, securities fraud, and conspiracy.

Broadway's Biggest Winner . . . Then Loser
ADELA HOLZER

🐛 Adela Holzer was a theatrical producer of at least a dozen Broadway shows, including the incredibly successful 1967 production of *Hair*, which multiplied her $57,000 investment to $2.5 million. But then in the 1970s, the Spanish-born entrepreneur switched her activities from investing her third husband's money to investing money contributed by many other people in a variety of importing and real estate schemes . . . at least, supposedly investing it. In 1977 her pyramidal house of cards collapsed, when new investors failed to provide sufficient funds to create "earnings" for earlier investors. The gig was up and Mrs. Holzer was indicted on 248 counts of fraud, eventually being convicted of grand larceny. All during the growing public scrutiny of her affairs, indictments, bankruptcy proceedings, and trials, the overconfident confidence woman was also at work on her autobiography with the somewhat worrisome title of *If at first. . . .*

Only Woman Reporter to
Report Her Own Rape
CAROLYN CRAVEN

🐛 For several years police in Berkeley, California, had been seeking a rapist they called Stinky, a large, black man with a memorable chemical odor on his body. Ms. Craven, a reporter on the staff of TV station KQED, had reported on Stinky's activities several times. Then, in January 1978, her bedroom was broken into early one morning by an odiferous man. For two hours or more Stinky assaulted the woman, threatened her six-year-old son's life, and ordered her to act as if she were enjoying it all. Ms. Craven kept her wits cool, consciously absorbed all the information she could about her attacker, and then when he left, she rushed to a neighbor and phoned the police. The reporter talked freely to the police and press, hoping by that to help other rape victims, publicly acknowledging the feelings of humiliation, guilt, violation. She even allowed herself to be hypnotized in the hope that police might gain additional clues about the rapist from her subconscious. She also went immediately into psychiatric care because the coolness she had maintained during the assault had left her with deep feelings of guilt. "I used to be an independent woman. But I've been robbed of my freedom to come and go." She told reporters, "Fighting back is the only way I can handle this violation of my life."

6

AMAZONS

First Example of
"I Did It with My Little Hatchet"
JEANNE LAISNÉ

❦ Jeanne Laisné, perhaps Fourquet, was best known as Jeanne Hachette for her heroism with a little hatchet. On a summer day in 1472, her French city of Beauvais was attacked by troops of Charles the Bold. That particular Duke of Burgundy was working to free his dukedom from the control of France, by, among other methods, trying to capture other parts of France. Beauvais was on the agenda. The populace of Beauvais, however, resisted mightily because Charles had a history of massacring all whom he conquered. The defenders of the castle were definitely losing. In fact, a Burgundian had reached the battlements and actually planted Charles's flag when a teenage girl pushed him off to the moat below and chopped down the hated flag with her little *hachette*. Heartened by her action, the soldiers and citizens succeeded in repelling the Burgundians, who called a halt to their intrusion into France. Louis XI promptly came to an agreement (albeit short-lived) with Bold Charles, organized a procession honoring Jeanne (which is still held in Beauvais), and rewarded her liberally.

Only Woman to Receive Papal Permission to
Wear Men's Clothing
CATOLINA DE ERANSO

❦ A Spanish convent girl who sought escape from her dull life, Catolina dressed as a boy and joined an expedition to the New World in the 1500s. She probably achieved the rank of lieutenant. On her return to Europe, the story of her adventure became known and she was called the Nun Lieutenant. Pope Urban VIII, charmed by her, gave her permission to wear male clothing for the rest of her life.

Most Useful Self-Immolation of a Woman
COUNTESS ZRINYI OF HUNGARY

❦ When Suleiman the Magnificent, leader of the Turkish Empire in its heyday, failed to receive a monetary tribute due him from Austria, he, though seventy-seven, set out to take Vienna. But something happened on the way: the troops ran into the fortress at Szigetvar (also called Szigeth) in

Croatia, where Count Zrinyi was in command. For weeks the Turks besieged the town and fortress, gradually taking over. The Count's men tried to escape but were killed in the attempt, leaving the fortress easily open to conquest. Three thousand Turks stormed the interior where the wives, or widows, of the soldiers waited their fate. Countess Zrinyi, unable to yield quietly to fate, stood at the powder magazine in the heart of the fortress. As the enemy slashed at her with their knives, she lit the powder. The fortress exploded and the thousands of invaders died with the Countess. As it turned out, Suleiman himself had died several days earlier and the mass deaths were sufficient to turn the Turks homeward.

Most Determined Female Fighter Against
European Colonization of Africa
NZINGHA MBANDE
(a.k.a. Ana de Souza Nzinga)

❦ Sister to the king of Ngola (now Angola), in 1621 Nzingha acted as her brother's representative in arranging a peace treaty with the Portuguese. A skilled negotiator, she succeeded in winning an agreement to keep Ngola an independent monarchy, even though at times she had to sit on the back of a maid-in-waiting when no chair was provided for her. She capped the negotiations by being baptized. But three years later, after her brother died and she became queen, the Portuguese reneged on the agreement, knowing that she would not be as easily manipulated as her brother had been. The Portuguese sent an army after her, and her own army retaliated (it is probable that her army was in great part female). Not liking the European examples she saw, Queen Nzingha renounced her earlier conversion to Christianity, and adopted ritual cannibalism. In coming years, she fought as she could, working all the time to build an alliance of other kingdoms sworn to support her (some, admittedly, joined the alliance only because she forced them to). Eventually, though, the might of Portugal triumphed. In 1635 she was returned to her throne but was again forced to flee into the jungle when she refused to swear allegiance to Portugal. Before Nzingha died at eighty-one years of age she saw the coasts of her land firmly in the control of outsiders, but she reverted to the outsiders' religion in her last years and was buried in the habit of a nun.

Only Pregnant Woman to Hold Off
a Siege of Her Castle
BRILLIANA, LADY HARLEY

❦ Lady Harley was resident in Brampton castle in Shropshire, during the English Civil War when being neighbors meant nothing if you had dissenting religious views. Continuously weak, ill with some unknown malady, and pregnant, Lady Harley made no effort to hide her Puritan sentiments from the Royalists who resided all around her. Her husband, Sir Robert, was often away, working with the Parliament in London. As the threats to the castle occurred more and more frequently, most of the servants abandoned Lady Harley. Occasionally messengers would enter the castle and be unable to leave because of the continuing siege. By February 1643 the castle was virtually a prison. Her husband and son had been indicted in absentia and she was charged with shielding enemies of the king. In July the neighborly sniping stopped and an army moved in to surround the castle—four hundred horse soldiers and three hundred foot soldiers. Brilliana refused to surrender. Her cattle were "taken into custody." The outbuildings were burned. One of Brilliana's spies reported that the Cavaliers were preparing fire grenades, so she had the building where the work was being done destroyed. Day by day, Lady Harley managed to protract the negotiations, forcing the Royalists to send to their superiors for responses to her offers. But as the men began to shell the castle in earnest, Brilliana's delaying tactics worked: Parliamentary forces drew up behind them and the enemy was routed, outdone by a woman. However, just a month later, the course of battle reversed itself, and as the Cavaliers drew near Brampton again, Brilliana died of the lingering illness that had troubled her for so long. Her people held out for six months before the castle was burned, and Brilliana's remains with it.

First Canadian Heroine
FRANÇOISE-MARIE JACQUELIN, MME DE LA TOUR

❦ A struggle between Mme de la Tour's husband and Charles de Menou d'Aulnay for control of the Saint John Region went on for a number of years in the mid-seventeenth century. In that time she served as courier, chartering ships to carry her rapidly to and from France where she hired soldiers and petitioned the king. In early 1645, her husband left the fort to go to Boston for aid. D'Aulnay, hearing that his enemy was gone, set on the fort with two hundred men. Mme de la Tour took command and, against overwhelming odds, kept the fighting going for four days. In the end, however, she was forced to surrender. D'Aulnay promptly forgot his promise of clemency, built a gallows, and hanged the men of the De la Tour fort. Mme de la Tour was forced to watch, a rope around her own neck. She died soon after, before her husband returned.

Indian Woman to Cause the
Pilgrims the Most Trouble
WETAMAO OF THE WAMPANOAGS

❦ Daughter-in-law to Massasoit, the Pilgrims' friend, Wetamao blamed the English when Alexander, her husband, died of a fever; she claimed the

English had poisoned him. The braves of her tribe regarded her as the squaw sachem, or chief, and followed her lead. Philip, Alexander's brother, spent years building resentment against the colonists, always encouraged by Wetamao. Finally, in 1675, King Philip's War began. Taken captive, Wetamao tried to escape but drowned in a swift river. And the upshot was that the Wampanoags and Narragansetts were broken up as tribes and the survivors sent to the West Indies as slaves.

First Woman to Receive a
Bounty for Killing Indians
HANNAH DUSTIN

❦ On March 15, 1697, just six days after the birth of her twelfth child, the Indians attacked Hannah Dustin's village of Haverhill in Massachusetts Bay Colony—as they were wont to do during King William's War. Mr. Dustin got most of the children to safety, but Hannah was captured, along with her newborn baby, the village nurse, and a few others. Marching the captives toward Canada, the Indians stopped only briefly to kill the baby by throwing it against a tree. Arriving at an Indian village, the captives found a young boy who had been a prisoner for several months. He and Hannah pretended to be friendly with some of the village Indians and they learned how to use a tomahawk. One morning before dawn, she and the lad attacked the sleeping Indians with hatchets. Hannah Dustin herself killed nine of them. The captives escaped, carrying the scalps of their captors, in case no one believed their story. In appreciation, the General Court in Boston granted Hannah twenty-five pounds.

Longest Lasting All-Woman
Army in Recent Times
THE AMAZON CORPS OF DAHOMEY

❦ It's not known how much reality there is to the legend of the Amazons, the tribe of powerful women who fought wars against ancient Greece. But the French learned in the eighteenth and nineteenth centuries of the very real existence of a corps of fighting women in the African nation of Dahomey. The Amazon Corps functioned as part of the king's fighting troops from at least the 1700s to about 1900. The women, selected as young girls, were generally the unattractive ones who, though officially ranking as the king's wives, did no duty as such. To protect their virginity, the death penalty was exacted when men were caught consorting with the female soldiers. At their peak in the mid-1800s, the Amazons may have numbered close to 10,000 officers and "men."

Only Female Sculptor/Spy
PATIENCE LOVELL WRIGHT

🐝 Around 1769, Patience Lovell Wright's husband died and she began sculpting in wax. Soon she was taking on commissions, which made her the first American professional sculptor. She quickly made a name for herself by the original idea of sculpting well-known, living figures instead of the previously popular criminals and allegorical figures. She left her home in Bordentown, New Jersey, for England in 1772 where her wax portraits became popular; her head of William Pitt was placed in Westminster Abbey. There she supposedly used her artistic success to mingle with the mighty and then relayed what she learned of war plans to Benjamin Franklin in Paris. Some stories have her concealing the information on written notes sealed inside the wax heads she shipped to Philadelphia for the wax museum her sister ran there. The true extent to which she passed on secret information is not clear. When Mrs. Wright later tried her luck in Paris, she came up against the beginning of the wax sculpture dynasty of which Mme Tussaud was a part.

Most Thirst-Quenching War Heroine
MARY LUDWIG HAYS McCAULEY
(a.k.a. "Molly Pitcher")

🐝 During the American revolution, Mary McCauley's husband was a gunner stationed near Monmouth, New Jersey. On June 28, 1778, during the Battle of Monmouth, Mary helped the men by carrying water from a stream to the hot, weary soldiers. When she saw her husband fall, she dropped her pitcher, ran to his gun, and commenced firing. She kept up the heavy work throughout the battle. Thirty-six years later the Pennsylvania General Assembly granted her a small annuity for her "war work."

Most Confusing American
Female War Heroine
NANCY HART

🐝 It seems that she lived a long, a very long, and active life. But actually there were two Nancy Harts. Nancy Hart I was a Georgia patriot who, one day during the American Revolution, had a beautiful dinner prepared when Royalist soldiers barged into her home. As they helped themselves to the dinner, she grabbed a gun, shot one, and held the rest at bay until Patriot help arrived and hanged the men. During the Civil War, the town of LaGrange, Georgia, had the only female Confederate militia company; the women called themselves the Nancy Harts.

Nancy II was a Civil War woman of West Virginia who appears to have had a great deal of fun. She was acting as a guide for a Confederate captain one night when she was captured; the captain ran off in fear of his life. She convinced the Union soldiers that she was just a simple, innocent, beautiful, six-foot-tall, country lass and was released. (The "six feet" may be an item of the confusion because Nancy I was also described as being six feet tall *and* cross-eyed.) Nancy's continued activities caused Union leaders to put a $500 price on her head. In 1861, for example, she was captured and held in the attic of a house in Summersville, West Virginia. One of her guards threatened to throw her to the troops. After she escaped, she remembered that guard and persuaded her friends to attack Summersville. As the town burned, she kidnapped the guard who had teased her, put him in one of her dresses, and marched him for hours tethered behind her horse. Nancy Hart later made raids with a more useful purpose, that of obtaining morphine needed by the South.

First Woman to Serve as a
Regular American Soldier
DEBORAH SAMPSON

❦ Raised as an indentured servant because her widowed mother could not afford to keep her family together, Deborah became free at eighteen to live her own life. And live it she did. She went to Bellingham, Massachusetts, in 1782 and, dressed in men's clothes, enlisted in the army as Robert Shurtleff. Working primarily as a scout, she fought in several battles of the Revolutionary War. Wounded in one battle, she managed to care for herself, thus keeping her secret. But eventually she became ill with a fever, and a surgeon in Philadelphia discovered her true identity. He told no one until she was through recuperating, during which time "Robert" had to contend with a girl falling in love with him and his strong, manly features. Finally the doctor informed the army that a woman had been serving as a soldier for two years, and Deborah received an honorable discharge. She married Benjamin Gannett and became a lecturer on her life as a soldier. The State of Massachusetts granted Deborah Gannett a small pension, which was later added to by the U.S. government at the behest of hero Paul Revere. After her death, a special Act of Congress gave her husband a pension to compensate for the medical bills that stemmed from her military service. The pension he received was twice the size hers had been.

Most Useless Self-Sacrifice to
End Political Bloodshed
CHARLOTTE CORDAY

❦ Appalled by the Reign of Terror, twenty-five-year-old Mlle Corday saw the conservative Girondists as the hope of France. But in 1793 they were overthrown in the National Convention by Robespierre, Danton, and Jean

Paul Marat, leaders of the radical and blood-thirsty Jacobins. Charlotte, deciding to kill Marat publicly, found he had retired to his bathtub to fight a skin problem with warm water; there he entertained his callers. She gained entry as a Jacobin sympathizer and murdered Marat with a butcher knife. Quickly caught and tried, Charlotte Corday, who sought eternal recognition for her deed, had her portrait painted by the German artist Hauer before she was guillotined. The Jacobins, of course, were able to use Marat's murder as a rallying point that brought many to their cause. The few remaining Girondists had to go into hiding until after Robespierre's own downfall the next year. In addition, reaction to Corday's deed started a revulsion toward women becoming involved in politics.

Only Western "Queen of the Arabs"
LADY HESTER STANHOPE

🐝 A niece of British Prime Minister William Pitt, Lady Hester Stanhope lived with him as a young woman, handling his affairs and serving as his official hostess at Downing Street. When he died in 1806 and the British government declined to recognize her services with more than a small annuity, she, bored, boarded a ship for the East, with a physician, companion, and servant. The ship was wrecked off the island of Rhodes, and Hester, who lost all her belongings, donned the Turkish male clothing she would wear the rest of her life. Her entourage made its way east through the desert, eventually reaching the ancient oasis city of Palmyra in Syria, making her the first European woman since Roman times to go to Palmyra. In Damascus she became, as she described herself, "the oracle of the place, and the darling of all the troops, who seem to think I am a deity because I can ride, and because I bear arms." Lady Hester was regarded, at least by her own reckoning, as the "Queen of the Arabs." Eventually she settled in Djonni, a half-ruined convent on the slopes of Mount Lebanon. In 1813 she became a victim of the plague, which probably left her further deranged. In following years it was her great delight to combat the authority of the British consul among the Arabs, but it was to the consul she would go when her bills needed paying. Gradually Parliament tired of having Lady Hester as a permanent, expensive ward and decreed the end of all financial support. The remainder of her life was spent in poverty. She beat her household slaves, so they often ran away. Probably food was provided her by the Arabs who came to regard the mystical mad woman as a kind of prophetess. When she died in 1839, her house was promptly looted by her neighbors. Only the forbearing British consul and an American missionary saw the "Queen of the Arabs" into her grave. (*The Dictionary of National Biography*, equally forbearing, more simply categorizes her as "eccentric.")

Only Woman to Single-Handedly Save a
Struggling New Nation
MATILDA NEWPORT

❦ Matilda Newport, an elderly but intrepid woman, was among the free American blacks who tried to form a new nation in Equatorial Africa. Neighboring West African tribes resented the colonists' presence and decided to destroy the community. On December 1, 1822, they were on the verge of massacring the colonists, when Mrs. Newport sauntered out of the stockade, pipe in hand. She strolled over to the part of the compound where native warriors were busily inspecting a cannon the colonists had been forced to abandon. Casually dropping a burning coal from her pipe into the powder chamber, the old lady moved off, unnoticed. The cannon boomed and those warriors who could still move fled. The offensive was broken, and the tiny but determined colony was saved, though it never became the "little black America" the original colonists had envisioned.

First Woman to Be Awarded
a Congressional Medal
MILLY FRANCIS

❦ Called the "Oklahoma Pocahontas," Milly Francis was rewarded by Congress for saving the life of Captain Duncan McKrimmon of the Georgia militia. Milly, three-quarter Creek Indian, was living at the time (1817) in Florida, which was not yet part of the United States. One day she heard the Seminoles' shouts of joy at taking a captive during one of their regular raids. She persuaded them to release him. Captain McKrimmon lived with her tribe until he was traded to the Spanish and then ransomed. Duly impressed by Milly, he later returned and proposed marriage to her. She turned him down, marrying instead an Indian from Georgia, whose tribe was soon forced to move to Oklahoma. Years later, an army major met Milly there and heard her story. The major reported her poverty to Washington where Congress granted her a pension and a medal. The bureaucracy, however, neglected to let her know until she was dying of tuberculosis, and even the funds arrived too late to help.

Largest Female Army
THE CHINESE ARMY OF NANKING

❦ During the T'ai P'ing Rebellion (1851–1864) the leaders of the insurgents established the "Heavenly Kingdom of Great Peace," which spent its twelve years of power at war. Men and women were regarded as complete equals but their armies were kept separate. A vast army of perhaps five hundred thousand women was formed in Nanking, the "heavenly capital." It was organized into thirteen thousand-member brigades that were fully involved in all phases of the war, including the retreat when the part of China the rebels had taken was recaptured.

Only Woman to Claim Personal Responsibility for Important Civil War Military Strategy
ANNA ELLA CARROLL

🐦 Anna Ella Carroll, currently heralded as a military advisor to Abraham Lincoln and originator of the plan to send Union troops into Confederate strongholds via the Tennessee River, is often described as a woman who never got her due recognition. The documents of the time, however, don't support that view of Ms. Carroll.

Basically a political pamphleteer, this daughter of the governor of Maryland flitted around Washington when war broke out, writing in favor of the Union and presenting a strong argument that Secession was an unconstitutional act. In 1861 she took a trip to St. Louis with Lemuel Evans of the State Department. There she met a river pilot who, accepting her erroneously as an official emissary, described his idea of invading the South through the Tennessee River instead of the proposed Mississippi route. She presented the plan—plainly acknowledging it as someone else's—to the War Department. Troops did, indeed, move up the Tennessee under General Grant (who, it was later seen, had proposed the plan himself). The Confederacy was broken in the West.

In 1868, Ms. Carroll, who had long been trying to get money from the government for her earlier Union-oriented writing, tackled Congress with a new claim: that she had originated the Tennessee River strategy. And she wanted payment and recognition for it. She spent the next fourteen years bribing and cajoling witnesses to support her claim, and then thoroughly exaggerating any sign of weak support she got. Congress never acted.

Most Popular Teenage Spy
BELLE BOYD

🐦 Prompted, at age seventeen, to actively help the Confederate side in the American Civil War, she began making up to Union officers near her home in Martinsburg, Virginia (now West Virginia), and sending any informational tidbits she picked up to Confederate officers. The official reprimand she received was not the first notice she had had from the Union side: it had earlier taken her side when the young, beautiful girl shot a federal officer who had abused her and broken into her home. Nor would it be the last. The next time she was arrested, she was acting as an official Confederate intelligence courier for which she earned a week of comfortable imprisonment. Nothing daunted, Belle celebrated her return to Front

Royal, Virginia, by alerting General Jackson, who was preparing to retake that town, to the strength and placement of Union troops. That earned her considerable Confederate gratitude and the honor of being arrested on direct order of the Secretary of War. A month later she was freed in a prisoner exchange. This time the North kept a closer eye on her; when federal troops returned to Martinsburg from Gettysburg, she was arrested again as a precaution. Her six-month imprisonment in Washington was marked by a severe bout with typhoid fever. The end of 1863 found her banished to the South, but soon she took off for England, carrying secret Confederate dispatches. Her ship was captured by a Union blockade and taken to Boston, giving her time to destroy the information she carried. The Union, hoping to get rid of her once and for all, banished her, not south, but north to Canada. Belle Boyd had indeed got in the Union's way, but its officers found her ever-enchanting. When she died in 1900 after a full career as an actress and lecturer, veterans from the Union side who remembered her fondly carried her coffin to the grave.

Only Woman to Be Awarded
the Medal of Honor
DR. MARY E. WALKER

❦ This doctor who had refused to take her husband's name was already wearing trousers as a matter of course when she was officially commissioned as an assistant army surgeon early in the Civil War. She followed several battles through the South, serving when and as she could. But she had no official standing until late 1863 when General Thomas in Tennessee appointed her an assistant surgeon, to the dismay of most other medical officers. The following April she was captured behind the Confederate lines and sent to Richmond, Virginia. After four months of imprisonment she was exchanged for a Confederate doctor in what was probably the world's first exchange of a female prisoner for a male of equal rank. That fall she was finally granted a real service contract as an acting assistant surgeon. In 1865, when medals were being granted by President Johnson in a flurry of generosity, Dr. Walker received the Medal of Honor for special valor (presumably for her excursions behind enemy lines). She wore the medal for the rest of her life. When the medal winners came up for review in 1916 in an attempt to preserve the Medal of Honor as truly the highest decoration, her name was among nine hundred and eleven removed from the list because she had not been cited for specific acts of heroism. She died three years later, after a fall on the Capitol steps, where she was trying once again to get her medal restored. In a voluminous government publication of 1948, *The Medal of Honor of the United States Army*, her name is not even mentioned. However, in 1977 at the urging of numerous

Baby Doe Tabor: when the dream
was gone

Marie Blanchard: airborne bureaucrat

"Maids for Wives" arriving at Jamestown; a moment of hope

Hetty Green:
photographed in 1899
in her familiar black

Nellie Bly: she travels
fastest who travels with lots
of money

Margaret Slocum Sage:
she made giving fun

Coco Chanel: her scents and designs made sense

The Edenton Tea Party: as a political cartoonist saw it

Mary Dunhill: she put the business in her pipe and smoked it

Carry Nation: with hatchet and Bible and a vaudeville gig

Maggie Kuhn and friends: gray power at work

The women of Wyoming cast their ballots, courtesy of
Esther Morris

From left to right: Queen Liliuokalani, *a.k.a.* Lydia Dominis: ruler for two years, composer of "Alohe Oe" forever; Jeannette Rankin: a lifetime of nay-saying to war; Mrs. Woodrow Wilson: her power lay in keeping a low profile

Well-to-do women voting in brand-new New Jersey: they lost their franchise almost before they knew they had it

A moment at Mount Vernon: from left, Jawaharlal Nehru; his daughter, Indira Gandhi, later virtual dictator of India; Frances Bolton, perennial congressperson from Ohio; and Mme. Pandit, ambassador to just about everywhere

Belle Starr: Queen of the Stolen Horses

Pearl Hart: she didn't know the heyday of the stagecoach was over

Jeanne Hachette: it takes only a moment to make a heroine

people—congressmen, feminists, doctors—Dr. Walker's Medal of Honor was reinstated.

First Major Female Revolutionary in Russia
CATHERINE BRESHKOVSKY

🐦 Sometimes called the "grandmother of the Russian Revolution," Catherine Breshkovsky tried to help educate a number of peasants when they were freed from serfdom, in theory at least, in 1861. But her efforts were suppressed and some of the literate peasants were exiled to Siberia: legal freedom was one thing, letting the peasants understand their rights was something else. She finally accepted the fact that no real reform was intended, and she left her children to join the revolutionaries who were beginning to talk of overthrowing the czars. In the late 1870s, she was arrested and sent to Siberia as a political offender, first woman to be so condemned. For twenty-three years she remained in the frozen wastes, first as a convict working in the mines, then as an exile. Freed for a brief time after the turn of the century, she went to the United States where she became a popular lecturer. Back in Russia, she was arrested again and remained in exile until released by the Kerenski government after the overthrow of the monarchy. She spent the remainder of her life in Czechoslovakia.

Only Madams to Duel Each Other
MATTIE SILKS AND KATE FULTON

🐦 Keepers of rival brothels in the silver-boom city of Denver, Colorado, Mattie Silks and Kate Fulton were also both attracted to the same man, Cort Thompson. Mattie, a newcomer to town, madam since age nineteen (she was very proud of never having been a "girl," always a madam), regarded the athletic Mr. Thompson as hers, but Kate pursued him with all her talents unleashed. One fine summer day in 1877, probably by prearrangement, a number of the girls and their fanciers went on an outing beyond the city limits. They consumed lots of food and liquor, then Mattie and Kate lined up, blasted away at each other . . . and both missed. But cohorts of each took up the cudgels and a massive brawl followed. The only real injury was to the cause of it all, Cort Thompson, who received a bullet burn on the neck. There might not have been a winner that day, but Mattie got Cort in the end. She married him in 1884.

First Woman to Go over Niagara Falls
in a Barrel
ANNA EDSON TAYLOR

🐦 Anna Taylor went over the falls in a barrel on October 24, 1901, as a publicity stunt to raise money to pay off the mortgage on her farm.

Only Major Female Combat Forces in the
Twentieth Century
THE RUSSIAN WOMEN'S BATTALION OF
WORLD WAR I

❦ In 1915, when German forces almost effortlessly destroyed the weak and inefficient Russian war machine, and with it vast numbers of male troops, a Women's Battalion was formed under Commander Maria Botchkareva (or Bochkaryova) to go to the front. The determination of these women earned them the name "Battalion of Death." In November 1917 it was a remnant of the Women's Battalion, plus a few male cadets, who were guarding the Winter Palace where Aleksandr Kerenski was nursing the new Russian Republic into being when Lenin's followers broke in and, that night, proclaimed the new Soviet Union.

First Woman, as a Woman, to Be Made an
Officer of a Male Fighting Unit
LIEUTENANT FLORA SANDES

❦ In Serbia in 1915 Flora Sandes was serving as a volunteer nurse attached to a Serbian regiment when the colonel jokingly recruited her into the regiment. As they retreated from the Bulgarian advance, however, the joke became distinctly less funny and she had to go into action as a real recruit. On New Year's Day 1916, the colonel really promoted her to corporal, and soon sergeant. She was given a platoon, which, she wrote home, "treated her like a mascot." At Bitolj in Macedonia, Flora Sandes was severely wounded by a hand grenade. It was almost a year before she was back in action, and then the action was in the reverse direction—the Serbian troops were finally retaking their own land. Parliament recognized her military prowess by elevating her to the officers' corps in 1918. In 1922, Lieutenant Sandes was demobilized, but she remained in Yugoslavia where she married. In 1939, as Captain Sandes, she was recalled into the reserves. Her second war widowed her, and she returned to England to live out her life.

Most Famous Disappearance of a Woman
AMELIA EARHART

❦ In May 1937, five years after the transatlantic flight that made her the first woman to fly alone across the Atlantic Ocean, Amelia Earhart and her navigator, Fred Noonan, took off on what was to be a round-the-world flight, the first undertaken by a woman. They left on the twenty-eight-thousand-mile journey from California, went to Miami and then down through South America, across to Africa, and into Asia. On July 3, the U.S. Coast Guard cutter *Itasca*, stationed in the Pacific for the purpose of maintaining contact with Earhart, picked up what was to be her last transmission. Communications had not been very good but her messages made it appear that she had overshot tiny Howland Island in the South Pacific. She was flying at one thousand feet and running out of gas. No sound was heard from her àgain. The *Itasca* sent the dreaded word: "Believe [her] down. Am searching probable area and will continue."

Thousands of ships and planes took part in the search for Amelia Earhart, but eighteen months later she was officially declared dead: "Lost at sea." But not dead was the speculation. A 1943 film, *Flight for Freedom*, had Rosalind Russell portraying a woman pilot as deliberately leaving her announced course to fly across Japanese-held islands and then crashing into the sea rather than be captured. Amelia's mother was convinced that she had been on a mission for the U.S. government. In the 1960s, one author completely switched direction and declared that Amelia Earhart was alive and well and living in New Jersey. But in 1975, reporter Adela Rogers St. Johns wrote that she personally had seen Navy documents showing that Amelia Earhart had made the journey at the urging of the U.S. government to see if she could discover the state of Japan's preparedness for war. Mrs. St. Johns also wrote that just before departure, the flier had said to her, "Don't worry about me," something that Ms. Earhart would never normally have said. Backing up such speculation is a passage in Amelia Earhart's own journal, written just before the flight, and which can be interpreted in several ways; "Whether I was right or wrong leave till the end of the flight. If it is successful, the merits and demerits can be threshed out then. If not, someone else will do what I have attempted and I will pass the problem on to him—or her."

Only Actress to Be Awarded a Patent
for a Weaponry Item
HEDY LAMARR

❦ In 1942, she and composer George Antheil were granted a patent for a communications system to be used in controlling the movement of torpedoes. Its details were secret.

Only Woman to Be Awarded the
German Iron Cross
HANNA REITSCH

❦ A test pilot with an ability to withstand pressures generally destructive to humans, Hanna Reitsch was asked to volunteer to test personally the flight of the V-1 "buzz bomb." Germany wanted to use the V-1 against England but there were developmental problems: its wings kept falling off. Though the V-1s were supposed to be pilotless, a seat was carved out in the nose of one for her and she rode through several flights at four hundred miles per hour analyzing visually where the stresses were that caused the problem. The problem was corrected on the basis of her reports, and Germany began launching the bombs—made terrifying by their pulsing buzz followed by silence so that there was no anticipating where they would fall—toward England in June 1944. Within two months, however, Allied troops had overrun the launch sites. After the war, Hanna Reitsch returned to her first love, gliders.

Most Unusual Woman Spy
"ANNE"

❦ "Anne" was a British spy who gained information from all over Europe during World War II without ever leaving London. A trance medium, she had the extraordinary ability to project her mind to anywhere she chose, leaving her body behind. Her traveling mind could listen in on conversations, read and memorize documents, and in general gather information with amazing accuracy . . . and no danger. Bernard Hutton, a journalist who met the woman later and actually saw her demonstrate her incredible skill, wrote that, "Anne was sent on many 'mind-travelling' expeditions. Any information she brought back to British Secret Service headquarters was treated as respectfully as information provided by other spies. British political and military strategy was influenced and helped by Anne's reports."

Only Stripper to Be Made an Honorary
Brigadier General
SHERRY BRITTON

❦ President Roosevelt, in bestowing the honor on her during World War II, said it was for "keeping up the morale of our boys." Pinup pictures of the stripper were found wherever the boys went.

Woman to Make the Most Wartime
Crossings of the Atlantic
FERN BLODGETT

❦ During World War II all Canadian radio operators were transferred into the military and female ones were no exception. Radio operator Fern Blodgett became eligible in 1941 to take up a merchant marine position on the Norwegian cargo ship *Mosdale*. The following July she married the captain and set up housekeeping among her radio gear. During the war *Mosdale* crossed the Atlantic safely ninety-eight times. Fern Blodgett Sunde was aboard for seventy-eight of those dangerous journeys.

First Woman to Fly a Jet Plane
ANN BAUMGARTNER

❦ Enchanted by having once seen Amelia Earhart, Ann Baumgartner had learned to fly, and when World War II started joined the WASPs—the

Women's Air Force Service Pilots. She was sent to Wright Field in Ohio, the Army Air Corps' aeromedical facility, to test equipment for the WASPs. Among other jobs, she designed the first relief tube for women pilots. Within months she had been transferred to the fighter section where she was doing major flight tests for the Air Corps. One of the projects being worked on was the twin-engined P-59, the first American jet. One morning, in October 1944, her boss casually said, "Ann, why don't you take up the jet today?" She did, and became the first woman to fly a jet.

First Woman to Fly a Helicopter
in a Combat Zone
CAPTAIN VALERIE ANDRÉ

❦ Assigned to duty in Indochina in 1949, French neurosurgeon Valerie André quickly realized that a helicopter was vital for bringing the wounded out of the jungle. She returned to France, learned to fly the unruly craft, and flew one back to Indochina. In more than sixty-five missions, she flew through Vietminh fire, landed in any available jungle clearing, and returned more than one hundred and fifty wounded men to safety. Twice she made parachute jumps to reach men who could not be moved without first being operated on. In 1976, she was promoted to general, the first Frenchwoman to reach that rank. Her husband had retired with the rank of colonel.

Only Woman in the Siege of Dien Bien Phu
LIEUTENANT GENEVIEVE DE GALARD-
TERRAUDE

❦ When the Indochinese fortress was besieged by Vietminh forces on March 28, 1954, Lt. de Galard-Terraude, a flight nurse, was just beginning her second tour of duty flying evacuation flights of wounded. While at the fortress to pick up more injured men, her helicopter was damaged and she found herself stranded, the only female to assist nineteen doctors with almost twelve hundred wounded. On May 7, Dien Bien Phu fell to the invaders and she elected to stay with the wounded. Among the other honors bestowed on the "angel of Dien Bien Phu" after her release nineteen days later, was an official invitation from Congress to visit the United States, making her the first woman foreign national ever to receive such an honor.

Most Recent Female Army
THE BANDA BRIGADE

❦ In the 1960s there were reports out of Africa of a female fighting corps formed by Hastings Banda, the first Premier of Malawi, formerly Nyasaland. Supposedly they helped in the fight for independence and later were put to work guarding the boundary with Tanganyika.

Last Known Woman to Head
a Major Spy Network
ANGELA MARIA RINALDI

❦ Angela Maria Rinaldi was both an artist and a parachutist. Her husband, also a parachute expert and instructor, traveled around Europe to various NATO and national military bases for exhibition work. Using techniques provided by the Russians, he photographed bases, recorded technical conversations, and microfilmed plans, when possible. All were relayed to his wife back in Italy, as was information garnered from her agents in most other European and North African nations. In the early sixties, Italian security began to have suspicions about the Rinaldis. They started a long, long surveillance program that came to a head in 1967 when Angela directed her spy ring to try to kidnap Svetlana Stalin on her flight to political asylum in the West. The increased activity of the group caused by the attempt allowed counterintelligence to arrest Angela, her husband, her number one assistant, and several lesser lights. Others with diplomatic immunity were deported. The thirteen-year-reign of the "red czarina," as Angela was called, was at an end.

Only Nurse to Be Court-Martialed by the U.S.
Military in the Cause of the Vietnam War
LIEUTENANT SUSAN SCHNALL

❦ While serving in the Navy in 1968, Lt. Schnall hired a small airplane and bombarded all military bases in northern California with leaflets announcing an anti-Vietnam march. The Navy was not pleased. She later said that she had had some trouble getting into the Navy in the first place: "Because I wore a peace symbol, I had to have an extra interview to determine my suitability as a member of the military."

Only Soldier to Be a Beauty Queen
RINA MESSINGER
Miss Universe of 1976

❦ An Israeli army instructor, Rina Messinger was chosen in Hong Kong. During her reign, she refused to consider seriously the need for guards against possible terrorists. She was determined to "have a wonderful year," living in New York and doing very different things from the usual aeronautics teaching she had been doing in the military. There were no incidents during the year of her reign.

7

WITCHES AND HOLY WOMEN

Only Female Pope
POPE JOAN

❦ Well, it really depends on what you care to believe. A legend has held for well over five hundred years that a woman who had always lived as a man was elected pope between Leo IV and Benedict III, in the mid-800s, and that she ruled for two and a half years until she miscalculated her timing and gave birth to a boy baby during a public ceremony. At various times called Agnes or Gilberta, today she is known as Pope Joan, and is thought to have probably been of English parentage though born in Mainz, Germany, and to have gone to Rome as the lover of a monk, becoming a priest herself after his death. Her rise to the top must have been extraordinarily quick. Her reign as pope went well until she fell in love with her chamberlain. Bad planning occurred when she failed to leave the Vatican in time to bear her child in secret, and the son was born during a grand procession. The watching crowds, horrified at the sight of a new infant emerging from their pope's robes, stoned Joan to death. Legend says that no papal procession has ever again taken that particular street in Rome. Numerous writers, including one Calvinist, have tried to demolish the story of Pope Joan ever since it began the rounds. Modern research, however, shows no gap between the two male popes that might have been occupied by Joan. The entire legend may have developed from the story of a papal mistress.

Most Enterprising Use of a Playing Card
MRS. EDMONDS

❦ One night at the end of Queen Mary's reign, Mrs. Edmonds, a landlady of Chester, England, overheard the mayor talking with an honored guest who was on an errand for the queen. The courier said he was bearing the order to execute all known Protestants. Mrs. Edmonds, herself a secret Protestant, opened the box containing the order and replaced it with a playing card, appropriately, a knave of clubs. The messenger, never checking his box, carried it to Dublin and presented it formally to the viceroy. The card was discovered and the chagrined messenger was ordered back to London for a new copy of the order. But before he reached the Capital, the Queen was dead and Elizabeth had ascended the throne. She rewarded the quick-thinking Mrs. Edmonds with a life-time pension.

Most Awful Wedding Present Given by a
Mother to Her Daughter
CATHERINE DE MEDICI

❦ In 1572, Catherine de Medici's Catholic daughter Marguerite de Valois married Protestant Henry of Navarre in a ploy to cement religious relationships within France. Coligny, a Protestant leader whom Catherine feared, came to Paris because he was a friend of the bridegroom. Catherine took the opportunity to try to eliminate him. Four days after the wedding the attempt took place but Coligny was only wounded. Rumors immediately began to circulate that the Huguenots would retaliate by killing the royal family. Catherine, not an avid Catholic but very serious about threats to her power, rather forcibly urged her not-so-kingly son Charles IX to agree that religious coexistence could not last and that as many Huguenots as possible should be killed. Before dawn on St. Bartholomew's Day, August 24, 1572, just six days after the wedding, Coligny was murdered as a signal for blood to flow. Before the massacre ended about ten days later, more than fifty thousand French men, women, and children had died. Henry promptly turned Catholic out of self-preservation and remained one until he and his wife escaped to Navarre two years later. Always easy in his religious conscience, Henry easily reconverted to Catholicism some years later in order to solidify his claim to the French throne.

First American Woman to Be
Excommunicated
ANNE MARBURY HUTCHINSON

❦ A follower of John Cotton, the theologian who believed that no matter what a person's deeds he must achieve a state of grace in order to be saved, Anne Hutchinson extended the idea to mean that when God chose to dwell in men, men need not worry about transgressions on Earth. This was heresy to the Puritans, who believed firmly that man could only be saved through work and good deeds (hence, the well-known work ethic of our culture). In what may be regarded as the first American club, Anne began sharing her beliefs at weekly meetings of Boston women (and soon, men). The church, regarding her views as advocating permissiveness, stepped in. Soon the town was divided over Anne Hutchinson. In 1637, the orthodox group gained control of the General Court and indicted Mrs. Hutchinson for "troubling the peace of the Commonwealth." Unfortunately, she ended her own testimony by shouting that God had told her that her persecutors would be destroyed. She was banished from the colony, but sentence could not be carried out until spring. Before she and her family could leave, Anne Hutchinson lost her reason, in what is now seen as probably a menopausal disturbance. She said things that brought her to trial again, this time by the church. During the trial she was told, "You have stepped out of your place. You have rather been a husband than a wife, and a preacher than a hearer, and a magistrate than a subject." Anne Hutchinson was excommunicated. It was at this point that Mary Dyer, later to be hanged (see page 100), proved a friend indeed and bravely joined Anne in a chin-high walk from the church. Taken by her husband to Rhode Island, she was joined by thirty-five families who agreed with her ideas. Anne Hutchinson later moved to New Netherland where she was killed in an Indian massacre in 1643.

First American Witch
MARGARET JONES

❦ In 1648, Margaret Jones of Charlestown (now part of Boston) was probably the first person to be tried and executed as a witch in Massachusetts. According to Governor Winthrop, "she was found to have such a malignant touch, as many persons . . . whom she stroked . . . were taken with deafness, or vomiting . . . she practices physic [with] extraordinary violent effects . . . some things which she foretold came to pass accordingly . . . she had (upon search) an apparent teat in her secret parts as fresh as if it had been newly suckled, and after it had been scanned, upon a forced search, that was withered, and another began on the opposite side." He further noted that on the day she was executed in Boston "there was a very great tempest at Connecticut, which blew down many trees."

Closest a Woman Has Come to
Running the Papacy
OLIMPIA MAIDALCHINI

❦ Known as the sister-in-law (sometimes called niece, sometimes other things not so nice) of Innocent X, around 1650, Olimpia's major purpose was to acquire as much money as she could, however she could. A prime source of funds was the selling of the curia. If no vacancies were available for her to offer, it troubled her little to create one through the use of a well-administered poison. She may have acquired the poisons from a chemist named Exili, who showed up later in the court of Christine, Queen of Sweden. Even the papal relationships in international affairs were dictated by Olimpia so as to keep foreigners from gaining any power in Rome. Olimpia's control of the pope and the papacy remained firm until his death in 1655.

First Women to Be Deported from America
MARY FISHER AND ANN AUSTIN

❦ Mary Fisher, an early convert of George Fox to the Society of Friends in England, experienced the horrors of imprisonment and naked, public flogging for her Quaker beliefs and for daring to reprimand the official clergy. In 1655, she left England for the New World. On a ship to Barbados in the West Indies, she met Ann Austin, a less tempestuous but just as committed older Quaker woman. On the island they made a number of influential converts and then headed for Massachusetts. Arriving in Boston in July 1656, they found that word of the Quakers' "heresies" had already reached the colony. Before they were allowed to land, their books were burned and they were stripped and searched for witch marks. Held for several weeks unable to speak to anyone, they were finally shipped back to Barbados. Only a few days later, the arrival in Boston of more Quakers led to even more repressive measures, culminating in the hanging of Mary Dyer.

Only American Female Religious Martyr
MARY DYER

❦ The strength of Mary Dyer's conscience first became known in 1638 when she publicly sided with Anne Hutchinson (see page 98). It wasn't until later, however, on a five-year sojourn back to England, that Mrs. Dyer (or Dwyer) turned Quaker. On her return to Boston in 1657, she was imprisoned under an act opposing Quakerism as heresy. She was jailed again two years later when the law had been strengthened to keep Quakers out of Massachusetts on penalty of death. Ignoring the law, she went to visit two jailed friends and promptly found herself also behind bars. Banished from Boston under threat of death, she and her friends elected to return to the city anyway, determined to confront the law. They were sentenced to die. The two male friends were hanged. Mary Dyer, already blindfolded and with noose around her neck, was suddenly reprieved and carried out of town. Shunning the reprieve, however, she again went back to Boston, knowing full well she was going to her death. On June 1, 1660, she spoke from the gallows: ". . . in His faith I abide faithful to the death." This time there was no reprieve for Mary Dyer.

First American Indian to Be Beatified
by the Catholic Church
KATERI TEKAKWITHA

❦ Called the "Lily of the Mohawk," Tekakwitha was the daughter of a Mohawk father and Algonquin Christian mother. Orphaned at age four by a smallpox epidemic, she remained with her Mohawk relatives who, as she grew, teased her for her badly pockmarked face and forced her to forget her early teaching. In 1675, when she was nineteen, Tekakwitha defied her uncle and went to a priest for religious instruction. Maltreated by her people, Kateri (which means Catherine), as she had been baptized, left the village with some visiting Christian Indians and went to Canada to Sault

St. Louis on the St. Lawrence River. There she adopted a fully religious life, including some degree of self-torture on her already disease-weakened body, and she became widely revered. When she died at age twenty-four, the reverence grew and brought forth many reports of her intercession with God on behalf of supplicants. In 1939 Tekakwitha was declared venerable. Then, in July 1980, she was beatified or declared blessed, a first step toward sainthood, even though no miracles by her have yet been proved. Her beatification ceremony, the first ever for an American layperson, was attended by five hundred North American Indians in full ceremonial dress.

Woman Responsible for the Most Havoc
Brought on a Colonial Community
TITUBA

❦ A West Indian slave, Tituba was brought to Salem, Massachusetts, in 1692 by the Reverend Samual Parris. She enjoyed teaching some of her voodoo tricks and telling tales to the adolescent girls of the neighborhood, who began to act as if possessed. When the doctors couldn't help, the ministers took over. The girls were forced to name their "tormenters." They pointed to Tituba, of course, but also some other women of the area. And so the mania began, with teenage girls as the chief witnesses— probably frightened but also exhilarated at their own power. Before the witch-hunt ended, nineteen "witches"—both men and women—were executed. The townspeople carefully followed the biblical injunction: Thou shalt not suffer a witch to live. Then Beryl Hale, wife of a minister of Beverly, was accused, and it became clear that no one was exempt. Other ministers and leaders began to question whether something might not be amiss with the proceedings when worthy church people were being accused as well as the more disreputable persons in town. A minister writing soon after pointed out that "it cannot be imagined that in a place of so much knowledge, so many in so small a compass of Land should so abominably leap into the Devils lap at once."

Many historians view the events at Salem as the last gasp in the spasmodic witch-hunts that had plagued Europe for centuries, killing hundreds, even thousands, of people—and often, perhaps, a few witches!

Last Woman to Be Convicted of
Witchcraft in Great Britain
JANE WENHAM

❦ Long after the witch-hunt fever of seventeenth-century England had died down, one lone woman, Jane Wenham, became victim of its memories in 1712 when a couple of servants in her Hertford town behaved somewhat strangely after being seen talking with her. The local magistrate, who still believed in witches and didn't like nonconformist Jane, put her through a test for witchcraft—a true witch cannot recite the Lord's Prayer—and she failed. Tried, she was found guilty, but the judge, who thought the whole sorry business a mistake, was able to prevent her execution and soon she received a royal pardon.

Longest Lived Sect Founded by a Female
Second Coming of Christ
THE SHAKERS

❦ A Quaker preacher, Ann Lee had been converted about 1758 by Jane Wardley, who firmly believed that Christ would come again as a woman. About 1770, Ann Lee suffered greatly after a fourth child died during birth; at one point in her anguish, she appeared to die but was reborn. The first major effect of her rebirth was, to the dismay of her blacksmith husband, her forswearing of sexual intercourse. The Shakers, an offshoot of the English Quakers known for their trembling trances, took her up as the long-awaited female spirit of Christ's Second Coming. Convinced that sex was the basis of human evil and that virginity was an essential qualification of an angel, she turned the Shakers into a celibate group that sought converts on the streets of England. Frequently jailed and persecuted, they left England for America after Ann Lee, now called "Mother of the New Creation," had a vision that directed them to the New World. Even her husband went along, although he later abandoned Ann and went to live with another woman. The first community of the United Society of Believers in Christ's Second Coming was established at what is now Watervliet, New York. They soon spread and enjoyed considerable growth, in part because women were recognized as wholly equal to men. When Ann Lee died in 1784, eleven Shaker communities had been started. The society began to die out, however, in the mid-nineteenth century because the orphans on whom they depended for the sect's continuation were now being taken care of by other, more conservative churches. There are reportedly a few Shakers still living, though they are quite elderly.

In 1776, Jemima Wilkinson of Rhode Island went through a similar rebirth. At age twenty-three this pious Quaker woman fell ill with fever (or died, depending on one's interpretation) and woke to declare that she had died but God sent her back to earth "to preach to a world." She was to be the Second Coming of Christ and to reign for a thousand years. She was to be the Publick Universal Friend. Her plans required that she be persecuted, so she went to Quaker meetings and taunted the congregations. They obliged by disagreeing with what she said; she had her "persecution." In preaching throughout New England during the next years, she gathered many followers, some quite wealthy and influential. It was no hardship for her followers to convert because she preached mainly standard Quaker doctrine. Mostly, however, they were fascinated by her personality, one that required she have only the finest, most costly things about her—which left her church in a state of perpetual debt. Feeling the pinch and looking for a clean, new place to live, she sent some disciples to western New York to found a Friends' Settlement. She followed when the hard work was done and she could live in some comfort at the village of what is now called Penn Yan (the U.S. Post Office rejected "City of Jerusalem" as a postal name). After Jemima Wilkinson's death in 1819, however, the settlement and sect fell apart.

Most Difficult Female Second Coming
to Be Faithful To
ELSPETH BUCHAN

❦ In 1783 the Scottish fanatic Elspeth Buchan declared the Second Coming of Christ and started a religious group that developed into a commune of about fifty people. Marriage was outlawed and the Buchanite Society as a whole owned the children. Elspeth Buchan, the "Friend Mother in the Lord," was, she proclaimed, the woman referred to in Revelation: "There appeared a wonder in Heaven: a woman clothed with the sun." Her followers were certain . . . at least they were initially . . . that Friend Mother was going to get them to Heaven. But as it became harder and harder to follow her way of getting there, enthusiasm waned and some tried to leave the group; she ordered the dissenters locked up and dunked in icy water daily. At one time she ordered the group to participate in a forty-day fast, the object of which was to become lightweight enough to fly to Heaven more easily. When they failed to fly, she said it was because they didn't believe enough. Some of the faithful may have actually starved to death; as one ex-Buchanite wrote, "a few expedients of this kind will leave her, in the end, sole proprietor of the Society's funds." After the fast, she had the ones still with her cut their hair, leaving only a small topknot by which the angels could pull them up into Heaven. But the angels must not have noticed them, and the Buchanites fell to earth.

Just before Elspeth Buchan died in 1791, her remaining followers heard her promise that she would return for them in six months. If they didn't believe firmly enough, she would leave and return again in ten years. If they still didn't believe enough for them to go to Heaven, she would reappear in fifty years to end the world. Hugh Whyte, her first and main adherent, quit adhering, packed up some other followers and disappeared to America. But a few stayed on to be near her body, which they packed in feathers. Fifty years passed. The day of her return came, went, and nothing happened. Her last faithful follower, who perhaps was just bound by inertia, asked friends to bury him on top of Buchan's feather-filled coffin so that he would know if she arose. There's been no sign that she did.

Female Perpetrator of the Greatest American
Literary Hoax of the Nineteenth Century
MARIA MONK

❦ In the 1830s, most of the immigrants to America were French and Irish Catholics. As has happened before and since, the economic pressures brought about by their willingness to work for low wages were manifested through religious prejudice against them. In the mid-1830s, a little book appeared, *Awful Disclosures of Maria Monk, As Exhibited in a Narrative of Her Sufferings during a Residence of Five Years as a Novice, and Two Years as a Black Nun, in the Hôtel Dieu Nunnery at Montreal*. Sometimes called "the *Uncle Tom's Cabin* of the anti-Catholic movement," the book swelled the ranks of the movement and the coffers of several Canadian and American anti-Catholic agitators. Maria, a real girl whose experience with the Hôtel Dieu convent probably consisted of a brief period of asylum offered any prostitute, just let her imagination run wild, and the agitators capitalized on it. Several astute Protestant ministers and editors began an investigation and found that not even Maria's description of the building was accurate. Even her family proclaimed her falsehoods. But, still, three hundred thousand copies were sold in the next twenty years. Long before that time was up, however, Maria Monk, abandoned by her backers who kept all royalties, returned to prostitution, and at age thirty-three died on New York's Blackwell's (or Welfare) Island.

First Spiritual Mediums
LEAH, MARGARET, AND CATHERINE FOX

❦ Strange rapping sounds started in the Fox house in 1848, and the consensus of all who heard them was that they were made by spirits trying to communicate. The teenaged Fox sisters first made contact on March 31, 1848, and soon worked out a language system (one rap meaning yes, two meaning no, etc.). They learned that they were in touch with the spirit of Charles B. Rosma, a pedlar who claimed he had been murdered long before in their house. News of their discovery spread quickly across North America and Europe, and a quasi-religious movement (spiritualism) started that hasn't yet died down, despite the fact that years later, Margaret exposed the whole thing. She claimed the girls had learned to crack their toes to annoy their mother. But the spiritualistic believers had the final word when, in 1904, the skeleton of a man was found buried in the house.

Only Medium to Be Fully Endorsed by a
Reputable Physicist
FLORENCE COOK

❦ In London in the 1870s, Florence Cook was renowned for her ability to materialize spirits. She was supposedly thoroughly investigated by the famed physicist and chemist, Sir William Crookes, discoverer of the element thallium. He found her materializations completely authentic, reported his findings to the public, and Florence Cook enjoyed great success as a medium. Later, it was revealed that Sir William and Florence were lovers.

Largest Religious Denomination Founded by a Woman
CHRISTIAN SCIENCE

❦ Founded by Mary Morse Baker Glover Patterson Eddy in 1879, the church is now established worldwide. The church forbids publication of its membership statistics, but there are approximately 3500 churches and societies around the world.

Mary Baker Eddy's belief in mental healing stemmed from two experiences of her own. After a series of discussions in 1862 on healing by mental suggestion with Phineas Quimby of Maine, she recovered from chronic invalidism, and, four years later, she began to walk only two days after a serious fall had convinced doctors she would never walk again (her spine did, however, continue to trouble her most of her life). She said, "I gained the scientific certainty that all causation was Mind." Soon she was visiting homes to discuss her ideas, and gained in the process of discussion a philosophical education that would provide the base for her beliefs. In 1870, she began a series of teaching lectures while working on a book, which would become *Science and Health*, originally published under the name Mary Glover. It propounded the basic belief of Christian Science—that both sickness and evil are illusions of the human mind, that they can be overcome by prayer to Christ who was the First Healer. The first sentence in *Science and Health* is the essence: "The prayer that reforms the sinner and heals the sick is an absolute faith that all things are possible to God."

In August 1879, her followers chartered the Church of Christ (Scientist), in Lynn, Massachusetts. And eighteen months later, the Massachusetts Metaphysical College, for teaching the scientific methods of healing, was also chartered. That fall, Mary Baker Eddy spoke prophecies during a trance and soon was named Pastor by her followers (Pastors would later be called Readers). The movement shifted to Boston after the death of Asa Eddy, her third husband, and it started to grow, becoming nationally organized in 1886. During these years, she wrote *Key to the Scriptures* and published her first newspaper. Mary Baker Eddy's last years were troubled by divisions in the church, often stemming from her own personality, arguments about doctrine, and occasional medical lawsuits. Not long before her death—from "natural causes"—she started publication of *The Christian Science Monitor*, now one of the most highly regarded newspapers in the world.

Without being certain of the number of Christian Scientists, it is probable that second in line for founding religious groups is Mrs. Ellen Gould (Harmon) White, the prime mover behind the Seventh-Day Adventists, who currently number about four hundred fifty thousand. Baptized a Methodist at fifteen, in 1842, she and her Maine family were expelled from the church for accepting preacher William Miller's belief that the world would end on a certain day. It didn't, and Ellen Harmon joined a prayer group to ask what they should do now. There she had the first of perhaps several thousand visions. She turned wholly Adventist and walked through much of New England spreading her belief. Her visionary trances became an important aspect of her preaching; witnesses claimed that she never breathed during them and that one had, in fact, lasted six hours. In one vision, she saw an angel telling her that the Sabbath should be on Saturday, the Seventh Day. Ellen Harmon married an Adventist preacher and together they made many converts. In 1860, a number of believers joined in officially organizing the Seventh-Day Adventist Church. During coming years, the doctrine of the growing group developed from Ellen White's visionary interpretation of the Scriptures.

Woman Exhibiting Most Faith in a Medium
SARAH PARDEE WINCHESTER

❦ Widowed by the firearms manufacturer in 1880, Sarah Winchester took her $20 million inheritance, moved to California, and discovered spiritualism. A medium told her that as long as she kept building her house she would evade death and her home would not be invaded by the spirits of those killed by Winchester rifles. So . . . first she built a basic house with cupolas and other time-consuming gimcracks . . . then she added a wing . . . then, unpredictably, more wings to form a square . . . then another off to one side. Every material was used, stairs rose into nowhere, ten thousand windows were cut on both inside and outside walls, doors opened to blankness. And the number thirteen abounded—thirteen windows in rooms, thirteen steps on stairways, thirteen panels in ceilings, and even thirteen bathrooms. For thirty-six years aging Sarah Winchester built— resulting in an edifice of more than one hundred sixty rooms, not counting hundreds more that were built and then destroyed. But she could evade death no longer, and the house as it stood when she died is on exhibit in San Jose, California, and is called the Winchester Mystery House.

Most Prolific Hymn Writer
FANNY CROSBY

❦ Blinded by an inflammation in early infancy, Fanny Crosby, a mid-nineteenth-century evangelist and teacher, wrote hymns in her head until perhaps thirty or forty had accumulated in her memory. She would then call in a scribe to record them. In this manner, she wrote over eight thousand hymns, many of them specifically for tunes supplied by her publisher. Perhaps the most famous is "Safe in the Arms of Jesus," which she reportedly created in twenty minutes.

Only Woman to Start a Society for the
Glorification of an Anglican Saint
THE HONORABLE MRS. GREVILLE NUGENT

❦ In 1894, Mrs. Nugent founded the Society of King Charles the Martyr on the grounds that though Queen Victoria and the House of Commons had abolished observances for him, the Convocation of the Anglican Church had, in 1649, officially sainted King Charles I for having been beheaded by Cromwell—thus making him the only Anglican saint. And, she thought, Queen and Parliament (only the "common" part at that!) had no right to downgrade the poor man.

Only Woman to Create a "Liberated" Bible
ELIZABETH CADY STANTON

❦ Early in her life, Elizabeth Cady Stanton felt that organized Christian religion had done much to keep women in an inferior position (one biographer attributes her antichurch opinion to a nervous collapse as a child while listening to a sermon). She had expressed this opinion first in the "Declaration of Sentiments" written for the Seneca Falls women's rights meeting in the 1840s. *The Woman's Bible*, published in two parts in 1895 and 1898, is a commentary reinterpreting the passages in the Bible (she used a translation from the Hebrew done by a woman, Julia Smith) that had long been used to keep women "in their place." In the introduction, she noted, "The only points in which I differ from all ecclesiastical teaching is that I do not believe that any man ever saw or talked with God, I do not believe that God inspired the Mosaic code, or told the historians what they say he did about women, for all the religions on the face of the earth degrade her, and so long as woman accepts the position that they assign her, her emancipation is impossible." An example of her comments of specific passages in the Bible relates to the Fifth Commandment: "In what way could [boys and girls] show their mothers honor? All the laws and customs forbid it." Even Mrs. Stanton's co-workers in the suffrage movement added to the ruckus caused by the book because they were afraid the church and its supporters would use it as a reason for delaying suffrage. The book was also one of the very few issues that ever divided Elizabeth Cady Stanton and Susan B. Anthony.

Only Woman to Travel to Mars
HÉLÈNE SMITH

❦ At the turn of the century, Swiss medium Hélène Smith, a pseudonym for Catherine Elise Müller, reportedly journeyed to Mars by leaving her body during a long series of seances. Through automatic writing she conveyed to the public full descriptions of the neighboring planet and its inhabitants, and even conveyed a full dictionary of the Martian language. No one has yet found the material of use except for Theodore Flournoy, a Swiss psychologist, who wrote a book exploring the woman's subconscious mental activity.

Strangest Religious Movement Started
by a Woman
THE PURGATORIAL SOCIETY

❦ Many women have started strange sects, but this society started in 1931 by Mrs. Luci Mayer Barrow of New York City conjures up the most fascinating "what if. . . ." No record of its following exists, but Elmer T. Clark reports in *The Small Sects in America* that he had seen a pamphlet she issued called "Warning Information." He describes it as "a somewhat incoherent 'revelation,' filled with irrelevant scriptural references . . . she was prepared to take charge of the world's affairs as the Lord's annointed. She proposed to move the royal family of Great Britain to Canada and install the returning Jesus in Buckingham Palace. John the Baptist is to be born again, under the sponsorship of a committee which included two United States senators, who were named. The pope will be brought to the United States to occupy the Capitol at Washington and summon a world-wide enclave of the churches. The Jews will at last come into their own, since Mrs. Barrow and her husband will collect all the money in the world and turn it over to them. The good woman herself will be President of the United States, her husband will be the Speaker of the House of Representatives, and a certain Jewish rabbi of Kansas City will be vice-president and 'king of the world.'" Mr. Clark corresponded with Mrs. Barrow about her program but was unable to gather more light on the subject.

Most Troublesome Convert to a Cause
NILA CRAM COOK

❦ In 1932 Nila Cook, an American, discovered Mahatma Gandhi and turned zealot overnight. She changed her name to Nagina Devi, which means something on the order of "Blue Serpent Goddess." The next year the convert caused the Mahatma, probably through her interest in disciples of the opposite sex, to carry out a twenty-one day fast to atone for her sins. Since he was in the Yerovda Jail at the time, being held by the British, he had already done considerable fasting. Nagina Devi quickly apologized to her leader in print and promised to obey his teachings. But her need to be different prevented her from keeping the promise. Some months later Nagina Devi left Gandhi's ashram, and he soon appealed publicly at a press conference for her return. During the next several weeks, she popped up at various Hindu shrines, often being thrown out, or even getting into well publicized fights. Finally the weird Blue Serpent Goddess showed up in New Delhi and held a press conference of her own, declaiming against the stern poverty of the Mahatma's way of life and declaring, "I want to attend orchestra dances!" She soon left India, with the Mahatma probably as relieved to have her gone as she was to leave.

Woman to Baptize the Most People
AIMEE SEMPLE McPHERSON

From the time her Angelus Temple ("The Church of the Four-Square Gospel") in Los Angeles was opened on January 1, 1923, until her death in 1944, Aimee Semple McPherson baptized, records show, at least forty thousand converts. Since she had been ordained by a Pentecostal community in 1909 and had started conducting the emotional revival services that made her famous by 1915, it is probable that she baptized as many as fifty or sixty thousand people in her checkered career. When director Frank Capra was preparing the movie *Miracle Woman*, supposedly based on her life, he changed reality somewhat to put her under the influence of an evil-minded business manager, because, he said, "The thought of a wicked evangelist deliberately milking the poor, adoring suckers for money in the name of Christ was just too much for my orthodox stomach. I weaseled. I insisted on a 'heavy' to take the heat off the evangelist."

Last Known Woman to Gain Fame
for Her Stigmata
TERESA NEUMANN OF GERMANY

For a period of almost twenty years in the 1920s and thirties, Teresa Neumann was the object of long journeys and awe when, each week, she went into a trance and began to bleed from nonexistent wounds on her hands, feet, side, and forehead. However, the Catholic Church made no claims for her and she was never thoroughly checked by reputable physicians.

Woman to Do the Most for Zionism
HENRIETTA SZOLD

An American-born Jew and leader in helping immigrants to America become "americanized" and naturalized, Henrietta Szold got her first sight of Palestine in 1909, when she was almost fifty years old. She found the Palestinian people in desperate need of medical help. In 1912, she reorganized a literary group, the Hadassah Circle, to which she belonged to give it a specific commitment to medical care but also to promote "Jewish institutions and enterprises in Palestine." (From the original thirteen members, Hadassah has now grown to more than three hundred thousand.)

Ten years after her first trip to Palestine, Ms. Szold returned there to head the organization, which soon took on all the work of resettling immigrants to Palestine. In 1935, old and weary, the seventy-three-year-old woman took on, instead of a comfortable retirement in America, the work of organizing Youth Aliya (immigration of youth) to get German-Jewish children safely out of Hitler's reach and into Palestine. Within its first five years seven thousand children were taken safely to Palestine and settled in *kibbutzim* or children's villages. Ms. Szold died in 1944 before seeing the almost million and a half of the world's Jews who would pour into the new state of Israel in the coming years. In 1976, Israel honored Henrietta Szold by placing her picture on the Israeli five-pound note.

Newest Religious Movement to Be Founded by
a Reborn Woman
THE LUMPA CHURCH OF NORTHERN
RHODESIA

❦ In 1953, Alice Lenshina followed Ann Lee's and Jemima Wilkinson's path (see page 102), "died" of a stroke, went to God, and returned to found a religious movement. The Lumpa Church, often called the Alice Movement, was nominally Christian but was against all whites and against any blacks who dealt in politics. Perhaps as many as seventy-five thousand followers acquired Alice's fierce dedication to guerrilla action against the African National Congress that was trying to create a new black nation. In 1964, the Lumpans killed some white policemen, and Kenneth Kaunda, the president of the new nation of Zambia, jailed Alice Lenshina. Released, she tried to set her remaining followers to work again and so, in 1970, the head of the Alice Movement was jailed again. She has not been heard from in recent years.

Only Nun to Become a Successful
Popular Singer
SISTER LUC-GABRIELLE

❦ Also called Soeur Sourire, Sister Luc-Gabrielle of Belgium is known for her bestselling composition and rendition of "Dominique" in the early 1960s.

Only Nun to Be Tried for Conspiracy to
Kidnap and Commit Sabotage
SISTER ELIZABETH McALISTER

❦ In 1971, Sister Elizabeth McAlister, an art history professor at Marymount College in Tarrytown, New York, and six other people, including Father Philip Berrigan, were indicted, at the well-publicized request of J. Edgar Hoover, on a variety of charges. These included conspiracy to kidnap Henry Kissinger, to raid a draft board, and to sabotage government installations. Sister Elizabeth's involvement came from a letter she wrote Father Berrigan during his imprisonment for burning Selective Service files. In the letter, which was smuggled into prison, she related an idea that Eqbal Ahmad had had for making "a citizen's arrest" of Henry Kissinger until demands to stop the bombing of North Vietnam were met. The prosecution, however, had tried to put such a mishmash of unrelated charges into one indictment that the jury finally voted a mistrial. Sister Elizabeth and Father Berrigan were, however, found guilty of the never-before-prosecuted charge of smuggling letters into a prison. After leaving the church, she later married Philip Berrigan and they remained protestors, being arrested again in early 1977 in a demonstration at the Pentagon against nuclear arms. The former nun served ninety days for throwing blood (which was duck blood) on the Pentagon's columns.

Largest To-Do over the Ordination
of Female Clergy
THE ORDINATION OF ELEVEN FEMALE
DEACONS BY FOUR "MAVERICK" BISHOPS

❦ In defiance of the hierarchy of the church, the ordination was performed at the Church of the Advocate in Philadelphia on July 29, 1973. One of the women, chemist, educator, ballooning pioneer Dr. Jeannette Piccard had, at seventy-nine, been working toward the moment for more than fifty years. But the struggle wasn't over. The ordination was declared invalid two weeks later and the women were ordered not to carry out priestly duties. Subsequently, however, the House of Bishops backed the ordination of women "in principle" and the eleven renegade priests decided they would have to go their own routes until the hierarchy made up its collective mind on their status. Reverends Carter Heyward, Alison Cheek, and Jeannette Piccard arranged to celebrate communion for the first time at Riverside Church in Manhattan on October 27, 1974. One male priest, when offered the Sacrament, said, "I hope you burn in hell." Reverend Cheek, a widow and mother of four, received an appointment the following August as an assistant parish priest in Washington, D.C., and later became a pastoral psychotherapist. Named one of the *Time* magazine Women of the Year, she said, "I am convinced that the only crime I have committed in this matter is to have been born female." All major changes in the Protestant Episcopal Church must be approved by the General Convention, made up of representatives of the three major groups: bishops, lower priests, and lay people. In September 1976 the Convention voted to include women in the canon on ordination, so the women previously ordained were free to seek approval by their own dioceses.

Last Known Woman to Be Killed by Demons
ANNELIESE MICHEL

❦ According to *People* magazine, twenty-three-year-old Anneliese Michel of Germany died in 1976 after being possessed for several years by five devils contending for her spirit: Hitler, Nero, Cain, an unidentified priest, and Lucifer himself. The possession had begun when she was seventeen. Soon the voices she heard in her head began to speak through her, screaming obscenities, in several different voices, at each other. The girl was forced to leave school. The activity the demons required of her kept her so occupied that she could neither eat nor sleep. For almost a year, a qualified Roman Catholic exorcist tried to rid Anneliese of the demons, to no avail. Finally one morning, the demon-ridden girl, weighing only sixty-two pounds, died. Her mother said, "This is what she wanted."

Woman to Evoke the Most Letters of Outrage
MADALYN MURRAY O'HAIR

❦ Somehow rumormongers mushroomed a criticism that Madalyn Murray O'Hair made against TV coverage of NASA astronauts reading the Bible during the Christmas flight of Apollo 8 into a demand that all mention of God and prayer be kept off TV. Then they proceeded to confuse a totally unrelated petition concerning religious broadcasting sent to the Federal Communications Commission into a petition from Mrs. O'Hair to remove all religious programming from the air. In just about one year—from December 1974 through January 1976, the FCC received 3.7 million letters protesting the petition. Many letters contained other petitions bearing thousands of additional signatures. The FCC had to hire extra people, as well as find great amounts of storage space, just to handle the burden of the anti-O'Hair mail.

Last Known Woman to Successfully Banish
the Devil
ELIANA BARBOSA

❦ Eliana Barbosa, a Brazilian teenager, announced one day in 1978 that Satan had been using her body and making her do terrible things to herself. Commanded by a vision to duplicate Christ's crucifixion, she took a ten-foot cross to the top of a distant hill and had herself bound to it (the police refused to let her use nails). There she remained for three days while crowds sang, prayed, and even bought souvenirs. Her helpful father cut symbolic but bleeding stigmata into her hands and feet, thus opening himself to a mutilation prosecution. At the end of the third day, hungry and tired, the teenager descended from her cross and announced herself at peace: "The Devil is gone." The bishop of her area, embarrassed by the whole display, said, "The Devil is evil, but in this case he wasn't guilty."

Strangest Evangelist
KELLIE EVERTS

❦ Although there have been several who might qualify as "strangest evangelist," perhaps the most mind-boggling is Kellie Everts, an excessively well-endowed (44–21–38) stripper who found God and now strips for Christ. A former government worker-turned-Miss Nude Universe and porno-film actress, she converted to a religious organization called One World Light. Soon she was hosting during daylight hours a come-to-God TV program encouraging people to stay away from the sort of places where she unclothes herself at night. In between times, she meditates on the mystery of it all.

Last Female Television Star to Be Publicly
Accused of Witchcraft
JACLYN SMITH

❦ In 1980 a besmitten young man sued Jaclyn Smith, of "Charlie's Angels" TV fame, for bewitching him via telepathy, working her wiles long distance until all he could do was think of her: She was, he claimed, ruining his life. To him, $20 million seemed a reasonable sum to demand for the mental anguish caused him. The judge threw the young man's problem out of court, refusing to accept old European witchcraft cases as legal precedent.

8

THE CREATIVE ONES

Woman Who Waited the Longest to Get a
Book Published
MARGERY KEMPE

❦ More than five hundred years passed between the time Margery Kempe of England had her story written down for her and the discovery in 1934 of the manuscript among some very musty papers. Margery Kempe, or Kemp, was a religious mystic who lived around 1400. Driven mad by her first pregnancy, she saw Christ and regained her equanimity. Thirteen more children later, she came to an agreement with her husband: She would pay off his debts and he would stay out of her bed. She took charge of her own life (or put it in the hands of Christ) and began to travel. She wandered through Britain, Europe, and the Holy Land, mostly walking, telling all whom she met of her experiences with Christ. Her journeys were often interrupted by sojourns in prison when authorities in various towns were disturbed by her apparently uncontrollable fits of weeping. In the last years of her life, she found scribes to take down her story as she told it, making *The Book of Margery Kempe* the first known autobiography written in English.

Only Major Castle Built by Women
CHENONÇEAU

❦ One of the famed chateaux of the Loire valley in France, Chenonçeau was planned and supervised by Catherine Briconnet in the early 1500s, while her husband, Thomas Bohier, a Royal Tax Collector, was away handling the financing of various wars. The castle is an elaborate, turreted, fairy tale dream that she and her husband planned on the site of an old mill, surrounded by woods and peace. It was probably the first castle whose prime *raison d'être* wasn't defense. But it was also very costly and by the time Catherine and Thomas died they were deeply in debt. Their son gave the castle to the king in exchange for cancelling some debts.

Called the "castle that women built," it was lived in and improved by Diane de Poitiers, who was given it by Henry II. Over his dead body, his wife, Catherine de Medici, confiscated it, enlarged it, and built the unique gallery over the river. One tourist legend says that Catherine started topless waitresses at Chenonçeau by holding a huge banquet and inviting beautiful noblewomen from all over France to do the serving à la nude. In the 1700s, Louise Dupin, daughter of a banker, acquired the castle from the court, shined and polished it, while Jean Jacques Rousseau practiced his theories of education on her sons. Mme Dupin was so well loved in the neighborhood that the peasants did not try to destroy the castle during the Revolution. One hundred years ago Chenonçeau was again restored by a woman, Mrs. Claudette Pelouze and, finally, during World War I, Mrs. George Menier turned it into a Red Cross hospital.

First Female Poet to Complain in Print of Criticism
ANNE BRADSTREET

❧ After a major volume of Anne Bradstreet's work, called *The Tenth Muse,* was published in the 1650s, the reaction in her Puritan community must have been acrimonious. In one later poem, Anne Bradstreet observed:

> I am obnoxious to each carping tongue
> Who sayes, my hand a needle better fits,
> A Poets Pen, all scorne, I should thus wrong;
> For such despight they cast on female wits:
> If what I doe prove well, it won't advance,
> They'll say it's stolne, or else, it was by chance.

First Bawdy Woman Writer
APHRA BEHN

❧ Widowed in 1666 at the age of twenty-six, Aphra Behn soon found herself in debtors' prison. Released, she sought a solution to her penniless condition and quickly took note of the new public passion for theater. Shunning the more refined themes of other women playwrights, Astraea, as she was called, turned to the raucous, "indecent," and "corrupt" themes (her own words) that drew Restoration audiences, and thus became the first female playwright to have her plays actually produced. Alexander Pope wrote of her:

> The stage how loosely does Astraea tread
> Who fairly puts all characters to bed.

First Known Fight Between a Female Author and Her Publisher
HANNAH WOOLLEY AND DORMAN NEWMAN

❧ Hannah was an orphan in seventeenth-century England who had the good fortune to be sent to school and then into service at various homes where she was able to learn quite a bit of cooking, medicinal botany, manners, clothing care, and so on. The "so on" in fact, is rather varied: At one time she made a list, "Things I pretend greatest Skill in," which is only partly shown here:

All kinds of Beugle-works upon wyers, or otherwise.
All manner of Pretty Toys for Closets.
Rocks made with Shell or in Sweets.
Frames for Looking-glasses, Pictures or the Like.
Feathers of Crewel for the corners of Beds.
Preserving all kind of Sweet-meats wet and dry.
Setting out of Banquets.
Knowledge in discerning the Symptoms of most Diseases and giving such
Remedies as are fit in such Cases.
Making Sweet Powders for the Hair, or to lay among Linnen.

Hannah married at twenty-four and began to order her own household, raise four sons and run a boarding house. Widowed in 1660, she looked for some way to make money and began to print up thin pamphlets of her best "receipts." The next year *The Cook's Guide* was published, soon followed by *The Ladies' Directory in choice experiments and curiosities of Preserving and Candying both Fruit and Flowers*. However, she soon got involved with Mr. Newman, who took her simple manuscript for *The Gentlewoman's Companion* and padded it with bad writing and dull discourses. Copyright law being rather in its infancy, she fought back by publishing a supplement to an earlier book, *A Queen-like Closet*, in which she told the public what she thought of Newman and urged them not to buy his versions of her books. She had no other recourse and one can only hope that her devoted readers went along with her. Perhaps so. From being one of the largest London publishers when he came across Hannah Woolley, Newman was reduced to bankruptcy in 1694.

First Woman to Write of Her Capture by and
Escape from Indians
MRS. MARY WHITE ROWLANDSON

❦ On February 10, 1676, Mary Rowlandson's home in Lancaster, Massachusetts, was invaded by Indians and she was held captive in the home of Wetamao (see page 83) until ransomed by her women friends for twenty pounds. Written originally for her children, the book was published in 1682 and eventually sold in thirty-one editions. It was called *The Sovereignty & Goodness of God, Together, with the Faithfulness of His Promises Displayed; Being a Narrative of the Captivity and Restauration of Mrs. Mary Rowlandson. Written by her own Hand for her Private Use, and now made Public at the earnest Desire of some Friends.*

First Female Artist to Go into
the Wilds to Paint
MARIA SIBYLLA MERIAN

❦ A forerunner of John James Audubon, both in ability and accuracy of observation, Maria had started painting the things of nature, especially insects, at a young age in Germany. Moving to Amsterdam after a bad marriage, she had access to the vast wildlife collections of the East India Company, and spent long hours studying and drawing the specimens. In 1699, she and her daughter sailed to Surinam in South America. There in the jungles she found enough interesting insects to keep her painting forever. A gift from one of them, however, sent her home with recurrent yellow fever after only two years. She was able to create a major illustrated work on the insects of Surinam and in 1705 published her greatest effort, *History of the Insects of Europe*. Its superb illustrations and descriptions of the insects, their food habits, and life cycles made it a basic reference for many decades.

Greatest Painting Done by a Woman That Was
Long Thought to Be the Work of a Man
CONSTANCE-MARIE CHARPENTIER OR
JUDITH LEYSTER

❦ It's a toss-up between two. About 1965, art historian Charles Sterling proved to the extent possible at the time that the portrait of Mlle Charlotte du Val d'Ognes, attributed to the great eighteenth-century French painter Jacques Louis David, was done by one of his pupils, Constance-Marie Charpentier. The proof in the second case is more definite. When *The Jolly Toper*, thought to be by Dutch artist Franz Hals, was cleaned recently by the Ryksmuseum in Amsterdam, the new brightness revealed the date 1629 and the letter J characteristic of Judith Leyster.

First American Bestselling Novelist
SUSANNA HASWELL ROWSON

❦ Born in England, Susannah was brought to America right away. At thirteen she returned to England where, while working as a governess, she later wrote *Charlotte, a Tale of Truth*, which was published in London in 1789. Three years later she returned to America with her husband, and *Charlotte*, now called *Charlotte Temple*, was published again. It was immediately popular and remained America's bestselling novel until *Uncle Tom's Cabin*, also by a woman, was published. *Charlotte*, which went through at least two hundred editions in its first century in America alone, is the heartrending tale of a respectable English girl. Drawn to an army officer, she overthrows her background and elopes with him to America. There the cad abandons her and her child. Together, they slide into destitution. At the end, the officer returns to save her, his real love, but it is too late and she dies.

Most Frequently Forged Woman Writer
MRS. ANN RADCLIFFE

❦ A late eighteenth-century novelist, Mrs. Radcliffe developed the gothic horror story that is often imitated even today. She grabbed her readers and kept them on the edge of a cliff, committed to plowing through page after page of unreal dialogue and rather stodgy characters. Perhaps because the last of her five novels was published after her death, forgers felt free to keep publishing books in her name. Alida A. S. Wieten, her literary biographer, has identified at least eighteen books published posthumously that were not by Mrs. Radcliffe.

Worst Example of a Woman's Own
Philosophy—Herself
MARY WOLLSTONECRAFT

❦ Wollstonecraft, whom Horace Walpole called a "hyena in petticoats," regarded independence as the road to happiness for a woman, and yet was unable to follow that road in her own brief life. Smarting from rejection by one lover, she left her job with James Johnson, a publisher of radical ideas, soon after the publication of *A Vindication of the Rights of Woman* in 1792 to watch the revolutionary struggle going on in Paris. There she quickly became involved with an American adventurer and speculator, Gilbert Imlay. He refused to marry her even after she bore his daughter, Fanny, and the prevailing scandal suspected him of keeping her only for the help she gave him in his business affairs. Imlay was widely unfaithful, to which Mary reacted at least twice by trying to commit suicide. They left Paris for London where Gilbert promptly disappeared. Mary, heartbroken, went back to work for Johnson. There she met and moved in with William Godwin, a political philosopher who soon ignored his antipathy toward human institutions long enough to marry her. As Dame Edith Sitwell wrote, "a long happiness was not for this fated creature": in 1797, Mary Wollstonecraft died soon after giving birth to a daughter, Mary, who would later be heard from as Mary Shelley, author of *Frankenstein* (see below).

Woman Writer to Have Had the Most Movies
Made from Her Book
MARY WOLLSTONECRAFT GODWIN
SHELLEY

❦ In 1818, Mary Shelley, daughter of early feminist writer Mary Wollstonecraft and wife of poet Percy Bysshe Shelley, published a novel called

Frankenstein, or The Modern Prometheus. Written for the amusement of friends who loved spooky stories, it is the tale of a scientist who creates a monster that destroys all the people the scientist holds dear. Mary Shelley herself called it a tale "to make the reader dread to look round, to curdle the blood and quicken the beatings of the heart." The book was popular immediately and remains so, enhanced by the many films that have derived from it since 1931 when the classic *Frankenstein*, starring Boris Karloff as the monster (Frankenstein is the scientist, *not* the monster), was filmed.

There have been at least twenty feature films since then and the number will probably rise before this book is published. Frankenstein has had a *Bride* and a *Son*—in two separate films—and has been *Young* himself. He has been both a *Teenager* and a *Ghost*, though that last episode by no means ended the saga. He has dealt with *Dracula, Wolf Man, Space Monsters*, and *Abbott and Costello*. He has been *Cursed*, had *Revenge*, and—all in all—found to be *Evil*. In short, *Frankenstein Must Be Destroyed*. But no. Instead he managed to *Conquer the World*. Perhaps his major feat, however, is one it seems unlikely that Mary Shelley could have anticipated: *Frankenstein Created Woman.*

Woman Who Performed the Most
Unsuccessful Ballet Performance in America
MME FRANCISQUY HUTIN

☙ On February 7, 1827, in her first ballet performance, Mme Hutin appeared in *The Deserter* at the Bowery Theatre in New York. The curtain rose on the exciting new art form. The audience gasped at the slight clothing the dancer wore and promptly removed themselves from the theater.

Most Fire-Proof Woman
JO GIRARDELLI

☙ An English performing fire-eater of the early 1800s, and seemingly totally nonflammable, Jo Girardelli ate fire, boiling oil or wax, even acid. She could drink molten metal and then spit out small, hard "bullets" into the audience. Any other person who holds candles to hand or feet will generally get burned. All that happened to Jo Girardelli was the collection of soot on her cool skin.

First Person to Be Exhibited by P.T. Barnum
JOYCE (OR JOICE) HETH

☙ Although Barnum had spent several years publishing an abolitionist newspaper, he had no qualms about purchasing the black woman who was rumored to have been George Washington's nurse. The tiny, shrunken woman had wrinkled, leathery skin, and her joints were fused with arthritis. Barnum quickly parlayed his $1000 purchase price into a weekly income of more than that by publicizing the "161-year-old slave who brought George Washington into the world." He added that he had the original bill of sale on the woman. Joyce Heth died the next year and autopsy revealed her age as no more than eighty, but Barnum had his first hoax and his first proof about suckers.

Most Dramatic About-Face Done
by a Woman Reporter
JANE CANNON SWISSHELM

As a young married woman, Jane Swisshelm gave up reading because it might make her appear to be brighter than her nonbook-minded husband. She had not even let her marriage announcement appear in the local paper because a proper lady's name should not appear in newsprint. But then Jane left her small corsetry business to take care of her dying mother. After her mother's death, her husband tried to sue the estate for Jane's nursing services, because he happened to be broke at the time. The absurdity of that gesture turned Jane Swisshelm into an avid married women's rights advocate. The dam broke on her use of her bright mind and she began writing anonymously for newspapers against slavery, capital punishment, and other wrongs. Determined to make her marriage work, she returned to her husband who urged her, since she appeared to be able to make money at writing, to keep writing for the newspapers and to use her own name. She was soon commenting in print on just about any subject that would allow her to attack established convention. Her witty and penetrating writing caught the attention of Horace Greeley, who hired her to report from Washington for his *Tribune*. She applied directly to Vice-President Millard Fillmore for a desk in the Press Gallery at the Capitol. He granted Mrs. Swisshelm's request, probably at the urging of his widely read wife. She kept the desk only long enough to feel that soon women would be able to work there without comment.

In one memorable column by Mrs. Swisshelm, she wrote about women doing men's jobs: "They plough, harrow, reap, dig, make hay, rake, bind grain, thresh, chop wood, milk, churn, do anything that is hard work, physical labor, and who says anything against it? But let one presume to use her mental powers—let her aspire to turn editor, public speaker, doctor, lawyer—take up any profession or avocation which is deemed honorable and requires talent, and O! bring cologne, get a cambric kerchief and feather fan, unloose his corsets and take off his cravat! What a fainting fit Mr. Propriety has taken! Just to think that 'one of the deah creatures'— the heavenly angels, should forsake the sphere—woman's sphere to mix with the wicked strife of this wicked world!"

Most Influential Novel by a Woman
HARRIET BEECHER STOWE'S *UNCLE TOM'S CABIN*

❦ Harriet Beecher Stowe started writing to soothe the family financial situation when her professor husband fell into fits of do-nothing depression. Her reading of books such as Lydia Maria Child's *An Appeal in Favor of That Class of Americans called Africans* led her to follow "the hand of God" (as she called it) in writing *Uncle Tom's Cabin*. The book showed the brutality and degradation of slavery and the institutions that supported it, written in a popular, grossly sentimental form that would catch attention.

First published in 1852 as forty installments in *National Era*, an antislavery newspaper, the articles were promptly brought out as a book, and the story made Mrs. Stowe a public figure, although it did little to help her finances—she received $300 for the rights. Within one year, three hundred thousand copies of the book had been sold. Numerous dramatic versions were staged, drawing to the theater even those who regarded the stage as immoral. Even P. T. Barnum staged one version. Not all versions were very faithful in their adherence to Mrs. Stowe's story, but their impact remained the same: shock, disgust, and a growing realization that slavery was an evil that must be attacked. Lincoln's famous comment on meeting Mrs. Stowe—"So this is the little lady who wrote the big book that caused the big war"—is probably apochryphal. But the fact is that by 1860 so many Northerners knew the shocking story of *Uncle Tom's Cabin* that they were willing—nay, eager—to become involved in a Civil War to right the wrongs of slavery.

Strangest Mother-and-Child Act
JOSEPHINE BOISDECHEME (MME FORTUNE CLOFULLIA) AND HER SON

❦ Josephine Boisdecheme was a Swiss lady born with a thick covering of hair over her entire body that gradually focused itself into a soft, curly beard. Her parents disapprovingly allowed her to go on display in France where she met a loving landscape painter, Fortune Clofullia. They were married and went to England together where the bearded wife appeared in the Great Exposition. Her first child was born hairless, but her second, a boy, had the soft down covering that presaged a lucrative career for him in side shows. In 1853, the family set off for New York, where P. T. Barnum quickly took charge. During the next nine months three and a half million people paid their fee to get into Barnum's American Museum where bearded mother and child were on display.

Greatest Proponent of the Bacon Theory of
Shakespeare's Plays
DELIA BACON (NO RELATION)

❧ A sometime lecturer and writer in New England, Delia Bacon first published her thoughts on the subject in 1856, calling Shakespeare "the Stratford Poacher." She held that the plays were written by a group of men led by Sir Walter Raleigh under the direction of Sir Francis Bacon. These men decided to convey their philosophy through puzzles and anagrams in the plays decipherable only by the most erudite scholar of the Elizabethan Age—presumably Delia Bacon herself. The strange Miss Bacon managed to go to England to be nearer the source of her fascination. While there she became increasingly leery of dealing with hard facts, and her supporters, some quite illustrious, dropped her as imagination usurped reality. She fell ill and help was requested from the American consul, who turned out to be Nathaniel Hawthorne. He helped her get her scribbling published as *The Philosophy of the Plays of Shakespere Unfolded*, and even wrote a foreword, though he didn't agree with her ideas. She persisted in contemplating Shakespeare's grave and may even have obtained permission to open it, convinced that she would find more direct messages from Sir Francis. At the last moment, however, she doubted her interpretation, lost her mind, and had to be carted back to America. More than one person evidently did read her garbled book because the controversy throws up ripples even today.

First Bestseller about a "Liberated" Woman
THE HIDDEN HAND, BY MRS. E.D.E.N.
SOUTHWORTH

❧ A sentimental domestic mystery published in 1859 of the heroine-in-danger genre, it featured a very innovative heroine named Capitola: Instead of waiting to be saved by a man she got herself out of her predicament. The public must have been ready for such a heroine, for the book was continuously in print for sixty-two years, during which time it was also produced as a play in at least forty different versions.

First Author of a "Dime Novel"
ANN SOPHIA STEPHENS

❧ When the New York firm of Irwin P. Beadle & Co. sought, in 1860, to bring cheaply produced novels to the general public, it selected for its first publication *Malaeska: The Indian Wife of the White Hunter*. Chosen for its "fine pictures of border life and Indian adventure," it was the product, published twenty years before, of Mrs. Ann Stephens, a New England writer and editor who had only briefly been as far west as Ohio. In the book, however, she found the balance of melodrama and sentiment that caused the ubiquitous dime novels to be snatched up in railway stations and coach stops. *Malaeska*, half a dozen other dime novels, many serials, and hundreds of other somewhat lurid stories and articles supported Mrs. Stephens' family after her husband's death in 1862. When *Malaeska* was reprinted (for the umpteenth time) in 1929, it was greeted with delight by reviewers who heralded it as true "proletarian" literature.

Only Woman to Be Presented with a Major Award Through a Ruse
ROSA BONHEUR

❦ Probably the greatest female animal artist, Rosa Bonheur was an independent soul who avoided marriage in order to maintain that independence. She bought a farm and stocked it with all the animals she painted, in order to study them in daily life, although she often traveled to fairs and circuses to see animals in more action. Once she kept a lioness on her farm in order to get to know it better. Her fame began when a picture of horses plowing won her the Gold Medal at the 1849 Salon. Traditionally, that award and others like it led to the bestowal of the French Legion of Honor. But the Emperor Napoleon III refused to grant the coveted award to a woman. Mlle Bonheur, continuing to work at her farm, ignored such matters. But one day in 1864, a servant fetched her from the muck of the farmyard to quickly change her clothing. Empress Eugenie was on her way to see the artist. Rosa just had time to change before the Empress, acting as Regent for her traveling husband, used her short-term authority to bestow the Grand Cross of the Legion of Honor on the woman who had earned it.

Youngest Artist to Be Awarded a Government Contract
VINNIE REAM

❦ At age eighteen, in 1866, Wisconsin-born Vinnie Ream, who had discovered sculpture only three years before, received a ten-thousand-dollar contract to do a full-scale statue of Abraham Lincoln to stand in the Rotunda of the Capitol. The first woman to receive a federal commission, she was accused of having used feminine wiles to gain the contract. Ignoring such rumors, she made her plaster model of the slain President and then went to Italy to acquire the finest Carrera marble. Although later critics have wondered if there were any body beneath the clothing of the President, the statue is still a favorite with visitors to the nation's capital.

Only Accused Murderer to
Become a Famed Sculptor
EDMONIA LEWIS

❦ A part black, part Chippewa Indian, Wildfire (Edmonia Lewis's Indian name) was sent to college with the aid of her brother who had succeeded reasonably well in the California Gold Rush. But her time at Oberlin College was tragically interrupted when she was accused of murdering two white friends. She was released because of insufficient evidence but did not return to the school. Instead, she went to Boston and discovered there the fascination of white marble that would hold her in thrall the rest of her life. In 1864, her portrait bust of a black Union war hero was repeated in one hundred plaster copies. She used the earnings from the popular reproduction to go to Rome, the contemporary mecca for sculptors. There she moved in the international art set and became, as recorded by Elizabeth Barrett Browning, "a great pet of mine and of Robert's." She drew on both of her heritages—black and Indian—in creating sculpture of silken beauty. By 1870 Edmonia Lewis could command several thousand dollars for sculptures done on request.

First Real Burlesque Show
"BRITISH BLONDES"

❦ Lydia Thompson of London brought her troupe of statuesque females to the United States in 1868, calling the show "British Blondes." Although it included skits and songs, it was the first show to devote itself primarily to the lucrative assumption that the female form, viewed for its own sake, will draw crowds.

Most Lasting Novel for Girls
LITTLE WOMEN, BY LOUISA MAY ALCOTT

❦ Already popular as a writer because of her torridly romantic serials, Miss Alcott was requested by her publisher to write a girls' story. She wasn't enthusiastic about the idea but managed to come up with a serial based on her own sisters which was published in 1868–69. Little did she realize that she was creating lastingly popular characters. Meg, Jo, Beth, and Amy are known the world over, each with her personal characteristics that are just as real today as a century ago. Elizabeth Janeway, in *Between Myth and Morning*, describes them this way: "Her girls are jealous, mean, silly and lazy; and for one hundred years jealous, mean, silly and lazy girls have been ardently grateful for the chance to read about themselves. . . . The real attraction is not the book as a whole, but its heroine, Jo, and Jo is a unique creation: the one young woman in nineteenth-century fiction who maintains her individual independence, who gives up no part of her autonomy as payment for being born a woman—and who gets away with it."

Woman with the Most Innovative Architecture
Plan to Receive a Patent
HARRIET MORRISON IRWIN

✓ A housewife and mother in the South in the mid-nineteenth century, Mrs. Irwin was untrained and unknown in the field of architecture until she developed her plan for hexagonal buildings. In "Improvement In The Construction of Houses," she developed her plan: "The objects of my invention are the economizing of space and building materials, the obtaining of economical heating mediums, through lighting and ventilation, and facilities for inexpensive ornamentation." In 1869, she became the first woman to receive an architectural patent, and she built an example of her hexagonal plan in Charlotte, North Carolina, where it still stands.

Only Mother of a President to Rear Her Son
in a House She Built Herself
JESSIE WOODROW WILSON

✓ In 1871, Jessie and Joseph Wilson moved to Columbia, South Carolina, where he became a seminary professor. They bought a plot of land on Hampton Street in Columbia and Jessie designed what was one of the most impressive houses in town—large, two-storied, set in a magnolia-filled lawn. She herself supervised the construction. Young Woodrow lived there until he left for Princeton University. Today the house is a Wilson museum.

First Writer to Have Her Work
Recorded in Sound
SARAH JOSEPHA HALE

✓ On December 6, 1877, Thomas Alva Edison recited Sarah Hale's vastly familiar children's poem, "Mary Had a Little Lamb," into the recording diaphragm as the first test of his new "Phonograph." She had written the poem almost fifty years earlier for a book of *Poems for Our Children*.

Woman Author to Do the Most Damage to the
Self-Esteem of Little Boys
FRANCES HODGSON BURNETT

✓ Mrs. Burnett's children's book, *Little Lord Fauntleroy*, was published in 1886 and immediately set a fashion in little boys' clothes—chosen, of course, by their mothers. Cedric, the hero who starts the book as a poor boy, finishes up as a peer of the realm clad in velvet and lace collars. The influence of the book was still apparent in early motion pictures with Freddie Bartholomew often dressed in frilly "Lord Fauntleroy" clothing.

Most Destructive Women Associated
with a Writer
THE MRS. BURTON, NIETZSCHE,
HAWTHORNE, AND STEVENSON

❦ Lady Isabel Arundell Burton, widow of Sir Richard Burton, explorer and translator who is best known for his elegant translation of *The Arabian Nights*, never approved of his bringing "dirty" Oriental stories to the English public. After his death in 1890 she burned his handwritten translation of *The Scented Garden*. That book had to wait sixty years before being brought to the English-reading public.

Elisabeth Förster-Nietzsche removed from her brother's unfinished manuscripts evidence of his growing insanity. He did, in fact, spend the last eleven years of his life with all reason gone. She managed to transform his image into one supportive of Nazism and her own into that of a self-made "high priestess" of his badly misinterpreted philosophy.

Mrs. Nathaniel Hawthorne, on the other hand, was requested by a publisher to prepare Hawthorne's *American Notebooks* for publication. She did so by changing names of real people, adding elegant Victorian phrases she happened to like, and deleting all unpleasantness, even to the extent of extracting a reference to having a tooth pulled.

When Robert Louis Stevenson's wife Fanny read *The Strange Case of Dr. Jekyll and Mr. Hyde*, she burned the manuscript, thinking it embarrassingly vulgar. He was, however, able to reconstruct it, thus rescuing one of the classics of literature.

Best Prepared Woman
SARAH BERNHARDT

❦ Suitcases are enough of an annoyance, but the fascinating and glorious Sarah Bernhardt complicated her travels by keeping as the central item of her baggage an elegant rosewood coffin. This curious good luck charm was made to her specifications when she was about thirty. The gift of an admirer, who gallantly said she could have anything she desired, it became her symbol "that my body will soon be dust and that my glory will live for ever." The coffin became a prop in one of the greatest publicity campaigns ever lived. She was often photographed in the casket and at times even slept in it. It had to be arranged in any hotel bedroom before the actress herself would enter. *Theatre Magazine* in a 1901 issue reported that the actress got in the coffin when the world became too much: "covering herself with faded wreaths and flowers, [she] folds her hands across her breast and, her eyes closed, bids a temporary farewell to life." The final farewell, too, was made in the travel-weary coffin. Sarah Bernhardt was buried in the gift of her admirer about fifty years after the gift was made.

Woman with the Frankest Motto
CLARIN DE BREUJERE

❦ "My Rights or I Bite" was the motto of Clarin de Breujere, a probably insane French writer at the turn of the century. She developed her own coat of arms on which to emblazon the motto.

Worst Sister Acts in Vaudeville
THE CHERRY SISTERS AND THE HILTON
SISTERS

❦ The Cherry Sisters took a straightforward approach to their talent: They knew they weren't good, so they advertised themselves as the worst and then performed behind a net to protect themselves from flying vegetables.

But perhaps worst in a different way were the Hilton Sisters, who together formed a small, and frankly not very good, jazz band. Literally together, since the girls were Siamese twins joined at the base of the spine. They both played saxophone, or sometimes Violet accompanied Daisy's sax on the piano. Violins, too, were in their repertoire. The girls, born in England, had been sold by their unwed mother to a couple who raised them from the word Go to be moneyspinners. Not until they were in their twenties were they able to reach a lawyer who sued the girls' "guardians" for their freedom and an accounting of all money earned by them through the years. The girls later appeared in a rather dreadful film called *Chained for Life*. They ended their lives working at a fruit stand in the South.

Only Woman to Have Two Popular Foods
Named for Her
DAME NELLIE MELBA

❦ When the Australian-born opera singer Nellie Melba was staying at London's Savoy Hotel in the 1890s, its well-known chef, Escoffier, created a special peach and ice cream dessert for her. He later added raspberry sauce and called it Peach Melba. The other food, Melba toast, was also developed at the Savoy, but supposedly for Madame Ritz. She preferred not to have her occasional need to diet known, and so the thin, dry toast was named for Melba, who frequently ate it herself.

Most Revolutionary Female Dancer
ISADORA DUNCAN

❦ Regarded by some as the first truly liberated woman, California-born Isadora Duncan's years as a dramatic dancer around the turn of the century were primarily years of rejection—*by* her rather than *of* her. She rejected ballet as unnatural for the human body. She rejected public school because it was more fun to teach dancing. She rejected marriage because, as she said in *My Life*, "Any intelligent woman who reads the marriage contract, and then goes into it, deserves all the consequences." (She later married a Russian poet who gave her all the hellish consequences that a wife could know.) She rejected America because its audiences were indifferent to her fluid modern dancing, and her bare feet were banned in Boston. Finally Isadora rejected dance and life itself for alcoholic oblivion and the ultimate automobile ride in 1927 during which her famous scarf caught in the wheel and broke her neck.

But her life, too, was a life of recognition by vast, enthusiastic European audiences and, soon, by the world that a new form of dance had arrived on the scene. Louis Untermeyer, who regarded Isadora Duncan as one of the *Makers of the Modern World*, said, ". . . her art was more than a vogue; it was a purging force. It cleared the stage of a clutter of false conventions and, freeing the body of corseted and petticoated absurdities, liberated its movements. Isadora Duncan brought about a revolution not only in the dance but in the modern mind, healthier for her pioneering art."

Only Woman Single-Handedly To Create a Major Art Gallery
ISABELLA STUART GARDNER

❦ Just for the fun of it, Isabella Gardner used the fortune her father left her to travel extensively in Europe. There she bought . . . and bought . . . and bought, often on the advice of her friend Bernard Berenson but just as often relying on her own instincts. Back in Boston she used the bits and pieces of old buildings she had found in Italy to design Fenway Court, a Venetian-style palace. She supervised every stage of the building, often to the dismay of the architect and his workers. She herself then arranged every item within—the furniture, the flowers in the courtyard, the window hangings, and, of course, the paintings: Vermeer, Fra Angelico, Cellini, Giotto, altogether one of the finest collections in the world. In 1903, Mrs. Jack, as she was known, opened the brick wall that had shielded the embryonic museum and admitted the public to her creation . . . but only when she felt like it—a fact that destroyed her credibility as a public museum and caused the U.S. Customs Service to charge high import fees on the works she brought into the country. At her death in 1924, her will demanded that every item remain exactly as she left it. Therefore Fenway Court still stands today, exquisite and unchanged. Aline B. Saarinen wrote of its creator in *The Proud Possessors*, "Like all egotists, she was driven by vanity. Hers was no mean variety: it was cosmic and insatiable. The ceaseless pursuit of its gratification . . . has enriched America."

Composer of the Largest Number of
Memorable Sentimental Songs
CARRIE JACOBS BOND

❦ Though now they seem almost painfully saccharine, Carrie Bond's songs have played a role in almost all American lives of the last eighty years, if only as remembered tunes played on grandmother's piano. They include "God Remembers When the World Forgets," "Just a Wearyin' For You," and the ever-popular "I Love You Truly." "The End of a Perfect Day," published in 1910, sold over five million copies and was sung by the composer at the White House. Mrs. Bond, widowed with children, was forced to try her hand at many things to earn a living. Although she herself couldn't sing well, she did earn more than a thousand dollars a week performing her own popular melodies.

Most Reproduced Portrait of a Woman
PAUL CHABAS'S ETHEREAL NUDE,
"SEPTEMBER MORN"

❦ It was a pleasant enough painting that won the Medal of Honor in the Paris Spring Show of 1912. Then a New York firm reproduced "September Morn" and placed it in their display window. The story goes that Anthony Comstock, the stern antipornographer whose name will forever mean killjoy, saw the picture, or at least saw young boys giggling at it, and promptly condemned the painting as obscene. One of his milder comments was, "There's too little morn and too much maid." The subsequent publicity made it one of the most famous paintings in the world. At least seven million reproductions were sold in the next few months, along with calendars (perhaps the first nude calendar), dolls, cane heads, statues, and even tattoos. There is a strong probability that the whole condemnation and consequent fame were engineered by a Hollywood publicity specialist named Harry Reichenbach. And the unknown model? Much of the to-do at the time revolved around a rumor that she was starving in a garrett in Paris. (Is it possible to starve in Paris without doing so in a garrett?) No, said the artist, she became the happy suburban wife of a French businessman. The original painting is now owned by the Metropolitan Museum of Art in New York.

Strangest Way to Get Your Message
to the People
PATIENCE WORTH

❦ Supposedly a seventeenth-century English immigrant to America who was killed by Indians, Patience Worth waited until 1913 to begin to communicate to the world through Mrs. Pearl Curran of St. Louis. At first,

Mrs. Curran wrote for Patience Worth through the tediously slow letter-by-letter process of using a Ouija board. Then the pair developed a technique by which Mrs. Curran, who never went into a trance, visualized actions or even pages of writing that she said aloud for someone else to transcribe. In this way, she/they wrote a number of novels including *Hope Trueblood* and *The Sorry Tale*. "They" were also an instant poetry machine—give Patience Worth any topic and instantly you could get back a quite readable poem on the subject.

First Person to Throw a Custard Pie in the Name of Entertainment
MABEL NORMAND

❦ In making a Mack Sennett comedy about 1913, silent screen star Mabel Normand gave into an ad-lib impulse typical of the early scriptless films and threw a pie at Ben Turpin. The rest is history.

Gladdest Woman
ELEANOR HODGSON PORTER

❦ Eleanor Hodgson Porter published *Pollyanna* in 1913, and the book promptly became a bestseller even though it was a children's book. Pollyanna's practical philosophy was to find a reason to be glad in any situation, no matter how dreadful. And from all accounts, her creator, too, managed to view all life through impossibly rosy glasses, perhaps because *Pollyanna* was such a huge success. The book was translated into many languages, made into a play, movies, a game, dolls, a spin-off *(The Yearly Glad Book)*—in all, a happy variety of immortality.

Most Imperiled Actress
PEARL WHITE

❦ Starting in 1914 with *The Perils of Pauline*, Pearl White starred in a number of movie serials that always left her hanging on a cliff, or in some other equally dangerous spot, until the next episode. In reality, she was not often required to utilize her acrobatic skills; stunt persons performed most of the trick work.

First Person to Appear in a Nude Scene on Film
ANNETTE KELLERMAN

❦ Australian swimmer Annette Kellerman was seen from the back in *Daughter of the Gods*, filmed in 1915. The first real sensation caused by nudity on film, however, was brought about by Hedy Kiesler, appearing in the German film *Ecstasy* in 1937. The actress did quite an extensive scene outdoors in her all-togethers. When the film was released, however, the scene had been edited down to where she just turned her back to the camera, walked toward the water, and swam. Even so, her financier husband, Fritz Mandl, tried to buy up all prints of the film. The scene enchanted Louis B. Mayer, movie tycoon, who brought the actress to Hollywood and changed her name to Hedy Lamarr.

Most Destructive Female Influence
on a Star's Movie Career
NATACHA RAMBOVA
(a.k.a. Winifred Hudnut)

❦ Natacha married Rudolph Valentino at the height of his slicked-hair, exotic fame. He trusted her to protect his privacy and guide his career. She did the latter by choosing Booth Tarkington's *Monsieur Beaucaire* as his next vehicle in 1924. The powdered wig hiding his famous looks and a rotten script allowed her to do the former: no one was terribly interested in invading his privacy. He sulked at home for two years and never really regained his popularity before he died in 1926, most unromantically, of a ruptured ulcer.

Woman to Most Thoroughly
Immortalize Her Uncle
MARGARET HERRICK

❦ Librarian at the Academy of Motion Picture Arts and Sciences, Margaret Herrick caught an early glimpse of the statuette created by George Stanley in 1928 for presentation to award-winning actors and film-makers. "Oh," she said, "it looks just like my uncle Oscar." The popular name caught on, perhaps encouraged by the fact that Margaret Herrick later became the Executive Director of the Academy. Just think, the lovely golden figure might as easily have become known as "Uncle." Or even "Fred."

Most Spectacular Structure Designed
by a Woman Architect
SAN SIMEON

❦ When William Randolph Hearst decided in the 1920s to turn his camp on land around the Bay of San Simeon in California into a "ranch," he called on Julia Morgan, a friend of his mother's. Miss Morgan was an architect who had graduated from the École de Beaux Arts in Paris (first woman to do so). He pictured a Spanish castle, and that's what she gave him—a huge Spanish-style main house with one hundred rooms, including thirty-eight bedrooms. Some guests were relegated to one of the Italianate palaces set around the grounds. All buildings shelter what is perhaps the most grandiose collection of art objects and artifacts ever assembled. The San Simeon estate is now a California State Historical Monument.

Before her death in 1957, Julia Morgan built numerous homes, offices and other public buildings, primarily in California. After the 1906 San Francisco earthquake, she worked on the rebuilding of the Fairmont Hotel. A newspaper interviewer asked her some puzzled-sounding questions about her work on the hotel, and she finally said, "I don't think you understand just what my work has been here. The decorative part was all done by a New York firm. My work was structural."

Only Actress to Have Her Legs Banned
MARLENE DIETRICH
❦ When posters showing Marlene Dietrich's lovely legs appeared in Paris subways, they were promptly removed as too distracting for rush-hour crowds. Even her husband of more than fifty years didn't see much of her legs—they lived together only a few days each year.

Most Learned Literary Hoax by a Female
DIARY OF A YOUNG LADY
OF FASHION, 1764-1765
❦ Supposedly kept by Cleone Knox, a well-traveled and sagacious observer of eighteenth-century English life, the *Diary*, published in England in 1926, went into nine printings within only two months. Critics compared it favorably with Pepys' diary and other great journals. But as literary types pleaded with the publisher for more information, a nineteen-year-old Irish girl, Magdalen King-Hall, daughter of a British Navy admiral, came forward and admitted writing the book. It was done purely for fun and to create something out of all she had learned reading up on the period in the library at Brighton where her father was stationed.

Only Performer to Take a Nude Bath in
Champagne on Stage
JOYCE HAWLEY
❦ In 1926, a party was held on stage at the Earl Carroll Theatre after a performance. Somewhat high, seventeen-year-old Joyce Hawley, a chorus girl, accepted Earl Carroll's offer to let her bathe in the wine for the delectation of several hundred party-goers. No one complained at the time but somehow the New York Grand Jury heard of the bath and started to investigate. It wasn't concerned about the nudity; it wanted to know where the champagne came from, since merely possessing the wine was a violation of the Volstead Act. Earl Carroll, as host, was indicted. Joyce Hawley thought nothing was wrong—after all, the champagne was only an inch and a half deep in the tub.

First Black Star of the Folies-Bergère
JOSEPHINE BAKER

❦ American singer and dancer Josephine Baker took Paris, which loves exotics of all varieties, by storm in 1925 (with a show in which her entrance was made in an upside-down split, wearing only a small pink feather for a costume). In 1926, she was invited to appear in the Folies-Bergère, the most elegant of skin shows. Her act at the Folies called for another dramatic entrance, this one made in a large, flowered ball descending from the ceiling. The ball opened like an egg and she danced, clad only in a string of bananas. Her popularity in Europe became so great that in just the first two years she received over two thousand marriage proposals.

Last of the Red-Hot Mamas
SOPHIE TUCKER

❦ On her own say-so, and without really defining a "red-hot mama," that's the billing this deep-throated café singer and entertainer used at the Palace Theatre in 1927, and it stayed with her. She had earlier been called the "World Renowned Coon Shouter," "The Queen of Jazz," and even the "Mary Garden of Ragtime."

Woman Who Received the Largest Sculpture
Commission Ever Awarded
MALVINA HOFFMAN

❦ In 1930, Malvina Hoffman received a commission to research and create one hundred and one life-size bronze statues of racial types of the world for the Hall of Man at the Field Museum of Natural History. An American student of Auguste Rodin and Janet Scudder, she was at that time best known for her portrait busts. She was selected from among three thousand sculptors for the Field commission. The research for the statues took five years and sent her, with her husband, to every inhabited corner of the earth. On her return to Paris, she oversaw all the work of casting the many statues in bronze. In *Heads and Tales*, the story of the journey, she described her work this way:

> Each race left its mark upon my consciousness with a vivid impression. I have tried both by the gestures and poise of the various statues, as well as by the characterization in the facial modelling, to give a convincing and lifelike impression. I watched the natives in their daily life, fishing, hunting, praying, and preparing their food, or resting after a day's work. Then I chose the moment at which I felt each one represented something *characteristic of his race, and of no other.*

First Guest Star in Broadcasting
GRACIE ALLEN

❦ Gracie Allen was first heard as a guest on a special broadcast by Eddie Cantor in 1931. Two years later she started a long-running gag of popping up on every possible radio program in search of her missing brother (her real brother had to go into hiding because of the publicity). In 1940, Gracie Allen entered the political arena as a Presidential candidate for the Surprise Party.

Most Famous Fan Dancer
SALLY RAND

❦ One of the many silent film actresses no one ever heard of, Sally Rand tried live play-acting but, in true theatrical tradition, found herself stranded in Chicago when the company went broke. She figured that fan-filtered nudity was better than starvation and soon appeared in a Chicago nightclub, initiating the costume that *Celebrity Register* described as "lipstick, rouge, slippers, two fluffy fans and a dim lavender light." She wanted to take part in the Chicago Century of Progress Exposition in 1933 but Streets of Paris, the biggest show at the fair, wouldn't have her. In retaliation, she appeared outside that show's doors on opening night, May 30, 1933, undressed as Lady Godiva. Streets of Paris took her in and she became probably the only memorable personality of that show. She was still fanning interest as a dancer in the 1960s when she would not tell what, if anything, she wore under the fans: "It doesn't much matter. The Rand is quicker than the eye."

Only Female Official Photographer of the
Hitler Regime
LENI RIEFENSTAHL

❦ Actress-turned-film producer and director, Leni Riefenstahl had a fan in Adolf Hitler, who asked her in 1932 to record his glory on film as he rose in power. She had to overcome (or ignore) the Nazi antifemale attitudes but managed to create a memorable documentary in *Triumph of the Will*, covering the 1934 Nazi Party Congress at Nuremburg. Her *Olympia*, beautifully documenting the 1936 Olympics, is regarded as one of the ten greatest motion pictures of all time. During World War II itself, she was inactive after refusing to make propaganda films. It was not until 1952 that Ms. Riefenstahl was acquitted of Nazi Party involvement and was free to return to her work. In recent years she has concentrated her skills on still photos of African tribal life.

Only Woman, Famed for Her Autobiography,
Who Didn't Write It
ALICE B. TOKLAS

❦ Alice Toklas was Gertrude Stein's companion, roommate, fellow salon-keeper, cook, whatever, from 1907 to 1946. In 1933, the overwhelming Gertrude published the *Autobiography of Alice B. Toklas*. In it she told her own story as if Alice were telling it from her point of view. Ms. Stein is said to have invented one of the most quoted phrases created by a woman: "Rose is a rose is a rose is a rose." The phrase is typical of her rather enigmatic, stream-of-consciousness writing, a style that led reporters who heard her somewhat more lucid speech to ask why she didn't write the way she spoke. Her reply: "Why don't you read the way I write?" In the *Autobiography*, "Alice" says, "Speaking of the device of rose is a rose is a rose is a rose, it was I who found it in one of Gertrude Stein's manuscripts and insisted upon putting it as a device on the letter paper, on the table linen and anywhere that she would permit that I would put it."

The real Alice had the distinction of being probably the first cookbook author to include marijuana in one of her recipes for brownies.

Only Woman to Appear in 1700 Movies
JANE CHESTER

❦ A Hollywood hopeful in the thirties, Jane Chester joined a number of other girls in having their pictures taken posed as the Statue of Liberty. She quickly gave up Hollywood as a lost cause and had moved away when Columbia Pictures chose the picture of her as the Statue for use as its trademark, opening every film it has released since 1938.

Only Singer Virtually to Own a Song
that She Did Not Write
KATE SMITH

❦ On November 11, 1938, during an Armistice Day radio broadcast, Kate Smith sang for the first time in public Irving Berlin's composition, "God Bless America." The enthusiastic response was so immediate and the song became so closely associated with Kate that Berlin gave her the exclusive rights to sing the song on the air. The right to sing it was later released to others, but there is still a large segment of America that believes Kate Smith wrote the national anthem, "God Bless America."

Most Frequently Misquoted Actress
GRETA GARBO

❦ Everyone knows that she said, "I vahnt to be alone," in a voice about which a *Picture Play* writer said, "for the life of me I can't decide whether it's baritone or bass." The Swedish actress who became known in Hollywood as "the Mysterious Stranger" (at the encouragement, or so he claims, of Lon Chaney, who found mystery helpful) is a greater success now than she ever was when making films. She retired in 1941 and has since been mostly alone. She recently told Allen Porter, film curator at the New York Museum of Modern Art, which holds SRO retrospectives of Garbo films, "I never said I wanted to be alone. I only said I want to be *let* alone."

Most Futile Campaign Designed to
Correct a Misconception

❦ The first holder of this award is the Daughters of the American Revolution. They tried to convince the public that they had not rejected Marian Anderson's request to sing in Constitution Hall in Washington, D.C., because she was black. When her manager asked for an April 9, 1939, date for a concert in the DAR-owned hall, the DAR turned him down. Miss Anderson recorded in her autobiography, *My Lord, What a Morning*, that they ". . . had decreed that it could not be used by one of my race." A national fuss ensued, during which Eleanor Roosevelt resigned from the DAR. She and others arranged for the concert to be held on the steps of the Lincoln Memorial. Thousands of people, who would not have been able to fit into Constitution Hall, which was the largest in Washington until the Kennedy Center was built, heard Miss Anderson's wonderful contralto voice. The DAR claims—but no one listens—that the National Symphony Orchestra had, six months before, reserved the hall for that April date, and that black tenor Roland Hayes had rented the hall eight years before, so they couldn't be against blacks.

A close runner-up in this category involves the space program. In March 1972 the Pioneer 10 spacecraft was launched from Cape Kennedy. The probe flew by Jupiter and then would slowly curve out of the solar system—the first earth-made object to do so. Attached to an antenna strut of the craft is a plaque bearing messages that it is hoped will be comprehended by some hypothetical intelligent life form who might come across the craft eons and light-years away. Part of the engraved message shows the outline figures of a human man and woman to indicate what kind of beings built the craft. The man has a penis. The woman has breasts but shows no line or other mark to indicate a vagina. When the plaque was first displayed to the public, a number of well-known columnists immediately spread the word that the hierarchy at the National Aeronautics and Space Administration had censored the female signs of sexuality. Government censorship! The people who designed the messages, including astronomer Carl Sagan and his wife, say the woman had never had external genitalia because the drawings were patterned after classic Greek statues and because they thought NASA *might* censor the figure. The censorship was on the part of the original artists, not the government. But NASA lives on with a reputation as the agency that was too puritanical to send a truthful message to other beings in the universe.

Only Major Woman Band Leader
in the Big-Band Era
INA RAY HUTTON

❦ A former Ziegfeld actress, Ina Hutton started her band career at sixteen in the mid-1930s, conducting an all-girl orchestra. The audiences liked it but the critics snickered and reminded Ina that "only men can play good jazz." By 1940 the all-girl band had become all men and her big jazz band was in wide demand. The sound was good and men in the audience appreciated the sight of a small blonde clothed in clinging evening gown leading a large group of men. The heyday of the big bands, however, couldn't last; there were too many of them with too few engagements to be had. In the one month of December 1946, eight of the best big bands sounded their last notes. Ina Ray Hutton's was among them.

England can claim the longest-lasting female-led all-girl dance band. Ivy Benson started her group about 1940 and it still plays, at least as an occasional curiosity.

Oldest Artist to Gain Fame
ANNA MARY ROBERTSON ("GRANDMA")
MOSES

❦ A New England farmer's wife, Grandma Moses began painting at age seventy-eight, only after her arthritic fingers could no longer do needle-work. Within a year, a New York collector had discovered her charmingly primitive work and entered a few pictures in a show of unknowns at New York's Museum of Modern Art. Her first one-woman show brought wide acclaim to her landscapes. By the time of her death in 1962 at age 101, her work was in demand by collectors all over the world.

First Widely Syndicated Female
Cartoon-Strip Artist
DALE MESSICK

❦ Dale Messick, born Dalia but forced to change it because she thought no one would support a female cartoonist, developed the idea for "Brenda Starr, Reporter" in 1940 with Mollie Slott, an executive with the Chicago Tribune-New York News Syndicate. Brenda's adventures as a stalwart advocate of the independent woman reporter were mostly derived from Dale Messick's own dreams, both night and day. At its height, the strip drew an audience estimated at forty million. The 1960s saw Brenda lose some of her popularity, but she has lately acquired folk-heroine status because of her liberated life. In 1976, Brenda Starr gained new impetus by forsaking thirty-six years of virginity in print and marrying Basil St. John, who had been after her for many years. Readers of one hundred fifty newspapers wished her well and even cheered when she later had a baby.

Only Sculptor to Design Pressurized
Flight Clothing
ALICE KING

❦ During World War II, the Aerospace Medical Research Laboratory called on sculptor Alice King because of her knowledge of the human body to design a special helmet that would pressurize a pilot's face and ears. A test proved it safe to one hundred thousand feet. That altitude might be needed for the special purpose to which her helmet would be put: Captain Charles Yeager wore it in 1947 in the flights in which he became the first human being to break the sound barrier. The sculptor remained in the research lab and eventually created the casts of the astronauts' heads used in guaranteeing a perfect fit for their individually made space helmets.

Woman to Photograph the Most Babies
CONSTANCE BANNISTER

❦ Constance Bannister became established as a photographer of "pinup" babies during World War II and soon every baby product firm wanted Bannister babies for their advertising. Several short films by and about her, numerous books, calendars, and pamphlets illustrated by her, and appearances on television made her the most sought-after baby photographer. By now she has viewed nearly one-quarter of a million diapered infants through her cameras.

Only Actress to Be an Actor
"ROBERT ARCHER"

❦ "Robert Archer"'s real name was Tanis Chandler and she went to Hollywood, like all would-be film stars, hoping to take the city by storm. Soon it was clear that all the studios wanted was men, and more men— because, in 1944, most of that sex were in the armed services. So she became a man, calling herself Robert Archer. But then one day on the set the director decided that a certain scene required lots of manly chest and called for the actors to remove their shirts. Robert Archer refused . . . and was found to be Tanis Chandler.

Only Opera Singer to Perform
Complete Roles While Seated
MARJORIE LAWRENCE

❦ In January 1943, only nineteen months after being stricken with paralyzing polio during a performance of *Die Walküre*, the Australian soprano Marjorie Lawrence sang in *Tannhäuser*, at the Metropolitan Opera, while seated on a divan. A few weeks later she did the long hours of *Tristan und Isolde* seated. Her courage had never been questioned since the night in 1936 when she made operatic history in *Götterdämmerung* by, instead of leading her horse offstage, galloping off through a ring of flame. She told the story of her struggle with polio in *Interrupted Melody*, which was later made into a film.

Youngest Composer to Perform His or Her
Own Work with the New York Philharmonic
PHILIPPA SCHUYLER

❦ An infant prodigy, Philippa Schuyler had been playing piano since she was three years old. She wrote *Manhattan Nocturne* for a young composer's contest sponsored by the Grinnell Foundation, and performed it with the Philharmonic in 1944, when she was twelve years old.

Only Female Leader of a Classical Japanese
Kabuki Dance Company
TOKUHO AZUMA IV

❦ Daughter of a long line of dancers in the traditional Kabuki style, Azuma was barred from the Grand Kabuki, *the* theater for this ancient style of voiceless dance and drama, because of her sex. Encouraged by her dancer mother, she prepared from childhood for the dance, and when her father died in 1945, the critical powers-that-be acknowledged her as good enough to inherit the leadership of his Azuma Kabuki troupe. She brought them to the United States in 1954 for America's first exposure to the seemingly alien but quickly absorbing style of Oriental dance.

First Child of a President to Sing
Professionally on Stage
MARGARET TRUMAN

❦ On August 23, 1947, with the encouragement of her father, Margaret Truman performed in the Hollywood Bowl, with the orchestra conducted by Eugene Ormandy. Several other concerts brought in audiences and similar reviews: pleasant voice, needs more training. She took the advice and even trained for a while with Helen Traubel. In 1950, however, Boston music critic Paul Hume wrote a scathing review of one concert. Margaret's father, Harry S. Truman, in never-forgotten fatherly feeling, wrote Hume a threat to destroy him if they should ever meet and denouncing him as "an eight-ulcer man on four-ulcer pay."

The world seems less interested now, when Ronald Reagan's daughter, Patty Davis, sings and acts professionally.

Most Famous Unknown Singer ... or Most Unknown Famous Singer
MARNI NIXON

❦ Originally a messenger girl on the Metro-Goldwyn-Mayer lot in Hollywood, Marni Nixon's voice was discovered somewhere along the line but seemingly no one wanted her body. In 1948 she sang for Margaret O'Brien in the film *Big City*. In 1956 Deborah Kerr in *The King and I* sounded remarkably like Marni Nixon, and five years later, Natalie Wood's voice in *West Side Story* was dubbed by the singer. Finally, in 1964, Audrey Hepburn's role of Eliza Doolittle in *My Fair Lady* was sung by the mystery voice. Nowhere on the record jackets of these movie sound tracks is it acknowledged that the heroine's voice is actually that of Marni Nixon. Just once did she herself get to appear on screen; she played a small role as a nun in *The Sound of Music*.

Only Cellist to Perform in Concert Topless
CHARLOTTE MOORMAN

❦ On February 9, 1967, Charlotte Moorman performed Nam June Paik's *Mixed Media Opera* at Town Hall in New York, minus a top. The spectacular concert ended in her arrest. The next year, she finished the concert in an effort to pay her mounting legal fees. This performance consisted of a variety of costume removals (starting from armor) and ending with her clad only in her cello, all with brief musical interludes.

Bestselling Novelist
JACQUELINE SUSANN

❦ Determined to make money, Jaqueline Susann, an actress-turned-writer, developed a formula for novels that included sex, drugs, thinly disguised celebrities, and the right of the reader to pity the unhappy heroes . . . and then sold them in probably the most relentless publicity tours ever undertaken by an author. Her *Valley of the Dolls*, published in 1966, has outsold any other novel, up into twenty million copies. The next two books, *The Love Machine* and *Once Is Not Enough*, made her the first novelist in history to have three consecutive books hit the top of the bestseller lists. Adela Rogers St. Johns says of Ms. Susann's work: "This is absolutely first-class, top-drawer trash, which the reading public requires, always has required, insists upon and righteously adores."

Ten years before *Valley of the Dolls* was published, the tradition that women should write genteel books was rudely shattered by Grace Metalious's *Peyton Place*. This first of the sexual blockbusters by female writers sold nine and a half million copies in the first twelve years. It spawned a movie, became the first soap opera shown on prime-time TV and the first television program to be shown on prime time three times a week, and has turned into a synonym for any place or situation where scandal underlies a surface niceness.

Strangest Way to Write Music
ROSEMARY BROWN

❦ About 1970, more and more talk was heard about new works by such composers as Liszt, Beethoven, Brahms, Chopin, Mozart, Grieg, and Stravinsky. The medium through which they reached the public was an unmusically trained (but from a family of psychics) British housewife named Rosemary Brown who wrote the music automatically as the dead composers relayed it to her. The method for transcribing it was taught to her by Franz Liszt, she claims. Some of the pieces have been recorded and the experts say that stylistically the numbers are pretty good and faithful to the predeath compositions but not as technically accomplished as the originals. The notes on the record album cover were also written by a spirit, that of Sir Donald Tovey, a musicologist who had been dead for thirty years. Oh—and Beethoven devotees will be glad to know that as a spirit he has regained his hearing. And Schubert *did* finish his Symphony.

Most Unusual Audience Participation
in a Play
KATHARINE HEPBURN

❦ Perhaps she felt that the particular matinee performance of *Candide* she was attending on Broadway in 1974 needed a pick-me-up. Or perhaps she just needed a brief rest herself. But anyway, there was this bed on stage, and in the bed was the leading man, Lewis Stadlen. Suddenly, there beside him, was the great Hepburn—just for a few brief silent seconds. Then she returned to the audience via the stairs up which she had come. She never explained what particular impulse she was following in making the stage appearance.

Only Aging Female Actor to Play Hamlet
DAME JUDITH ANDERSON

❦ In 1971, at age seventy-three, Dame Judith took on the famous role. The critics had difficulty getting across the credibility gap. No great actress had performed the role since Sarah Bernhardt at the turn of the century when she was perhaps fifty.

Oldest Actress to Sign a Long-Term Contract
JUDITH LOWRY

❦ At age eighty-five, in 1975, Judith Lowry was asked to sign a five-year contract to play Mother Dexter on the CBS-TV comedy series, "Phyllis." Ms. Lowry was flattered. The series folded before the actress did.

Most Efficient at Making
Her Dream Come True
CHARLOTTE BERGEN

🦃 Several times each year Charlotte Bergen, an elderly, wealthy New
Jersey woman, rents the famed Carnegie Hall, hires the American
Symphony Orchestra, as well as some soloists of her choice, sends
invitations to a growing coterie of fans, and holds a free concert, with
herself at the baton. Raised on pleasant parlor music, which she played on
her cello, she didn't discover an urge to conduct until in her seventies when
she began to help an ailing church choir. She discovered the glories of
wielding a baton and began to feel every musician's dream—to be at the
head of a great symphony orchestra. So she also discovered a very soul-
satisfying use for her money. Between public concerts she practices by
conducting recorded symphonic music. Her public has come to respect her
determination, if not her skill.

Highest Paid Female Journalist
BARBARA WALTERS

🦃 In April 1976, Barbara Walters, the longtime mainstay of NBC's early-
morning "Today" show, left her job for ABC and the chance to be
America's first woman regularly to anchor an evening network news
program, not to mention a contract calling for a million dollars a year for
five years. Reaction in the industry was swift and vocal, much of it
expressing dismay at the news media acquiring "game show standards," at
the division between news and entertainment being compromised, at
"grotesque amounts of money"—all reactions that probably would not have
been voiced about a man earning such a contract. The whole point of the
move for ABC was to try to bring its always-in-third-place-among-the-
networks news division into stronger contention for the advertising dollar;
ABC executives thought Barbara Walters and her million-dollar salary
could make the difference. (It turned out not to: not until an entirely
different format was developed did ABC's ratings go up. Ms. Walters's
great interviewing skills were used on a variety of other programs.)

Biggest User of Gumdrops
ANN FITZPATRICK

🦃 A resident of Stockbridge, Massachusetts, Ann Fitzpatrick sculpts
figures out of candy, using a sugar paste as the base and then decorating
with carefully chosen shapes and colors of gumdrops. Her business, called
Gum Drop Square, goes through ten or twelve tons of the stuff each year,
turning them into cars, dolls, Santas, castles, and window displays for
Bloomingdale's.

Most Prolific Female Mystery Writer
DAME AGATHA CHRISTIE

❦ "Give me a nice deadly phial to play with and I am happy," declared Agatha Christie. By her death in 1976, this bloodthirsty but always genteel English creator of such popular detectives as Hercule Poirot (with his "little grey cells") and the neighborly Miss Jane Marple, had over one hundred books and plays to her credit. Starting with *The Mysterious Affair at Styles*, published in 1920, Dame Agatha created most of the techniques of mystery novels that are now commonplace. Most of her books continue to be republished as each new generation of mystery addicts comes along. By 1976 her books had been translated into 103 languages and well over 300 million copies sold. Many have been made into films and TV shows, and several plays have been produced both on stage and on film. One of these, *The Mousetrap*, is the longest continuously-running play in history. It opened in London's West End in 1952, passed the record for performances in London in 1963, and was still running eighteen years later. At least one actress has made her entire career from the one play.

9

GLAMOUR GIRLS

Woman Who Worked the Hardest
to Be with Her Lover
BERTHA

❦ It seems Charlemagne refused to be separated from his children. He insisted that they dine with him, travel with him, ride with him—above all, that they must never marry because he would not let them leave nor permit a stranger to come reside with them. Predictably, Bertha and her sister Rotruda grew restless under these constraints, and found passing pleasure with various nobles of the court. One winter, Bertha's love was a courtier named Angilbert. In order to avoid leaving male footprints in the snow leading to her tower bedroom, Bertha would go to the main castle, pick Angilbert up on her back, and carry him to her chambers. After their dalliance, she would return him across the courtyard in the same fashion.

Most Unusual Coronation
IÑES DE CASTRO

❦ Iñes de Castro was crowned queen of Portugal in 1357. There was, however, one irregularity: She had already been dead for two years, murdered by the order of the new king's father and predecessor, Afonso IV. She and Dom Pedro, Afonso's son, had been lovers for many years, and perhaps were secretly married. Her influence over Dom Pedro grew over the years and through several children, until Papa didn't approve. He ordered the assassination of Iñes. Pedro swung back into line, at least until he ascended the throne two years later. The first thing he did was order Iñes to be exhumed. Her body was robed, seated, and crowned, and, it is said, the members of the court were ordered to kiss their new queen's hand.

First Publicly Acknowledged Royal Mistress
AGNES SOREL

❦ Agnes Sorel was mistress to Charles VII of France, but oh, so much more in the legends of France. In the mythology that developed around certain lives, Agnes played a vital role in the seemingly infinite struggle between France and England called the Hundred Years War. When the English king, Henry VI, was declared king of both nations, indolent Charles just decided to live and let live, letting the loyalty of his subjects wither. Not even his coronation, forced by the ill-fated Joan of Arc, got him off his couch. Legend has it, however, that a maid of honor, Agnes Sorel, became his mistress and shamed him into taking to horse in battle. She got friends to advance him funds for war and she encouraged brave young men to pledge themselves to knighthood in the cause of their king. Charles regained his kingdom, and the influence Agnes had over him became public knowledge. The poet in every French breast took over, elevating her to a position of inspiration for all. When she died suddenly in 1450, probably of dysentery, her followers would have none of so banal a death and insisted she had been poisoned.

First Known Woman to Be Given
a Diamond Wedding Ring
MARY, DUCHESS OF BURGUNDY

🐦 In 1477, Mary received a diamond wedding ring from her betrothed, Maximilian of Austria, who needed to impress the woman because competition for her hand was pretty stiff. She brought with her marriage much of France and the Netherlands, which passed into the domain of the Hapsburgs with her marriage to Maximilian.

First White Woman to Live Alone in America
MARGUERITE DE LA ROQUE

🐦 Perhaps as a lark, in 1541 Marguerite and her maid accompanied Roberval, leader (with Jacques Cartier) of an expedition into the heart of Canada. On board the ship Marguerite became pregnant by another man. In retaliation, Roberval abandoned her, the lover, and a maid on an island in the St. Lawrence River. The baby, the lover, and the maid all died. Marguerite was left alone, subsisting on berries and expecting death any moment, when a fishing boat found her and took her back to France. No more is known of the adventurous woman, but another Marguerite, the Queen of Navarre, wrote up her story as a popular romance.

First American Woman Presented at Court
MATAOKA
(a.k.a. Pocahontas)

🐦 Mataoka, playfully known to her family, and then the world as Pocahontas, was the Indian wife of John Rolfe, the first tobacco man. She went to England with this strait-laced English gentleman who went through much soul-searching before marrying the Indian girl. He, she, and their son went to meet his mother (and women today think that's an ordeal!) and to promote the colony. On January 6, 1617, Pocahontas was presented to the King and Queen by Lord and Lady de la Warr, under the name Rebekah, which she had taken at her christening. Her health began to fail but she joined Rolfe aboard ship to return to America. Before the ship left the Thames, however, Pocahontas was dead, probably of the dreadful chills of Thameside London. She is buried at Gravesend. Her son, Thomas, remained in England until adulthood.

Longest Running Beauty Contest
THE CZAR'S WIFE

❦ Over a number of centuries the Russian czars brought aristocratic virgins to Moscow from all over the Russias to be poked, proded, posed, and peered at during a week of strenuous girl-watching. The strain, however, was worth the prize: marriage to the czar and life in luxury as a czarina. The custom died out under Peter the Great, whose own parents had wed that way. He developed a mistrust of women, perhaps because his half-sister had tried to have him assassinated and his mother had forced him to wed a woman he couldn't stand. After he divorced her, he secretly married his mistress, who became Catherine I. Many succeeding years of rule by women effectively killed the beauty contest approach to imperial marriage.

Most Famous Sex School
SCHOOL OF GALLANTRY

❦ A seventeenth-century Parisian girl (originally named Anne) who discovered quite early that sex and love were insatiable needs for her, Ninon de Lenclos decided to turn what she wanted to do anyway into profit. No ordinary prostitute, she demanded the same *joie de vivre* from her lovers that she herself had: "One needs a hundred times more esprit in order to love properly than to command armies." All the best men came to her salons, both for love and wit, and Ninon became known as the expert on love. Always thinking, she opened the School of Gallantry, a polite name for something much more intimate. Young men of the aristocracy were enrolled by wise parents to learn the correct ways of love. Ninon's lessons developed into widely known aphorisms concerning love; for example— "Men are more often defeated because of their own clumsiness than because of a woman's virtue." She saw it as her job to eliminate all chances of clumsiness. Not all was just talk. Ninon was happy to demonstrate her lessons in bed, though perhaps not with every student. In later years, after a tragedy in which her own son, not knowing who she was, fell in love with her, she left Ninon behind and became the still loved Mlle de Lenclos. Even at 80 she inspired passion in more than one male breast. Her death at 90 occurred in the company of old friends and lovers.

Only Royal Mistress to Be Betrayed
by Her Own Pet
MME DU BARRY

❦ A milliner's assistant taken in hand by a roué who introduced the young beauty to King Louis XV of France, Mme du Barry let all the glories of wealth and power go to her head. She kept as a pet a young, dark-skinned boy from Bengal whom she named Zamore, requiring that he share a basket with her favorite dog and sit quietly at her feet. She was often painted with him to sharpen, by contrast, her pale beauty. But boys grow up and kings pass on and mistresses lose power when their protectors die. Came the French Revolution and du Barry went to England, taking much of her funds to safety. For some reason she returned to Paris. Zamore, remembering his childhood of humiliation, reported her return to the decapitating Revolutionary Tribunal. As one biographer, Stanley Loomis, put Zamore's action: "The adder of resentment must long since have sunk its fangs into Zamore's inscrutable heart." He testified at her trial and she was found guilty of consorting with the aristocracy (difficult not to do when one is a royal mistress). Du Barry, undignified to the last, was taken screaming to the guillotine.

Most Persuasive Diplomatic Gift
LOUISE DE QUÉROUALLE, OR KÉROUALLE,
EVENTUALLY CARWELL

❦ When Louis XIV was trying to achieve an alliance with England in 1670, he sent a gift that he knew would most readily catch the eye of his brother monarch, Charles II. That gift was Louise de Quéroualle, a maid of honor to the Duchess of Orleans, Charles's sister. Charles, who was in the process of removing Barbara Villiers, his Duchess of Cleveland, from his bed, was ready for new sport. Louise played her game well and kept the king at bay for several months until he had agreed to Louis's plan: France would provide military defense for England if England would declare itself a Roman Catholic nation. Carwell's role in international affairs went to her head and she spent her later years with Charles (she remained his Duchess of Portsmouth until his death in 1685) frequently playing spy for France and living to the hilt on huge amounts of money collected for patronage favors. She also produced one of Charles' fourteen illegitimate children. After Charles's death, she returned to France.

Woman with the Largest Wardrobe
EMPRESS ELIZABETH OF RUSSIA

❦ Empress Elizabeth reportedly had at least fifteen thousand dresses, each with its own accessories and undergarments. Much of her wardrobe was pink, a color she usurped as her own, outlawing its use by any other woman. She was a little more practical in the matter of shoes: she had only five thousand pair.

Woman Loaned Out by Her Husband
for the Silliest Reason
MARGHERITA GUAZZI

❧ A beautiful and shapely model and wife to the mid-eighteenth-century Prussian artist Raphael Mengs, Margherita Guazzi was loaned by him to Johann Joachim Winckelman. Purpose: to test the elevation of that man's mind. Winckelman, an archeologist and art historian who had turned Roman Catholic while living in Rome, was rewarded for his religious zeal by promotion to the rank of Abate: not quite priest but more than a layman. He wanted to demonstrate the strength of his will in resisting bodily temptation. So good friend Mengs loaned him Margherita to lie naked by the abate's side. They spent hours carrying on high-level artistic discussions ignoring the closeness of their naked bodies. Winckelman was just showing off—he would have found the demonstration much more difficult if Margherita had been a smooth, adolescent boy.

Footnote: Winckelman was later murdered by a young lad whom he invited to his hotel room to "see some coins."

Another footnote: In 1946, Mahatma Gandhi in India announced that he had often slept beside young girls in order to strengthen his resistance to sexual temptation.

Last Woman to Have Her Breast Serve as the
Mold for Drinking Goblets
MARIE ANTOINETTE OF FRANCE

❧ The Sèvres porcelain factory still displays in its museum one from a set of goblets made from a mold of Marie Antoinette's breast, a custom that was more popular in antiquity than in recent times.

First Couturier
ROSE (ORIGINALLY ROSE-JEANNE) BERTIN

❧ Dressmaker ("Secretary of Fashion") to Marie Antoinette, about 1780, Rose Bertin had an establishment in London as well and did a great deal of business with ambassadors' wives. When the Revolution forced her into exile she took all the royal ladies of Europe as clients. Even today many dressmakers call themselves "Mme Rose."

Most Immortalized Consumptive
LA DAME AUX CAMÉLIAS

❧ La Dame aux Camélias was patterned after Alphonsine (later Marie du) Plessis, a runaway from a small Normandy village who became one of the most popular courtesans of Paris. By age nineteen she was being kept by seven different men, one for each night. Men found her sparkling eyes particularly disturbing, though the sparkle was caused as much by tuberculosis as her *joie de vivre*. Her relationship with Alexandre Dumas *fils* was short but memorable. When he heard of her death at age twenty-three in 1847, he immortalized her as Marguerite Gauthier in *La Dame aux Camélias*, which later became the play *Camille* and then Verdi's opera *La Traviata*.

In 1927, Janet Flanner reported in *The New Yorker:* "Camille is buried in the cemetery of Montmartre. A special fund has been raised to care for her grave, most of the money going to erase signatures of unhappy lovers who scrawled their names on her tomb."

Only Woman Whose Morals Were an Official Agenda Topic of a Cabinet Meeting
PEGGY O'NEALE EATON

❦ Peggy O'Neale had just married Senator John Eaton, in September, 1829, though they had been friends for many years before her first husband's death. Or had they been much more than friends? The Cabinet wives certainly thought so and when President Jackson appointed Eaton Secretary of War, they were outraged. Gossip said that Peggy had traveled as Eaton's wife before they were married, that she had had a miscarriage at least a year after her first husband had gone to sea, and more. The Cabinet wives, refusing to socialize with Peggy, egged their husbands into a Cabinet split right down the middle. Peggy's supporters were led by Secretary of State Martin van Buren, the detractors by Vice-President John C. Calhoun. President Jackson, who thought his own wife had been killed by gossip, supported Peggy fully, and called at least one full Cabinet meeting specifically to try to deal with the rumors. It didn't work, and what began as a wives' social crisis became a governmental Cabinet crisis. Finally in 1831, Eaton resigned and Jackson retaliated by demanding the resignation of his entire Cabinet.

In 1859, three years after Eaton's death, Peggy dumbfounded Washington society by marrying her granddaughter's nineteen-year-old dancing teacher. When he had run through Peggy's money, he eloped with the granddaughter herself.

Only King's Mistress to Cause Her King to Abdicate
LOLA MONTEZ

❦ The Andalusian, as Lola Montez was known, was actually Eliza Gilbert of Irish birth. Her fame started with her breasts—bared, that is, to King

Ludwig I of Bavaria. Separated from her husband in the early decades of the nineteenth century, outcast from her family, she took up dancing in Spain. She traveled the European capitals and acquired many lovers but little success. Finding herself in Munich, she decided to go right to the top to gain support and permission to dance in a particular theater. Planting herself firmly, and without appointment, in the royal ante-room at the palace, she conned her way past a footman and a major domo into the presence of the king himself. His eyes were caught by her superb bosom. Real or artifice? She grabbed a pair of scissors and tore open her dress. Real! And so began the sixty-year-old king's infatuation with the adventuress of whom one newspaper writer lyricized, "How am I to describe Lola's breasts when I cannot find words to describe even her teeth?" Ludwig promptly made Lola both the Baroness Rosenthal and Countess of Landsfeld.

While the king's countrymen eyed her breasts Lola occupied herself by dabbling in Munich politics, persuading the king to take a liberal, anti-Jesuit stand as well as decorating the luxurious home Ludwig presented to her. Pride of position made her sign bills for goods received "The King's Mistress" . . . and they were paid. As she herself wrote: "To be beautiful! What power and what good fortune!" But few appreciated her dancing and the genuine aristocracy ignored her, despite the king's wishes. The king's people convinced him she might be possessed by demons. He sent her to a mesmerist, both to be treated and to get her out of wrathful Munich. He failed on both counts and in 1848, the king yielded to public opinion and published a decree that Lola, the Countess of Landsfeld, "has ceased to possess the rights of a Bavarian subject." But it was too late for the king. Hatred of Lola had united two major forces, the university students and the Jesuits. Ludwig himself was forced to abdicate. Lola went to London, married, abandoned that husband to whom she may not have been legally married anyway, traversed America and Australia, failed at acting, married yet again in San Francisco, and took up the lecture platform, advising her audiences on beauty and love. Even though her platform debut in 1853 in San Francisco had tickets selling for as much as $65 each at auction, her success was minimal. Lola Montez returned to New York, found a religious faith, and died at age forty-one. Poor and alone, she was buried simply as Mrs. Eliza Gilbert.

Creator of the Most Famous Woman's Pants
ELIZABETH SMITH MILLER
❦ For her own use in gardening, Elizabeth Miller of Petersboro, New York, designed in 1851 a pair of ankle-length trousers, topped by a skirt descending just below the knee. Perhaps neglecting to change one day

before making a visit, she wore her costume to Elizabeth Cady Stanton's house. Visiting at the time was editor Amelia Bloomer, who promptly wrote up the idea in her publication *Lily*—and won for full pants ever after the name of "bloomers." Eventually the women's rights leaders dropped bloomers as their costume because of the ridicule they caused.

Only Woman Whose Mild Flirting Produced a New Type of Wine
ANNA BONACCORSI

❦ Anna Bonaccorsi was the wife of Italian Baron Bettino Ricasoli, a stern and proud man, who was briefly Prime Minister of a united Italy in 1861. One evening, they attended a ball during which a young man asked Anna for several dances. She politely granted them and returned after each to her husband's side. Nevertheless, the Baron, feeling his family honor had been attacked, called for his carriage and promptly set off through the night to Broglio, his ancient—and long deserted—family seat. He kept his wife at Broglio the remainder of her life (not for nothing was he called the "iron baron"). He used his own time as jailer to experiment in grape-growing and wine-making and devised a new method of fermentation that produced Chianti, a new type of wine.

Most Famous Courtesan with Other People's Money
LA PAÏVA

❦ Originally Thérèse Lachmann, mistress to dukes, Napoleon III, etc., La Païva was quite willing to be lover for an hour or so to anyone who yielded to her incredible demands, all of which went into good investments. After her one-night marriage, she told her husband, "I am a harlot and I intend to remain a harlot." And very lucrative it was, too. The prime Païva legend concerns one young man who implored her for a brief time of love but could not really afford her. She told him to gather all the money he could in ten-thousand-franc notes, and they would make love as long as it took for the money to burn. He returned a few days later. The notes flamed, so did their passions. As the fire died she chuckled over a young man who would burn his own wealth for her. But the laugh was his because he had brought counterfeit money. (As Cornelia Otis Skinner tells the tale, the lover was a banker and even though the notes were fake, the sight of money burning made him impotent.) Eventually she was forced out of Paris on suspicion of being a Prussian spy, but she left with another grand gesture of oneupwomanship: she, a prostitute, purchased one of the grandest of former Empress Eugénie's diamond necklaces with her nefariously acquired funds.

Only Stripper Whose Act Ended in a Death
"MONA"

❦ An artist's model named Mona is sometimes credited with starting the vogue for striptease in 1893. She and her friends, while attending a student's carnival ball, got carried away with an unplanned but riotous beauty contest. Mona evidently felt that there was only one really good way to display her charms. She leapt on a table and proceeded to remove her clothing in a very sensuous manner. When the students involved were arrested, reprimanded, and lightly fined, rioting broke out. Eventually troops were called in and one student was killed.

If it seems a very late and mild way for stripping to start, it should be recalled that at the "infamous" Moulin Rouge in the same part of Paris, gentlemen got their erotic jollies, in public at least, by catching a glimpse of an inch or two of bare flesh fleetingly exposed during the can-can. In private, however, nude photos were all the rage.

Greatest Jewelry Showoff
LIANE DE POUGY

❦ There have been many jewelry showoffs throughout history but perhaps for sheer subtle ostentation there have been few like Liane de Pougy . . . and the maid who walked behind her. A dancer, Liane guaranteed the success of her debut at Paris's Folies-Bergère by writing Edward, the Prince of Wales, that he must come and applaud her. Charmed by her audacity, he did so and soon all Paris was at her feet, or, as Janet Flanner reported years later, "Every Parisian who could afford it fell in love with her." For the price of adoring her was always a major addition to her jewel collection. Liane had a running battle going with Caroline Otéro, the other top-of-the-heap demi-monde in Paris at the end of the nineteenth century. It was important for her to appear more successful than Otéro. On one occasion when Otéro appeared in public dripping with jewels, Liane quickly rearranged her own apparel for the evening and strode into L'Opéra shorn of all jewels but with her maid stumbling behind under the weight of her entire collection. On another occasion at Maxim's, Liane also carried off the honors of the evening by again dressing in simple basic black. She made her entrance and then stood aside so the crowd could see that she was accompanied by her maid: every inch of the maid's uniform was covered in diamonds. La Otéro stomped out of the restaurant.

Longest Haired Women
THE SUTHERLAND SISTERS

❦ Each of the seven Sutherland sisters, a family of farm girls from New York State, had hair that reached the floor. Among all of them, the hair totalled the staggering length of 36 feet 10 inches. At the turn of the century, their papa, no fool, capitalized on their hair by creating a basically ineffective brew of alcohol and rainwater and selling it as Sutherland Sisters Hair Grower and Scalp Cleaner. Pictures of his daughters shone on the bottles and in the ads. The firm proved unsuccessful, however, and the girls moved on to appearances with the Barnum and Bailey Circus.

The longest known hair from the head of one woman belonged to Jane Bunford, a British turn-of-the-century woman who is often called the tallest woman in the world. If she hadn't had a spinal curvature, she would have measured 7 feet 11 inches. Her hair at its longest topped that: it was 8 feet long.

First Famous Woman to Advertise
Chewing Gum
ANNA HELD

❦ Around 1900, the manufacturer of Yucatan peppermint-flavored gum wanted a star to help publicize their new product. Anna Held, Polish-born Ziegfeld star (and Ziegfeld's wife) agreed to chew it in public, and to mention its name, for the price of a string of perfectly matched pearls. Incidently, Ms. Held, renowned for her perfect hourglass figure, had achieved that shape by having her lower ribs removed.

Most Expensive Woman's Bicycle
LILLIAN RUSSELL'S

❦ Lillian Russell's bicycle was given to her about 1900 by friend Diamond Jim Brady, at a cost at the time of about $10,000. Oh, it was gold-plated all right, but so were the dozen or so others that Brady had had made for himself. Lillian's had to be something special. Its handlebars were mother-of-pearl. The spokes were covered with rubies, emeralds, diamonds, sapphires, and other nice little bits to make them sparkle colorfully as she rode in Central Park. And when Lillian wasn't riding it, it reposed in a specially molded, velvet-lined, leather traveling case.

Only Woman to Make Clothing from a Wright
Brothers Aircraft
MRS. WILLIAM TATE

❦ After completing a series of tests on control surfaces, the pioneering Wright brothers abandoned one of their early gliders in Kitty Hawk. Because one Wright had boarded briefly at Mrs. William Tate's home during the tests, she felt entitled to the sateen fabric used to cover the wings. There was sufficient material to make durable dresses for her daughters.

Worst Example of "The Poor Little Working
Girl Who Married a King"
DRAGA MASCHIN OR MASIN

In 1900, Alexander of Serbia took Draga Maschin out of the red light district and made her his queen. Draga hadn't always occupied the red light district. In fact, she had been a lady-in-waiting to Alexander's mother (good help must have been hard to find). She lost her job and references when the queen found her in bed with the king. However, she seemed to be just what Alexander needed: "This is the only woman with whom I can be a man." Many of her earlier clients wrote Alexander demanding money to keep them from publishing "I knew her when" stories. But he didn't care . . . all he wanted was marriage. But when the marriage finally took place it was greeted by dead silence from the populace. Quickly tiring of the lack of joyous parties, Queen Draga, hoping to get the people on her side, announced that she was pregnant: the news was received by the loud guffaws that her lie deserved. But figuring that if she couldn't get friendship, she could at least get luxuries, Draga went on a vast spending spree, primarily on funds milked out of her countrymen by forcing them to support something called "Queen Draga Cavalry Regiment." All, of course, encouraged by Alexander, who loved to see his queen happy. Soon the people had had enough. Even the king's father (whom he had earlier forced into abdication and then made commander of the armed forces) recognized his son was "a criminal with a psychopathic disposition." Months of plotting on the part of the military culminated in June 1903 in the murders of Alexander and Draga. But no simple murders: their bodies were shot, then stabbed, and then trampled. Queen Draga, the girl who wanted it all, was shot thirty-six times and stabbed forty. So much for fairy tales.

Last Woman to Own the Hope Diamond
EVALYN WALSH McLEAN

Evalyn McLean, the Washingtonian who said her only important role in life was deciding "what amusing thing" she should do next, thought, in 1908, that it would be amusing to challenge the legend that the Hope Diamond—previously among a Sultan's harem jewels—brings bad luck to its owners. She had a priest bless her $154,000 purchase just to make sure. Mrs. McLean often wore the spectacular blue gem with another necklace bearing the ninety-two and a half karat, $120,000 Star of the East. (She felt there was therapeutic value in buying gems, just as other women might buy hats.) The Hope diamond, however, seems not to have lost its dreadful efficacy. Evalyn's husband, Ned, was an alcoholic. She herself became addicted to drugs prescribed to ease the pain of a badly set broken leg. Ned was involved in the Teapot Dome scandal and eventually died in a mental institution. Her daughter died of an overdose of sleeping pills. Upon

Evalyn Walsh McLean's death, New York jeweler Harry Winston, unable to find a purchaser for the incredible blue stone, presented it to the Smithsonian Institution in Washington, D.C.

First Prominent Twentieth-Century Hair Bobber
IRENE CASTLE

❦ The shearing of their "crowning glory" has gained currency among women at various times in history, but the twentieth-century episode, inaugurated by dancer Irene Castle in 1915, appears to have lasted longest. Irene Castle also shook up the public by dispensing with her whalebone corsets, and many women breathed a sigh of relief.

Seventeenth-century England saw an episode of bobbed hair, which became a matter of serious public outcry. A male (of course) member of Parliament described women who would cut their locks as: ". . . gonne so farre past shame, past modesty, grace and nature, as to clip their haire like men with lockes and foretops."

Youngest Miss America
MARGARET GORMAN

❦ Margaret Gorman was chosen at age fifteen from almost one thousand contestants in the first Atlantic City contest, held on September 7, 1921. The daring event—probably the first bathing beauty contest ever—was held in an attempt by the businessmen of Atlantic City to stretch the summer season beyond Labor Day. The winner was given no title—the name "Miss America" was not used until 1940—and nothing but eye appeal counted. Ms. Gorman stood 5 feet 1 inch tall and measured 30-25-32. The beach ban against tight bathing suits and naked knees was dropped for the occasion. Talent and poise didn't enter into the picture until years later after strong complaints from churches and the YWCA.

In 1919, at the Chu Chin Chow ball in New York, a contest was held to select the most beautiful among a large number of costumed women. The winner, Edith Hyde, was given the title "Miss America" but this contest held no connection with the later Atlantic City event.

Last of the Infamous Royal Mistresses
MAGDA LUPESCU
(a.k.a. Helen or Elena Wolff)

❦ Magda Lupescu became mistress to Prince (later King) Carol II of Rumania, in about 1924, and stayed with him through one marriage, an annulment, another marriage, and a divorce. His political enemies and father forced him into exile in France, and he left his wife behind in Rumania but took Magda. He lived near Paris with his "Cleopatra of the

Near East" until 1930. Then, when a group of leftists gained control of Rumania, he just walked back into the palace at Bucharest and reclaimed his throne from his young son in probably the quietest coup ever. Lupescu was not far behind, although those in control had ordered him to leave her. No one wrote or spoke aloud about the frequent presence of the red-haired Jewess in a small cottage on the palace grounds. But rumors flew, many making her the decision-maker behind the throne. The king's opponents marked her for assassination, blaming her "Jewish influence" on "almost every evil in this country." But, instead, they found themselves arrested. In 1938, at her behest, King Carol abolished political parties and became a virtual dictator. The anti-Semitic and anti-Magda forces grew until, in September 1940, the king was forced to expel her from the country. A few days later he himself was forced by the Nazis to abdicate in favor of his son, and he followed Magda Lupescu into a second exile. In 1947, in Brazil, King Carol married her, making her Princess Elena. He died six years later in Portugal among other ex-royalty. Princess Elena died in 1977, also in Portugal, where it took a major governmental decision for her to be buried next to her husband among the other royal graves.

Woman to Cause the Most
Difficulty for Brunettes
ANITA LOOS

❦ In her 1925 novel *Gentlemen Prefer Blondes*, which became a play, a musical, a movie, a boon to beauty shops, and seemingly a fact of life, Anita Loos cast in concrete the image of the dumb but beautiful blonde, in the character of Lorelei Lee. H.L. Mencken saw the book as the first time an American writer had poked fun at sex. Philosopher Santayana, without cracking a smile, called the book "the greatest philosophical work of the century."

First "Best-Dressed" Woman
MRS. HARRISON WILLIAMS

❦ In 1933, Balenciaga, Mainbacher, and a few other Paris designers chose a "Best Dressed" list from among their favorite clients. Mrs. Williams, wife of a New York businessman, was selected first. The Associated Press then wanted a finger in the pie and the selections became a publicity free-for-all, with such popular but hardly sartorially elegant figures as Eleanor Roosevelt making the list. When World War II wiped out communications, Eleanor Lambert, a New York press agent, took over the task of running the decision-making process. Suggestions are made by designers and others in the clothing industry, then balloting is done by fashion editors, with a final review by a committee to prevent Eleanor-types from creeping in. The results are announced with a great deal of ballyhoo and cheers or tears by manufacturers. James Brady, author of *Superchic*, wrote, "There is a good deal of otherwise valuable newspaper space and even television time given to the Best Dressed List, which itself is nonsense, and perhaps some sort of press council should investigate this waste of newsprint in a time when trees are in short supply."

Only Actress to Be Officially Requested by the
U.S. Defense Department to Change
Her Hair Style
VERONICA LAKE

❧ Veronica Lake's long-hair-in-the-face style was immensely popular with young women all over the country during the early 1940s. Those same young women, however, were running the machinery in weapons factories, and their hair kept getting caught. She agreed to make a change, and the safer upswept hair-do was the result.

First Publicized Woman Who was
Originally a Man
CHRISTINE JORGENSEN

❧ As George Jorgensen, Jr., he grew up more attracted by things that were stereotypically feminine than masculine. A stint in the U.S. Army further convinced him that he was quite different from other men, and he began to look into medical solutions. George went to Denmark in 1950, and after a series of operations and other treatments, he emerged, two years later, as Christine. Christine Jorgensen became an actress, radio and TV personality, and lecturer, always charming, witty, and frank about the change that had been wrought in her life.

Oldest Homecoming Queen
RITA REUTTER

❧ At age fifty-eight Rita Reutter, a grandmother of fourteen, was elected the 1976 Homecoming Queen at Florida Technological University in Orlando. A graduate student in guidance and counseling, she wanted to liven up the homecoming weekend. She ran on the slogan of "You can have a cutie pie any time. Let's have something different."

Last Royal Mistress to Finally Wed Her Prince
MRS. LILLIAN CRAIG

❧ Lillian Craig, a Welsh divorcee who had been living with Prince Bertil of Sweden for thirty years, was finally able to marry him in 1977. His father, King Gustaf Adolf, had made the prince promise not to marry a commoner until after the heir to the throne was grown and married himself. Bertil's other brothers had each married outside of royalty and relinquished their claims to the throne. Somebody had to stay eligible! So Mrs. Craig discreetly moved into a house in the suburbs of Stockholm, never participating in his official life. Gradually the people of the kingdom came to know of her existence but said nothing about her. Even the press never took official notice. Bertil said of her during those years, "I call this a rare love." Finally in 1975 the old king died. Three years later, the new king, who had not even been born when Bertil and Lillian met, married himself—and to a commoner! The way was now clear. On December 7, 1977, Mrs. Lillian Craig and her prince were married in a royal ceremony. She came away a princess. "This is a real fairy tale," her prince said happily.

Most Covered Up Beauty Pageant Contestant
MALAK NEMLAGHI
❦ Malak Nemlaghi was Miss Tunisia in the Miss World Pageant of 1978. But even though she had appeared publicly in a bathing suit to win her country's title, she wasn't about to remove the traditional Moslem yashmak that covered her face when publicity photos were to be taken in London. She was disqualified, got lots of publicity, and reappeared in the pageant the next day, dressed appropriately. One of her sponsors admitted that Malak had more respect for the value of publicity than for tradition. She didn't win.

Best Example of Who-Do-You-Believe
QUEEN NOOR
❦ In one week in 1978 the name of Queen Noor of Jordan appeared on both the International Best Dressed List and on Richard Blackwell's Worst Dressed List.

Most Expensive Bra
ELSA PERETTI
❦ The bra created by designer Elsa Peretti is a halter design, made of eighteen-karat gold mesh. The bra is available at Tiffany's in New York for about four or five thousand dollars (depending on the price of gold). It is worn, preferably, with a skirt that is slit all the way up.

Most Public Acceptance of a Madam
FRAN YORK
❦ When Fran York, a brothel-keeper in Beatty, Nevada, lost her seventeen-room place of business due to a fire, the Women's Auxiliary of the Veterans of Foreign Wars remembered that Fran York had always been quick to contribute generously to any fund-raising event in town, and the women decided that it was their turn to help her. The group held a

dance that raised $5000 toward a building fund. In the meantime, Ms. York's business is being conducted on an abbreviated scale in a three-room mobile home, where most of her clientele is from California, a fact which makes the local women more friendly to her than they might otherwise be.

Most Memorable Way to
Celebrate an Inheritance

❦ Passengers aboard a National Airlines flight from Miami to Los Angeles in 1978 were jarred out of their travel-induced trances by the sight of a "blond, lovely, very happy—and completely nude" young woman prancing through the aisles and over the seats of the tourist class section. As reported by one woman passenger to The Associated Press, "She perched on top of Row 27, guzzling champagne, and the passengers started laughing and clapping. She said she had just inherited $5 million." It took the crew fifteen minutes to capture the elusive celebrant and encase her in a blanket back in first class. Her male escort reportedly spent the whole time under his seat.

10

TEST TUBES AND TELESCOPES

Only Woman to Create a
Dictionary Out of Spite
CATHERINE THE GREAT

❦ About 1772, the Russian empress Catherine the Great made an old but no-longer-quite-so-faithful friend, Princess Catherine Dashkova, president of the Imperial Academy of Sciences. At the same time, the learned empress created a language academy, making Dashkova head of it too. As a leisure-time activity between lovers, the Empress wrote articles published under pseudonyms in the academy's *Organ of the Friends of the Russian Tongue* . . . at least until Dashkova started printing items critical of Catherine. Gradually Dashkova's great success at running both academies made her old friend jealous. When the language academy announced a program to create a major Russian dictionary and failed to consult the Empress on each detail, Catherine quickly announced that she herself would develop and supervise a better dictionary than the academy was capable of doing. In 1787 the first volume was published. It was poorly designed, incomplete, showed inadequate scholarship, and, to top it off, cost far too much.

Woman Whose Idea for an Invention Had the
Most Far-Reaching Historical Repercussions
CATHERINE LITTLEFIELD GREENE

❦ In 1792, Catherine Greene, the widow of General Nathanael Greene, with a plantation in Georgia to run, met a young tutor, Eli Whitney. Knowing first-hand the problems of producing usable cotton in quantity, she suggested to him that he might devise a machine to separate the sticky seeds from the fiber in the cotton boll. She financed and supported him during the six months it took him to accomplish the task—and there is the possibility (backed by the fact that she received royalties) that Mrs. Greene gave Whitney the basic idea of how to do the job, just leaving him to work out the mechanics of it. The short-term effect of the invention on her was loss of her plantation because of patent lawsuits (the gin, once made, proved to be so simple that anyone could make one). The long-term effects on the South and the United States as a whole were more drastic. The South developed a viable economy based on cotton, but that economy was dependent on a revival of the previously dying slave trade to pick and handle the vast quantities of cotton soon required by the world. The slavery, of course, led to the Civil War.

Longest Known Medical Career of a Female Disguised as a Male
"DR. JAMES BARRY"

❦ "Dr. James Barry," whose real name was possibly Miranda Barry, received a medical degree from Edinburgh University about 1812, at age fifteen. He/she served in the British Army at Waterloo and rose to be Inspector General of Hospitals in Canada and elsewhere in the world. An autopsy after the doctor's death revealed a woman. Dr. Barry must, at times, have let the charade drop because the autopsy showed she had had a baby. Even so, the British Army buried her as a male to avoid having to admit that a woman had been among its ranks for fifty years.

First Computer Programmer
ADA AUGUSTA, COUNTESS OF LOVELACE

❦ The Countess had a somewhat strange friend, Charles Babbage, who was obsessed with the idea of creating a machine that would calculate mathematical problems far faster than man could. During his development work on an "analytical engine," about 1815, she helped with translating problems into forms the "engine" could handle.

Only Female Teacher to Go to Prison for Teaching Blacks
PRUDENCE CRANDALL

❦ In 1833, Quaker Prudence Crandall admitted a Negro girl as a student in her Female Boarding School in Canterbury, Connecticut. The parents of the white students objected, so she closed her school and promptly reopened . . . with a completely black student body. This time the whole town and countryside objected, to the extent of quickly getting the state to pass a law making it illegal to teach "any black person . . . not an inhabitant of any town in this state." Because she and abolition leaders had garnered her black students from all over New England, she was vulnerable to the new law and was promptly jailed. She was convicted, but the decision was overturned by a higher court on a technicality. Released, Prudence Crandall returned to her home school, where angry mobs made life hell for her. In September 1834, she gave in and closed the school.

First Important Female Astronomers
MARY SOMERVILLE AND
CAROLINE HERSCHEL

❦ Mary Somerville, a self-taught Scottish woman, for whom Somerville College at Oxford is now named, first gained recognition in 1826 by reading a paper before the Royal Society on "The Magnetic Properties of the Violet Rays of the Solar Spectrum." It was reinforced in 1831 by a comprehensive book, *Celestial Mechanism of the Heavens*, a popularized English version of Laplace's *Mécanique Céleste*. Caroline Herschel, on the other hand, worked for the most part in the shadow of her brother William, court astronomer to George III. She did, however, receive acceptance in her own name for the discovery, with a homemade telescope, of three nebulae and eight comets and for publication of a catalog of stars. In 1835, the two women were accepted into membership, albeit honorary membership, in the Royal Astronomical Society, the first women to be so recognized. The society's council reported to the membership, "On the propriety of such a step, in an astronomical point of view, there can be but one voice: and your Council is of opinion that the time is gone when either feeling or prejudice, by whichever name it may be proper to call it, should be allowed to interfere with the payment of a well-earned tribute of respect."

First Blind, Deaf, and Mute Person
to Be Educated
LAURA D. BRIDGMAN

❦ Left almost without senses by scarlet fever in her early childhood—even her senses of smell and taste were affected—Laura Bridgman could have expected the well-nigh contactless life of other blind deaf-mutes, but the Perkins Institution in Boston heard about her in 1837 and asked her family to send the eight-year-old to them. The director felt, against all advice and experience, that education should be possible. For weeks Laura uncomprehendingly fingered objects and matching raised letters until one day the stunning moment of understanding—the one made famous in *The Miracle Worker* about Helen Keller—occurred for Laura Bridgman. Once that moment comes, the rest is the tough, daily slogging to build vocabularies and train muscles to write and to spell out words. Unfortunately for Laura, the thousands of people who came to marvel could do nothing for her progress, and the school itself accomplished nothing more after she was twenty. Unable to cope with living at her family's home, however, Laura Bridgman returned to Perkins and spent her remaining forty years there, carrying out simple tasks and a huge correspondence.

Only Librarian to Have a Comet
Named for Her
MARIA MITCHELL

❦ On the night of October 1, 1847, Maria Mitchell, twenty-nine-year-old daughter of a Nantucket Island bank cashier, went, as she usually did, to the roof of their apartment over the bank. Days belonged to housework and her job as the town librarian, but nights had belonged to the skies ever since she had absorbed her amateur-astronomer father's enthusiasm. Part of their work was official, as an observation station of the U.S. Coast Survey, but all, for Maria, was sheer heaven. That cold night when she put her eye to the two-inch telescope, something seemed to be out of place in the sky. She blinked and looked again. Yes, there was a point of light just above Polaris, where she had certainly never seen one before. Summoning her father, he confirmed her discovery of a comet—a visitor from beyond the solar system—and officially recorded the entry that, to the chagrin of better-equipped male astronomers around the world, made her the first woman to qualify for the King of Denmark's standing offer of a gold medal to anyone who discovered an unknown comet with the aid of a telescope. Librarian Maria Mitchell became astronomer Mitchell with a comet named for her. A few years later she moved to the mainland and became American's first female astronomy professor, teaching at Vassar College.

Only Woman Doctor Whose Education was
Decided by Student-Body Vote
ELIZABETH BLACKWELL

❦ Challenged by the knowledge that no woman had knowingly been admitted to the medical profession in the English-speaking world, Elizabeth Blackwell, a British-born American teacher, decided to take up the cudgel. She spent several years working as a governess in doctors' homes in order to use their libraries and to have private tutoring, all the while writing applications to medical schools around the United States. She refused the suggestion, made by several schools, that she change her name and dress as a man. Finally, in 1847, the Geneva Medical College in New York decided to put the matter to the student body rather than reject her out of hand. An uproarious meeting was held, resulting in a resolution, perhaps meant as a joke, by the class: "Resolved—That one of the radical principles of a Republican Government is the universal education of both sexes: that to every branch of scientific education the door should be open equally to all; that the application of Elizabeth Blackwell to become a member of our class meets our entire approbation; and in extending our unanimous invitation we pledge ourselves that no conduct of ours shall cause her to regret her attendance at this institution." Elizabeth Blackwell graduated at the top of that generous class on January 23, 1849. The school, however, refused to accept Ms. Blackwell as a precedent and immediately shut its doors to females.

Ten years later, after Dr. Blackwell had spent considerable time in England, *Punch* wrote the following tribute to her:

> Young ladies all, of every clime,
>   Especially of Britain,
>   Who wholly occupy your time
> In novels or in knitting,
>   Whose highest skill is but to play,
>   Sing, dance, or French to clack well,
> Reflect on the example, pray,
> Of excellent Miss Blackwell!

First Woman to Be Kicked out of Harvard
HARRIOT K. HUNT

❧ In her quest for a medical education to supplement the experience she had from practicing as a doctor, Harriot Hunt had applied in 1848 to Harvard College (male since its founding in 1636), and had been refused. Emboldened by what she heard and saw at the national woman's rights convention in 1850, she again applied and this time was admitted at the behest of Oliver Wendell Holmes. But so, too, were three black men. Two shatterings of precedence in one term were too much for the white, male students. In a mass meeting, they made their views known, and Ms. Hunt was removed from the school. Three years later she received a medical degree from Female (later Woman's) Medical College in Philadelphia.

Woman to Make Most Basic
Scientific Discovery
AGNES POCKELS

❧ According to Dr. Florence Sabin, herself a remarkable woman, a German girl named Agnes Pockels discovered surface tension in 1881. Though unable to go to college, she carried on research at home. While working with salts, she discovered that salts in solution gave the surface of the solution a greater "pull" than plain water had. She brought her observation to her brother's attention and he told his professor, who ignored the new but seemingly irrelevant information. Ten years later, in correspondence with the English scientist Lord Rayleigh, she told of her observations, and he printed her letters in the journal *Nature*. She began to receive credit for the discovery, though you'll still only rarely see her name mentioned in physics texts or histories.

Astronomer to Classify the Most Stars
ANNIE JUMP CANNON

❦ The use of the spectroscope in astronomy was just getting started when Miss Cannon, a graduate student at Radcliffe, was hired by the Harvard College Observatory in 1896. She was fascinated by stellar spectra—the characteristic light given off by a star interpreted by the way it is broken up by a prism. Thus began the catalog of the heavens, called *The Henry Draper Catalogue* (which was financed by Mrs. Mary Anna Palmer Draper), the only comprehensive descriptive catalog of all visible and not-so-visible stars. So two women were really responsible for *the* major stellar reference book. Annie Jump Cannon photographed and studied almost four hundred thousand stars during her forty-five years at Harvard, in addition to building the Observatory's library and photo file to among the most reliable and extensive in the world. Annie Jump Cannon, justifiably called "Census Taker of the Skies," received in 1925 the first honorary doctorate ever conferred by Oxford University on a woman. In 1933 she established for the American Astronomical Society the Annie J. Cannon Prize, given every three years to a distinguished woman astronomer.

First Person to Analyze the Economic
Implications of the Status of Women
CHARLOTTE PERKINS STETSON (LATER
GILMAN)

❦ When Charlotte Stetson's marriage crumbled, she had only her skill as a writer to rely on for support. Gradually her articles and poems brought her a reputation that turned her into a popular lecturer on subjects such as social organization. All she saw and felt led her to the conclusion that nonworking women were parasites and that it was economic dependence that kept women in a submissive position. All a woman had to give in return for support were her sexual favors—not a description of the "partnership" that marriage was touted to be. In 1898, she published her views in *Women and Economics*. Mrs. Stetson was among the first to propose that baby care, cooking and cleaning be turned over to those women who were good at it—specialists, in other words—leaving most women free for other jobs. When she married her cousin Houghton Gilman, they lived such an existence, residing in a boarding house and eating all meals out. Later in her life, however, she wrote, "wifehood and mother-hood are the normal status of women, and whatever is right in woman's new position must not militate against these essentials."

First Person to be Psychoanalyzed
BERTHA PAPPENHEIM
(a.k.a "Anna O.")

❦ A woman in her early twenties, Bertha Pappenheim was the patient of Dr. Joseph Breuer in 1880. He found her mute and almost totally paralyzed for no discoverable neurological reason. Such hysteria was being "treated" then by post-hypnotic suggestion, but Breuer realized that a different Anna was speaking when she was hypnotized. He decided to keep talking to that Anna, the one who gradually told him about how each of her various symptoms first appeared, what she was thinking, and so on. As he learned in his almost daily sessions, her physical symptoms related primarily to guilt feelings about her father's illness and, once aired, the symptoms cleared. Breuer related his cure of the patient he called "Anna O." to a friend, Sigmund Freud, who spent a lifetime exploring the unconscious through the psychoanalytic technique. Bertha, who may have spent some years as a drug addict, later became a crusader against white slavery, a writer, and feminism advocate.

Woman to Do the Most Physical Labor for an
Intellectual Achievement
MARIE CURIE

❦ Along with her husband Pierre, Marie Curie discovered the radioactive elements radium and plutonium. She knew that radium existed theoretically, but she wasn't satisfied until she had actually isolated some of the incredibly elusive material from the ore pitchblende, which had already yielded uranium. Day after day, summer and winter, for four years, working in the courtyard of an abandoned shack at the University of Paris, she shoveled huge quantities of the heavy ore from the storage pile into a giant cauldron. Then she stirred the thick, sticky substance as it heated over a fire. As portions of it rose to the top, she scooped off part, poured it into vast jars, and wheeled them into the shack, where her husband carried out the intricate crystallization procedure. Ultimately they were able to isolate an invisibly minute quantity of radium from the tons of mining waste that Marie had moved. They fully described the physical properties of the element and even proposed a variety of medical uses for it. In 1903, the Curies were awarded the Nobel Prize for Physics, sharing it with their friend Henri Becquerel, who had discovered radioactivity. Ironically, it turned out later that what she had slaved to isolate was only a salt of radium. She then spent more years (though rather less arduous ones) truly isolating the dangerous element. And as a reward beyond the honors of the world, she eventually died of leukemia, brought on by exposure to her own discovery.

Countess Zrinyi: courage at the heart of the matter

Nancy Hart the First: an example to housewives everywhere

Belle Boyd: a gnat in the Union's eye

Dr. Mary Walker: she never parted from her Medal of Honor

Flora Sandes as a Sergeant Major

Mary Baker Eddy: "All things are possible to God"

Catherine de Medici urging her son to do her dirty work

Fanny Crosby: though her eyes
were blind, her heart saw the world
as a hymn

Elizabeth Cady Stanton *(left):* she
parted with friend Susan B. Anthony
(right) over *The Woman's Bible*

Henrietta Szold in her later years: she sought and got cooperation wherever she went

Mary Wollstonecraft: ahead of everyone else with her ideas; slow to learn about love

Harriet Beecher Stowe: she walked softly and carried one hell of a big stick

Rosa Bonheur

Vinnie Ream with a bust of Lincoln

The divine Sara Bernhardt, *sans* coffin but with a definite sense of the dramatic

Mary, Duchess of Burgundy: my kingdom for a ring!

Anna Held: chewing gum had no
place in her famed Peacock gown

Irene Castle, before haircut

Lola Montez about 1851 when she took American by storm: you had to be there to believe it

Catherine the Great: in the midst of love and power, a dictionary!

Elizabeth Blackwell, M.D.: persistence rewarded

Marie Curie with husband Pierre and daughter Irène in a rare moment of relaxation

National Air and Space Museum, Smithsonian Institution, Washington, D.C.

Harriet Quimby: her skill stirred the hearts of American women

Annie Oakley: making accuracy count

Joan Whitney Payson: mother of the Mets

Most Contagious Woman
MARY MALLON
(a.k.a. "Typhoid Mary")

❦ Although she herself never came down with typhoid fever, Mary Mallon, a New York housemaid of the early 1900s, infected, directly or indirectly, at least thirteen hundred people. For nine years the New York health authorities hunted her, confined her, tested her, lost her when the courts ordered her release, hunted her again when her trail could be discerned through new typhoid cases. Because she was a not very clean person who often worked where food was served and because she refused to stop working in such places, the city authorities finally used unusual powers to place her in permanent detention. She was isolated, though in some comfort, for the twenty-three years until her death in 1938.

Only Female Physician to a Harem
DR. BROIDO

❦ A Russian-born Frenchwoman, Dr. Broido was appointed in about 1908 by Sultan Mulai Hafid as doctor to his harem at Fez. She had previously spent several years as a ship's doctor (probably the world's first female one) on Russian ships sailing out of Casablanca.

Only Woman to Obtain a U.S. Patent for a
Device to Prevent Masturbation
ELLEN E. PERKINS

❦ A nurse, Ms. Perkins of Beaver Bay, Minnesota was convinced that masturbation caused insanity, imbecility, and feeblemindedness, so she invented a preventative armor for which she received a patent in 1908. Her device was an armor-like suit that fit over the whole torso. The crotch had a lock for which the key was retained by an attendant—presumably only inmates of institutions were to use it. It wasn't necessary for the armor to be unlocked for the inhabitant, male or female, to urinate. Nurse Perkins claimed the device caused little if any discomfort.

Most Helpful Invention by a Woman If You
Happen to Have It with You When You're
Stranded on a Deserted Island
HANNAH ROSENBLATT

❦ In 1923 Hannah Rosenblatt, an American living in Manila, patented a message-carrying bottle stoppered by a cork with a small bell attached for calling attention to it. Stacy Jones recorded this marvelous device in *Inventions Necessity is Not the Mother of*.

Most Important Woman in Saving a Nation's
Economic Base
DR. JEAN MACNAMARA

❦ In the 1920s on a trip through America, Australian Dr. Macnamara learned that rabbits could be killed with myxomytosis bacteria. Rabbits were a seemingly ineradicable pest in Australia, where their sheer numbers destroyed so much grazing land that the sheep industry— Australia's prinicipal crop—was in serious danger of collapsing. The samples of the bacteria that she sent, however, were dumped into the sea by overzealous customs officials. It took Dr. Macnamara fourteen years to convince the government to give myxomytosis a real trial, and then it was not totally successful until they discovered that mosquitoes were vital to carrying the bacteria (which, by the way, is harmless to all species save rabbits). Then, almost 90 percent of Australia's rabbit population was destroyed and the sheep industry, with its attendant wool export, was saved.

Curiously enough, the merino sheep industry in Australia got its start primarily through the work of a woman. In 1801, Elizabeth Macarthur's husband was refused permission to reenter Australia for eight years. That left her in control of their farm. She extended it and introduced merino sheep to her lands. They were hardy and produced fine, thick wool. Mrs. Macarthur's merinos soon became the principal Australian breed.

First Woman to Save Her Life by Jumping
with a Parachute
MRS. IRENE MacFARLAND

❦ Mrs. MacFarland was the first woman member of the exclusive Caterpillar Club (an unorganized group of people who have saved their lives using parachutes; they receive pins from a parachute manufacturing firm) when, ironically enough, she was testing a parachute she was developing. Running her tests at an Army base at Cincinnati, Ohio, she was refused the use of an airplane unless she wore a proven chute along with the experimental one. In jumping, the test chute became tangled on the plane. The pilot could not land because she dangled below the craft. Mrs. MacFarland calmly analyzed possibilities and then used the opening of the proven chute to jerk herself free and land safely.

Woman to Do Most to Eradicate Tuberculosis
Among the Navajo
ANNIE DODGE WAUNEKA

❦ Annie Wauneka, daughter of an important Indian chief, acquired early his devotion to helping his people, especially in encouraging them to accept the assistance of the U.S. government. She won the respect of the Navajo and was the first woman elected by them to be a delegate to the tribal council. As chairperson of the health committee for the council, she challenged the hold tuberculosis had on her people. To do so, she learned all she could about the disease and then, beginning in the 1930s, had to convince the medicine men to encourage the sick ones to accept white men's aid. Because of her, more than twenty thousand Navajo went through the mysteries of being X-rayed, and two thousand of these accepted hospitalization when they were discovered to have the disease. This was just the beginning for Mrs. Wauneka. Her influence led to homes being cleaned up, children being vaccinated, and many young people going to college. In 1963, Annie Dodge Wauneka was presented with the Freedom Award by President John F. Kennedy.

First Woman to Experience Weightlessness
MARGARET JACKSON

❦ A high-altitude specialist at the Aero Medical Laboratory in Ohio, Margaret Jackson was charmed by pilot reports of the pleasant feeling caused by the brief weightlessness of an aircraft put into a special arcing trajectory. So she donned a flight suit in 1941 to try it herself. Her reaction: "It was fascinating. One feels completely buoyant. Like floating on sea water, only completely free."

Most Innovative House
Constructed by Women
SOLAR HOME AT DOVER, MASSACHUSETTS

❦ The participants in construction were Dr. Maria Telkes, a physical chemist at Massachusetts Institute of Technology, who conceived the idea for a solar-heated home and developed the actual heating plan, one different from any used before; Eleanor Raymond, an architect who designed the five-room house around the heating requirements laid down by Dr. Telkes; and Amelia Peabody, owner of the land, who offered to have the house built on her property and to pay the $20,000-plus construction cost—the house was to be hers at the end of the project. Dr. Telkes lived in the house through the winter of 1948-49 and found it totally comfortable, as have Ms. Peabody's tenants ever since.

Only Woman to Be Granted the Title
"Great Woman Doctor"
DR. PIERRA HOON

❦ After earning her medical degree in Paris and studying veneral diseases there, Thai-born Dr. Hoon returned to her own country in 1937 and went to work for the Ministry of Health. During the next years, while working on women's diseases and prostitution, she also adopted forty-five orphans. In the early 1950s, the government officially added *Vejjabul*, meaning "great woman doctor," to her name, in recognition of her status as the first woman doctor in Thailand.

Most Influential Woman in the Treatment of a Major Disease
SISTER ELIZABETH KENNY

❦ "Infantile Paralysis. No known treatment. Do the best you can with the symptoms presenting themselves." This was a doctor's telegraphed response to a query by a nurse in the Australian outback when she was confronted with symptoms she did not recognize in a two-year-old girl. Elizabeth Kenny did the best she could, using moist heat and massage to combat what she saw as the spasm of muscles involuntarily contracting in pain. She didn't know that doctors the world over would have immobilized the little girl's legs to keep strong muscles, unaffected by the disease, from displacing weak, damaged ones. But her "best," which included retraining of weakened muscles, got the child, as well as others in a small epidemic, on their feet again. When Nurse Kenny finally reached the city, her reports of her "best" threw the medical profession into an uproar, all save the man she had originally telegraphed, who became her supporter. Thus began the struggle to keep children from being permanently crippled by their physicians, a struggle that would last until her death in 1952. The people of three nations—Australia, Great Britain, and the United States—would adore her for making their children walk again . . . but medical commissions of those same three nations would condemn this upstart nurse for challenging the best medical advice and theory of physicians. Throughout those years she never accepted payment for her work, living off the royalties from a special patient-stabilizing stretcher she invented as a transport nurse in World War I (when she gained the title "Sister"). She died before her conflict with the medical profession was fully resolved, died while Dr. Jonas Salk was preparing the vaccine that would, for the most part, put an end to crippling by polio (infantile paralysis).

In the closing passage of her autobiography, Sister Kenny wrote:

> In these pages I have striven to set down the brief record of a life that has little claim to distinction beyond the fact that within its narrow limits a battle has been fought against forces entrenched in precedent and armored with tradition. A measure of victory has been won, and honors have been bestowed in token thereof. But honors fade or are forgotten, and monuments crumble into dust. It is the battle itself that matters—and the battle must go on. One human life alone cannot encompass the full extent of the struggle.

First Woman to Visit the North Pole
LOUISE A. BOYD

❦ Born to wealth, Louise Boyd was able to support her interest in polar exploration by financing her own expeditions of scientists. The work done by many of her expeditions fed the growing need for understanding of the area by the military; some of the work was done in secret for the Pentagon. For years, however, her personal dream of reaching the North Pole had to be put aside. Then, on June 16, 1955, she flew to the Pole with a photographic expedition and landed there. She had at last the "personal reward" that she wrote scientists seek "aside from the contribution which every scientist makes to our nation's welfare."

Biggest Female Winner of TV Game Shows
DR. JOYCE BROTHERS

❦ Psychologist Dr. Brothers answered questions about boxing on "$64,000 Question" and "64,000 Challenge" in the years 1955 through '57, winning a total of $134,000. She came out clean when those shows were investigated for dishonesty—and so she should; she went through a six-week cram fest as well as memorizing a boxing encyclopedia before appearing on the shows. Since then she has been a regular on TV, both on her own programs and as a popular guest, working in her real field of psychology. Her husband calls her "the greatest self-promoter who ever came down the tube."

Only Female Personal Physician to a
President of the United States
DR. JANET G. TRAVELL

❦ A pain-relief neuromuscular specialist, Dr. Travell had served as President John F. Kennedy's doctor since 1955 when, among other treatments, she had prescribed the famous rocking chair for him to relieve the pain from two operations on a back injury suffered in World War II. When Kennedy became President, she moved to Washington along with him. Kennedy recognized her value and said, "She's the reason I'm alive today."

Most Important Woman in Space Programs
DR. ALLA G. MASEVICH

❦ Originally an expert in the structure of red giant stars and in solar evolution, Dr. Masevich of the U.S.S.R. was given, in 1957, six months to develop a way to keep track of the Soviet Union's first satellite, which would be launched that autumn. Working with no precedent, she developed a simple tracking network that followed Sputnik when it was launched in October. As earth satellites became more complex and were launched more frequently, she developed the network that kept them in communication with Earth. *Saturday Review* called Dr. Masevich "the Erudite Shepherdess of Home-Made Moons." The network she has now developed to keep track of all objects in space consists of more than one hundred ground-based stations and three tracking ships.

Only Woman to Discover Fossils
Important to Understanding the Evolution
of Human Beings
MARY LEAKEY

❦ Since 1931, Mary Leakey and her husband Louis S. B. Leakey had spent some part of almost every year in the hot, rocky isolation of Olduvai Gorge in northern Tanzania searching for fossil remains of man. They and their sons frequently found new types of fossil animals, and Dr. Leakey found man-ancestral bones elsewhere. Still they were convinced that Olduvai should yield signs of early humans. On July 17, 1959, Mary Leakey gently uncovered some teeth and a palate bone of a manlike creature. Five years later, a son found a piece of jaw. The man-creature, called Zinjanthropus, is, according to the Leakeys, probably an offshoot of human development that died out. Zinjanthropus, which may have flourished about a million years ago, was about five feet tall, large-chested, and small-brained with a barely distinguishable brow.

In 1975, several years after L. S. B. Leakey's death, Mrs. Leakey discovered, about twenty-five miles from Olduvai Gorge, the jaws and teeth of at least eleven manlike creatures. The fragments have been dated as 3.75 million years old. That is almost a million years older than any previous humanoid fossils had been reliably dated.

Woman to Invent Most Widely
Used Equipment
EDITH OLSON

❦ An inorganic chemist with the United States Army, Edith Olson worked with three other scientists to shrink the required size of electronic parts for missiles, thus creating great savings in size and consequent fuel requirements. She equated the task with needing to print all the volumes in the Library of Congress on a grain of rice. For accomplishing the impossible, Mrs. Olson became, in 1959, the first woman to receive the Department of Defense's $25,000 prize, awarded because an estimated $200 million a year would be saved by her printed circuits. The photographic and lithographic techniques she devised to print the circuits are now used worldwide.

Oldest Woman to Be Required by
Law to Go to School
MRS. SOFIE MADSEN

❦ In the early 1960s, at age 104, Mrs. Madsen of Denmark received an official order to begin school . . . because the computer punch cards in the system that kept track of citizens had no information bit for an age beyond ninety-nine. Her age was thus translated as four.

Most Influential Scientific Book by a Woman
SILENT SPRING BY RACHEL CARSON

❦ Published in 1962, *Silent Spring* changed our entire view of earth, and of the industries and governments that irresponsibly do things to it without proper regard for the consequences. After Rachel Carson's book became known, thinking people could no longer accept with equanimity the idea that those in responsible positions would do nothing to jeopardize earth. It became clear that solutions of the minute could do eternal and irreparable harm to life on our planet. As she wrote, "As crude a weapon as the cave man's club, the chemical barrage has been hurled against the fabric of life."

Ms. Carson, a writer at heart, became a biologist in order to have something interesting to write about, a subject that could reach readers beyond the scientific community. One of her early magazine articles, called "Help Your Child to Wonder," has become a classic. Her first full-length bestseller was *The Sea Around Us*, published in 1951. Its success allowed her to quit her position with the U.S. Fish and Wildlife Service and devote her time to study and writing. She spent four years quietly researching and writing *Silent Spring*, an eloquent study of the insidious effect of pesticides on the permanent balance of life. She had to keep the project quiet because she was well aware that government and industry pressures against exposing little-known truths could be formidable. It was published in 1962, and the furor began. Even as she was dying of cancer, she made the effort to testify before a Senate committee in support of her thesis. Rachel Carson died in 1964, before the space program produced photos of earth as a beautiful blue ball in space, photos that reemphasized her idea that earth is finite and fragile and must be protected. British naturalist Sir Peter Scott, testifying before the House of Lords, said of her, "Future generations will regard Rachel Carson as a great benefactor of the human race for the impact of *Silent Spring*."

Only Woman to Orbit the Earth
VALENTINA TERESHKOVA

❦ A Soviet textile worker, Valentina Tereshkova made a hobby of sky diving. When Yuri Gagarin made the first manned space flight, she wrote to the authorities asking if a woman could participate in the program. Invited to join the ranks of candidates for cosmonaut training, this laborer who had no higher education but a great deal of determination impressed everyone. On June 16, 1963, she was launched into orbit in Vostok 6 to rendezvous with Vostok 5, which had been launched the previous day for a duration-testing flight. She was originally to stay in space only one day but the time was extended to three. Later that year, Tereshkova married fellow-cosmonaut Andrian Nikolayev. In 1969, at the World Congress of Women meeting in Helsinki, Finland, she claimed that she took the most pride in giving birth to her children.

Woman Who Inspired First Public Discussion
of Students at Women's Colleges Living
Openly with Men
LINDA LECLAIR

❦ The housing rules in 1968 at Barnard College in New York City decreed, in part, that women living off campus could do so only with a relative or for a live-in job. Ms. LeClair contravened the latter requirement by having a friend call the placement office asking for a girl to live in and take care of her young children. She got the fictitious job . . . and moved in with her boyfriend, a student at Columbia. When her whereabouts were discovered, the real issue, sex, was disguised by citing her for a violation of college regulations by giving a false address. Barnard students came out heavily on Linda's side. At her hearing so, too, did religious counselors and various professors. In the end, Ms. LeClair's punishment consisted of a reprimand, loss of school cafeteria privileges, and a prohibition against attending dances and other school functions. But she didn't mind: she was busy elsewhere. School housing hasn't been the same since.

Only Woman to Head a Test of Long-Lasting
Underwater Living
DR. SYLVIA EARLE MEAD

❦ A marine biologist and fully qualified diver, Dr. Mead was selected to lead a team of women aquanauts who, in 1970, stayed two weeks at the bottom of the sea near the Virgin Islands. It was one of the tests of the Tektite project, which investigated both the sea itself and people's ability to live and work in tight, underwater quarters for long periods. The sixteen other teams in the extensive project were all made up of men.

Most Knowledgeable Person about Fleas
MIRIAM L. A. ROTHSCHILD

❦ A British zoologist, Miriam Rothschild has no formal degrees but has received honorary recognition from both Oxford and London universities. Most curious about the flea's fantastic jumping ability, she has photographed flea leaps with special cameras that allow her to obtain ten thousand frames per second. Having inherited her father's incredible collection of over ten thousand flea species, she has spent numerous years cataloging the tiny insects. In 1977, Dr. Rothschild invited the world's specialists to an international flea convention at her country estate.

Only Archeologist to Excavate Her Own Home
(She Thinks)
DOROTHY EADY

❦ Dorothy Eady tells a story of being declared dead as an injured child of three but waking to look for her home—not her father's house in Plymouth, England, but a great stone temple where she knew she belonged. She didn't find the home she remembered for more than forty years when, as a staff member of the Egyptian Antiquities Service, she went to the ruins of the city of Abydos, where the god Osiris was worshipped. There she identified the temple of Seti I as her prior home. She had been, several thousand years before, an orphaned girl dedicated to the temple and was able to tell her modern day colleagues things about it that, on excavating, they found to be true. In 1979, Om Seti, as she is called in the Egyptian village where she lives, told the *New York Times*, "I can't remember any ordinary life, so I think I must have been stuck in the temple. I have a vague memory of the processions. I can remember an awful old killjoy of a priest."

Strangest Museum Started by a Woman
THE SPIDER MUSEUM
AT POWHATAN, VIRGINIA

❦ The Spider Museum was founded by Ann Moreton, probably the only woman in America who doesn't look for a dust rag or broom when she spots a spider web, for her new webs just increase the size of her collection. The exhibits extend to the outdoor world where special nature walks take visitors through the webs and to the nests of numerous more living specimens. Originally a photographer who became challenged by photographing spiders and their webs, Ms. Moreton has also started the National Arachnid Society to get young people interested in spiders.

11

PROWESS WAS A LADY

Only Sportswriting Nun
JULIANA BARNES, OR BERNERS
❦ Prioress of Sopwell Nunnery in England around 1481, Juliana drew on her own aristocratic background to write (in her own hand instead of through a scribe, as was more usual at the time) of fishing, hunting, and hawking, for "the gentill men and honest persones." Supposedly Izaak Walton of *Compleat Angler* fame was a devotee of *The Book of St. Albans*, which contained her essays on fishing, fly-tying, and hunting.

First Queen of the Green
MARY, QUEEN OF SCOTS
❦ She broke her "mourning"—such as it was—to play golf soon after Lord Darnley, her husband, was murdered. Even to the Scots, who invented the game and played it avidly, that seemed a bit callous.

Most Successful Female Hunter
PRINCESS CHARLOTTE
❦ In 1755, Princess Charlotte, with two companions, joined a hunting party of twenty men led by Emperor Francis. The hunt, through the forests of Bohemia, lasted eighteen days. During that time it was recorded that the princess fired 9010 shots. In all there were 116,209 shots fired—no easy task in those days—and the bag was 47,950 head: 19 stags, 77 roebucks, 10 foxes, 18,243 hares, 19,545 partridges, 9,499 pheasants, 114 larks, 353 quails, and 454 other birds. Not mentioned is the number of bearers needed to lug it all home.

First Woman to Make a Parachute Jump
JEANNE-GENEVIÈVE LABROSSE
❦ Setting aside the possibility that there may have been women acrobats among those in old China who entertained audiences by leaping from buildings and trees holding on to large umbrellas, Jeanne-Geneviève Labrosse was the first female parachutist in France in 1799. She was a seamstress who sewed together the panels of the parachutes used by the inventor of parachutes, André Jacques Garnerin. She made one descent

from a balloon and then married the inventor. Their niece Elisa later became the most famous parachuting woman balloonist in Europe.

First Woman to Hold Gym Classes for Women
CATHARINE BEECHER

❦ This innovative educator, sister to Harriet and Henry Ward, was sternly the traditionalist regarding education for women, except in this one respect. Catharine Beecher started in 1823 what became, four years later, the Hartford Female Seminary in Connecticut to get girls out of the factories and turn them into teachers and to prepare girls to be women "worthy" of their husbands. This last purpose, however, called for women to be physically healthy, not languishing around all day in garments drawn so tight as to make them faint—a rather revolutionary thought in those days when, as she noted, "A woman who has tolerable health finds herself so much above the great mass of her friends . . . that she feels herself a prodigy of good health." Catharine Beecher later introduced special classes, which she gave the appealing Greek name of "calisthenics," into her current school, the Western Female Institute in Oxford, Ohio. The theories she developed on the subject were published in 1850 in *Physiology and Calisthenics*. Strictly a conservative otherwise, she "spoke" in public only when her brother could accompany her and read her speech aloud while she sat next to him on the platform.

Only Major Sport Invented for Women and
Promoted by Them
TENNIS

❦ During the 1860s and seventies, several people pioneered a game that would give women more exercise than the quickly boring one of croquet; basically it was an outdoor, wall-less version of the court tennis game that had been played for several centuries. Most often credit is given specifically to British Major Walter Wingfield, who introduced a version using an hourglass-shaped court at a house party in Wales in 1873. He patented his version but the rectangular court quickly became standard. A fellow officer took some of the equipment with him to Bermuda, where the game was played by a visiting American, Mary Ewing Outerbridge. She bought the equipment and took it home with her to New York. The Staten Island Cricket and Baseball Club agreed to set up a court, where she and her friends were quickly playing. Her brother, a director of the club, formed the U.S. Lawn Tennis Association in 1881 to establish uniform rules and tournament regulations.

First Female Long-Distance Swimmer
EMILY PARKER

❧ In 1875, Emily Parker of Britain swam the ten miles from the London Bridge to North Woodwich in less than two and a half hours and received a gold medal for her efforts.

Only Memorable Female Sharpshooter
ANNIE OAKLEY (PHOEBE ANN MOSES)

❧ Annie Oakley was already renowned in Cincinnati farm country for her accuracy with a gun when she beat the well-known Frank Butler in a shootin' match. Chagrined, he married her in 1876, when she was fifteen, and they remained together for fifty years. Eventually, she became the bigger name and he became her manager, wrangling her appearances in Buffalo Bill's Wild West Show. She stayed with the show on and off for much of her life. Sitting Bull called her "Little Sure Shot." European royalty marveled at her, and Crown Prince Wilhelm of Germany let her shoot the ashes off his cigarette. Thomas Edison filmed Annie Oakley in 1894 in one of his first experimental motion pictures. Even in World War I, soldiers at army camps were treated to the spectacle of little Annie Oakley's skill. This lady of the Wild West—which she was never really part of—died in 1926, back in her home territory of Ohio.

Least Successful Ladies' Day Baseball Game
HELD BY THE WASHINGTON
SENATORS IN 1897

❧ Thirteen years after the New York Giants had pioneered the audience-gathering day, the Washington Senators held a Ladies' Day baseball game. The ladies at that Senators game were so incensed at the decisions of the home-plate umpire that they stormed the field, rioted, and tore apart the stadium.

Most Important Sports Maneuver
Discovered by a Woman
THE BACKHAND IN TENNIS

❧ Bertha Townsend, second American woman champion when tennis was just evolving, developed the backhand in 1886. She was left-handed and found that she could play better by holding the racket across her body instead of reaching for the ball from the other side. Other players quickly followed suit, destroying her short-term advantage.

Only Woman to Knock Out a
Major Boxing Champion
HESSIE DONAHUE

❦ In an 1892 boxing exhibition in Arkansas, there weren't any takers one night to try their fists against the legendary John L. Sullivan. So Hessie, wife of Sullivan's promoter, climbed into the ring for a little crowd-pleasing sparring. John L. made the mistake of bopping Hessie's nose a little harder than usual. Hessie got mad and swung before the boxer had recovered his own balance. A fluke hit to the jaw and the great John L. went down, out cold. That might have been a taste of things to come: later that year Sullivan lost his championship to Gentleman Jim Corbett.

Only Woman to Launch a Career on the
Failure to Swim the English Channel
ANNETTE KELLERMAN

❦ Crippled by polio as an infant, Australian-born Annette Kellerman had turned to swimming as a therapeutic exercise. At seventeen, in 1905, she attempted to swim the Channel, which had previously been swum only by men. After six and a half hours, however, she was forced to give up; the high waves made her seasick. The interest in her brought about by the attempt, however, was sufficient to launch her career as a professional theatrical swimmer, and she started the first successful aquacade. Many years later, her spectacular life was portrayed on film by Esther Williams, *Million Dollar Mermaid*. (See also page 130.)

Strongest Woman
KATI SANDWINA

❦ Born to a circus family at the end of the nineteenth century, by her teen years Kati Sandwina was twisting steel bars in a vaudeville act. By the age of twenty, she stood six feet one inch tall and weighed about two hundred ten pounds, all smoothly distributed on an attractive figure. She liked to support half-ton cannons on her back, demonstrate the correct way to weight-lift three hundred pounds, and carry her smaller husband over her head with one hand. She liked the spectacular and so did circus audiences . . . like the time she served as the support for a bridge while forty men and horses trotted blithely across it. Kati gave up weightlifting and twisting steel in the 1940s when she turned fifty-six and then retired in New York.

Only Woman to Fly a Powered Aircraft Before
the Wright Brothers
AIDA DE ACOSTA

❦ An American attending a convent school in Paris, Aida de Acosta met, through friends, Alberto Santos-Dumont, the Brazilian aviation pioneer.

She became an eager follower of his ideas for flying machines, and day after day she watched him work on the development of his lightly powered dirigible. Flattered by her interest, he gave her some lessons on how to maneuver the unwieldy craft, and then on June 29, 1903, five months before the Wrights successfully flew their airplane, let her take it up alone. She spent an hour and a half piloting the strange craft over Paris, finally landing, dramatically, in the middle of a polo game. Aida's family was so aghast at her exploit that they made both her and Santos-Dumont promise never to tell a soul. He kept his word, never giving the name of the woman who appeared over Paris skies, and so did she until 1932 when she mentioned the episode at a dinner party in Ohio. A reporter heard about it and then revealed the whole story.

By the time her flight became public knowledge, Aida de Acosta Breckinridge had lost most of the sight in both eyes through glaucoma. In 1945 she founded the Eye-Bank for Sight Restoration, an organization that led the great strides made in corneal transplants.

First Woman to Drive Cross-Country
ALICE HEYLER RAMSEY

❦ In 1909, Alice Ramsey of New Jersey drove across the United States with three friends, the first woman to do so. She was president of the Women's Automobile Club of New York, and her friends were fellow members who went along to help drive and change tires. The 3800-mile trip from New York City to San Francisco was made in an open Maxwell and took the women forty-one days.

A year later, Blanche ("Betty") Scott, made the first drive across the nation by a woman alone. Driving an Overland, she maintained a comfortable pace between the same two cities but stopped in each state along the route to be greeted by the governor.

First American Woman to Fly an Airplane
BLANCHE STUART SCOTT

❦ During a lesson from Glenn Curtiss in September, 1910, Betty Scott was taxiing along the ground when, as she related it, the wind caught the plane, giving the lift necessary to get the airplane airborne. (There were rumors that she planned the "accidental" flight, the first made by a woman in America.) But two weeks later, Bessica Raiche, wife of a Long Island aircraft designer, deliberately soloed her airplane, if only a few feet off the ground. The Aeronautical Society of America recognized Mrs. Raiche as America's first female pilot because her flight was not a matter of chance.

Betty Scott, however, did go on to make the first accepted flight by a woman in public, at Fort Wayne, Indiana, the following October. She rose all of twelve feet into the air. This intrepid flier never did get a pilot's license because she felt the requirements were too stiff.

First American Woman to Earn
a Pilot's License
HARRIET QUIMBY

❦ At age twenty-seven Harriet Quimby was drama critic of *Leslie's Weekly* in New York. Enchanted with the idea of flight, she asked John Moisant of the Moisant Flying School of Long Island to teach her to fly. John was delighted but was killed in a crash at New Orleans before he could keep his promise. Alfred, John's brother, agreed to follow through. Her lessons took place in secrecy until a spectacular forced landing revealed to the public that a woman was learning to fly. Sherwood Harris, in *The First to Fly*, observed, "It is difficult for us to comprehend now just how much the news of America's first women pilots must have meant to a generation of women trapped in the hopelessness of sweatshops and menial labor or suffocated by the respectability of a middle-class life that permitted no step—not even a glance—beyond certain narrow, circumscribed patterns of life." Harriet Quimby and fellow students Blanche Scott (see page 180), who had already been flying but felt she needed more lessons, and Matilde Moisant (who figured that if her brother was going to reach women she better be among them) became heroes to many imaginative women everywhere. On August 1, 1911, Harriet Quimby was awarded license number 37 by the Aero Club of America, which was authorized by the Fédération Aeronautique Internationale to issue licenses. Matilde Moisant received hers thirteen days later.

In 1912 Harriet Quimby persuaded the *London Mirror* newspaper to back her effort to be the first woman to pilot an airplane across the English Channel. As with swimmers and balloonists, early pilots were challenged by the thought of crossing the Channel. In July 1909, Louis Blériot had made the first crossing in an airplane, winning the prize offered by the London *Daily Mail*. Quimby decided within months of receiving her pilot's license that she would be the first woman to accomplish the feat. With the *Mirror* backing her, she laid her plans in secret. Before she was ready, an Englishwoman, Eleanor Trehawk Davis, crossed the Channel as an airplane passenger on April 2, 1912. Fourteen days later, Harriet Quimby was ready, flying a Blériot plane she had never flown before. Unlike Blériot, who flew from France to England, she took off from the cliffs of Dover. Fog eliminated visibility so she could rely only on her compass. When she judged that she was halfway across, she descended below the fog. Ahead she saw the beaches of France with fishermen waiting to greet her. Three months later, during an exhibition flight to a lighthouse in

Boston Harbor, Ms. Quimby's airplane flipped out of control. She and her passenger were thrown into the harbor; neither survived.

Longest Working Female Big Cat Trainer
MABEL STARK

❦ A nurse who first began to work with big cats in 1912 and retired only in 1967, Mabel Stark was nicknamed "the Tiger Woman." Only five feet three inches, she was the first woman to work with a cage full of tigers, reputedly much harder to train than lions. She became obsessed with the idea of the superiority of her intelligence over the brute force of the big cats, and always looked for new ways to demonstrate it to audiences. When her first employer, the Al G. Barnes Circus, refused to buy her a whole cage of tigers, she moved to Ringling Brothers and soon became a center ring feature act. Often wounded, she was once knocked unconscious by a single blow from the paw of an 800-pound Bengal tiger. Before her death she was scarred from head to toe, often twice in the same place. She retired at age seventy-eight but had no interest beyond her cats, and she soon died.

Worst Score for a Single Hole
in a Golf Tournament
160

❦ An unnamed woman was on the sixteenth hole of a qualifying round for the Shawnee Invitational for Ladies at Shawnee-on-Delaware, Pennsylvania, in 1912. Her first stroke on the normally four-stroke sixteenth sent the ball into the river. It floated, so she boarded a rowboat powered by her husband, and proceeded to take stroke after stroke, faithfully recording each one, trying to get the ball back to dry land. Two hours later, the other players looked up incredulously as the missing woman hit the ball from the woods onto the green. The honest golfer had taken one hundred and sixty strokes to move her ball the one hundred thirty yards to the hole.

First Person to Free-Fall Sky Dive
GEORGIA ("TINY") BROADWICK

❦ Mrs. Georgia Thompson, otherwise known as Tiny Broadwick, was hired by Glenn Martin to demonstrate over Los Angeles the parachute he was developing. It opened by a tug from a cord extending from the airplane. On June 21, 1913, she made her first jump, and landed safely. Not all her jumps were so successful, however, and her frequently broken bones snapped the enthusiasm of potential buyers. The next year, on September 13, 1914, Tiny, as part of a parachute stunt team, made the world's first free-fall sky dive at San Diego, possibly not on purpose, when her chute failed to open at first.

Best Female Basketball Team
THE EDMONTON GRADS

❦ Between 1915 and 1940, the all-women Canadian basketball team, the Edmonton Grads, won 502 games, including an unbroken streak of 147 games. Each of the four times they appeared in the Olympics, they won every game they played.

First Women to Cross America on Motorcycles
ADELINE AND AUGUSTA VAN BUREN

❦ Adeline and Augusta Van Buren wanted to prove that women could be as useful as men in the coming war, and so set off to become the first women to cross America on motorcycles. They left New York on the Fourth of July, 1916, and traveled 5500 miles all told. They ventured to the top of Pike's Peak (first women ever to top it in motor vehicles), through desert, through cities, where they were several times arrested for wearing men's clothing, and they arrived in San Francisco sixty days later. When Adeline, having shown that "woman can, if she will!" volunteered for the army, they said she couldn't. She returned to teaching. Augusta took up flying and, according to Adeline's daughter in *Ms*. magazine, kept flying almost until her death in 1959.

Greatest Woman Circus Gymnast
LILLIAN LEITZEL
(LEOPOLDINA ALITZA PELIKAN)

❦ A center-ring circus aerial-gymnast with Ringling Brothers-Barnum & Bailey in the 1920s, the minute (four foot, nine inch, ninety-five-pound) German-born Lillian Leitzel commanded absolute silence during her performances, holding thousands in thrall as she maneuvered on the rings fifty feet above their heads. The silence stopped when she started her famed "Leitzel Twist," in which she spun her whole body around one hand gripping a swiveled rope. The audience would count and gasp as she neared . . . and topped . . . 100, although legend insists she once achieved 249 of those extraordinary one-arm swings. The amazing Lillian is also credited with twenty-seven consecutive one-arm chin-ups, followed immediately by seventeen more done with the other arm, performed in Philadelphia in 1918; later writers, however, are skeptical about that record. Lillian Leitzel died in Copenhagen on March 15, 1931, after a thirty-foot fall from a broken ring.

Woman to Hold a Tennis Championship
the Longest
ORA WASHINGTON

❦ From 1924 to 1936 Ora Washington of Pennsylvania was undefeated for the American Tennis Association (the black tennis organization) singles title, and in the last seven of those years was also in the championship doubles pair. She may well have been better than any of the white women of the time, but there's no way to tell. Helen Wills Moody, who spent only seven years undefeated, refused to play Ora Washington (see Althea Gibson on page 189). Forty years after she lost her title, Ms. Washington gained recognition by being inducted into the Black Athletes Hall of Fame, but no current trace of the champion could be found.

Only Successful Golf Club Owned and
Operated by and for Women
THE LADIES' GOLF CLUB OF TORONTO

❦ The Ladies' Golf Club was started in 1924 by Canadian and U.S. golf champion Ada Mackenzie, who was, at eighty years old in 1970, still going around the course in par 73. Men are admitted to the club only as guests and at off-peak hours.

Only Female Mountain Climber to Have a
Mountain Named for Her
ANNIE SMITH PECK

❦ American archeologist, Greek scholar, and lecturer Annie Peck gained her first fame in 1895 by climbing the Matterhorn clad, scandalously, in knickerbockers. Having conquered most of the really tough climbs in Europe—many of them for the first time by a woman—she turned her sights to South America in quest of mountains never conquered by anyone. In 1908, at age fifty-eight, she reached the summit of the north peak of the twin-peaked Huascarán in the Andes. She claimed that the never-measured peak was 24,000 feet, making it the highest altitude so far reached by a woman. But Fanny Bullock Workman, who had climbed high in the Himalayas, had the peak measured by triangulation and proved it was only 21,812 feet, 1500 feet less than the height attained by Mrs. Workman. Nevertheless, in 1927, the Lima Geographical Society officially named the north peak of Huascarán Cumbre Aña Peck.

Winningest Basketball Coach, Male or Female
MRS. BERTHA TEAGUE

❦ Mrs. Teague was coach of the Byng High School basketball team in Ada, Oklahoma, from 1927 to 1969. During forty-two years of coaching, her teams won eight state championships, lost only one hundred fifteen games, and even had one winning streak of ninety-eight straight games. In all, her winning record was two hundred and twenty-eight games better than any other coach.

Most Versatile Woman Athlete
BABE DIDRIKSON

❦ Early in her life, Babe Didrikson decided that although it might not be the thing for a nice Texas girl to do, she was going to be a great athlete. Her friends teased Mildred Didrikson by calling her Babe Ruth, a name that stuck, but they stayed out of her way when she practiced hurdles by leaping across neighborhood hedges. In 1930 she joined the Golden Cyclone Athletic Club girls' basketball team and was twice elected All-American basketball forward. A company track team gave her the chance to compete in preparation for another goal: the 1932 Olympic Games at Los Angeles. At the Olympic trials, where she was the whole team representing Employers Casualty Co., the five-foot-tall, one-hundred-five-pound Texan ran and hurdled off with thirty points. The closest competitor was the entire twenty-two woman team from Illinois, who, between them, managed to scrape together twenty-two points.

The 1932 Olympics brought eighteen-year-old Babe Didrickson to international acclaim, though she was allowed to enter only three events. Her javelin throw made a world record, as did her running of the 80-meter hurdles. A third gold medal disappeared when one judge disqualified her high jump, insisting that her shoulder had gone over the bar first. By some strange reasoning, the judges awarded her a silver for the disqualified jump. But she had no time—or inclination—to repine: sportswriter Grantland Rice had introduced "the Babe" to golf, and within a year she made the longest drive ever achieved by a woman. Before she got up a full head of steam in golf, however, she went into vaudeville to earn money for her family. The athlete performed in music halls, demonstrating hurdles, singing, and playing the down-home harmonica. She established a professional basketball team with herself as the only woman. In between these events, Babe Didrikson took up swimming (missed setting a new record by one second) and lifesaving, played baseball (making the longest throw achieved by a woman and pitching in spring training to the Boston Red Sox), held every record in Southern AAU track and field event she entered, did well at figure skating, performed in billiards exhibitions, and even tried her hand at designing sports clothes. She later said that table tennis was the only game she didn't get along with.

Golf, however, became her ruling passion, especially after 1938 when she married wrestler George Zaharias ("The Crying Greek from Cripple Creek"), who encouraged her. She turned professional for a while but found fewer tournaments available to the pros than to the amateurs. Forced to sit out a three-year waiting period to regain her amateur status, the Babe lent her time and name to sports exhibitions for selling war bonds and adding bowling to her exhibition-level skills. War over and amateur status regained, Babe Zaharias took on and won a phenomenal seventeen golf tournaments in a row, topping off the run by becoming the first American woman to win the British Women's Amateur. That same year, she and Patty Berg formed the Ladies Professional Golf Association, which encouraged the development of moneyed tournaments for professional players.

The end for Babe began in 1953. She was found to have cancer of the colon and had a colostomy performed. In three months she was back on the course at Tam O'Shanter, near Chicago, but came in an appalling fifteenth place. Determined to make a complete comeback, she worked very hard and regained her health and conditioning. The next year she won the U.S. Women's Open. Soon, though, an X-ray of a ruptured disc in her back revealed that the cancer had spread. Babe Didrikson Zaharias died in 1956 at age forty-two, called by many the greatest woman athlete the world had ever known.

Longest Running Champion Athlete
STELLA WALSH

❦ A Polish-born American world-class sprinter and long jumper, Stella Walsh (originally Walasiewicz) first began winning in 1929 and the next year won three gold medals in the 1930 Women's World Games. In 1932 and '36 she ran for Poland in the Olympics, winning a gold the first time and a silver the second. The 1938 European championships brought her two golds and a silver, the latter in the long jump. And in 1948, eighteen years after she achieved the first of her records, she won additional Amateur Athletic Union titles in the one-hundred-yard dash, two-hundred-twenty-yard dash, and the long jump. In all, she won about forty championships, including six world records, many of them in years long after most runners have felt their legs to be too old for championship races. Mrs. Walsh could not, however, outrun urban street crime. She was murdered by a mugger in Cleveland, Ohio, in 1980.

Person to Swim for the Longest Time
MYRTLE HUDDLESTON

❦ The very persistent Myrtle Huddleston of New York City swam in 1931 in a pool for eighty-seven hours and twenty-seven minutes without a rest. There is no way to equate that sort of record with the marathon open-water swimming being done these days, in which waves, sharks, jellyfish, cold, darkness, etc., all take a toll on the swimmer.

Highest Earning Athlete
SONJA HENIE

❦ Before Norwegian ice skater-turned-skating movie star Sonja Henie turned professional in 1936, she won ten world titles (most ever until 1980 when Irina Rodnina of the Soviet Union achieved her tenth in pairs skating—with two different male partners) and three Olympic gold medals (first woman to win three in a row). She started skating spins and jumps at eleven in the first Winter Olympic Games when women were hemmed in by long, full skirts; as a child, she got away with knee-length skirts. The judges, however, were marking down women skaters for attempting moves that were considered unladylike. Sonja finished last. Two years later, she came in second and then, introducing balletic movements into free skating for the first time, she began her still unbeaten chain of ten successive world titles (Rodnina didn't compete in 1978). The controversy over the first of those wins (granted by a panel of five judges, three of them Norwegian) led to the ruling that no nation could have more than one judge. When she turned professional after the 1936 Olympics, her father, always her manager, forced Darryl F. Zanuck to view a skating show, and his enthusiasm helped to launch her movie career. From 1938 on she was star and coproducer of the Hollywood Ice Revue. When Sonja Henie died of leukemia in 1969, her estate was worth more than $47 million.

Only Concert Pianist to Win
Olympic Gold Medals
MICHELINE OSTERMEYER

❦ In 1946 Micheline Ostermeyer began her concert career in Paris, continuing her habit of practicing most of every day. But much of every night she practiced something else—track events. In 1948, at the London Olympics, she won gold medals in discus throw and the shot put (it was the first time she had ever competed in that event), plus a bronze in the high jump. Although she later became one of France's greatest pianists, for many listeners she was always remembered as an amazing phenomenon: an athlete who amazingly enough played the piano.

Organizer of the Most Elaborate
African Safari
LAURA CORRIGAN

❦ Laura Corrigan, whose life followed the classic American rags-to-riches pattern, felt challenged by a safari made by Mrs. Stotesbury in which that woman had killed enough alligators for a complete set of luggage. Mrs. Corrigan decided that her safari would be humanitarian in nature. In order to present fourteen animals to the Cleveland Zoo, she mounted a safari made up, according to Cleveland Amory, of "three airplanes, a newspaper-man, a photographer, two maids, two secretaries, a doctor, a nurse, two cooks, three waiters, a hairdresser, a manicurist, and a dressmaker."

Most Sport Championship Titles
Won by a Woman
JUDITH DEVLIN HASHMAN

❦ A former Baltimore, Maryland, schoolteacher, Judith Hashman took up badminton with her father as instructor. She won her first juniors title in 1949. From 1953 to 1967 she won fifty-six national titles in the United States, Canada, and England, plus numerous others in the Netherlands, Ireland, Scotland, and Jamaica. Her phenomenal record includes ten singles titles and six doubles titles (played with her sister Sue) in the All-England Championship, the top of the heap in badminton. Called the best woman player in the history of the game, her instructor father is called the best male player—but he won only six All-England championship singles titles. Since 1970 Mrs. Hashman has represented Great Britain when playing.

First Person to Swim Lake Ontario
MARILYN BELL

❦ The Canadian National Exhibition hired Florence Chadwick of English Channel fame to try to be the first woman to swim across Lake Ontario from Youngstown, New York, to Toronto on September 9, 1954. Her fee was $2500, plus another $7500 if she made it. Sixteen-year-old Marilyn Bell of Toronto and Mrs. Winnie Leuszler challenged Chadwick but the CNE would have none of it. Nothing loth, Marilyn and Winnie dove in at Youngstown when Chadwick did. Chadwick and Leuszler gave up the thirty-two-mile swim in the middle, but Marilyn swam on alone, watched over by her coach. Twenty hours and fifty-nine minutes after diving in, Marilyn Bell was pulled out of the water at Toronto. Lake Ontario was not swum again until 1975, when Diana Nyad swam the distance in twenty hours.

Most Generous Tennis Player
MARY SUTTON BUNDY

❦ The first American to win at Wimbledon, Mary Sutton Bundy is equally renowned for her display of sportswomanship in 1930. In that year at Forest Hills, she was playing Hazel Hotchkiss Wightman for the Women's Singles National Championship. One point away from victory, May, as she was often called, had a freak accident which broke her left leg and dislocated her right shoulder. If she had left the game, Hazel Wightman could not have won because the game would have been declared a default. May Sutton put the racket in her left hand and finished the match on a borrowed crutch. Then she went to the hospital. In 1956, Mary Sutton Bundy became the first woman named to the National Lawn Tennis Hall of

Fame, which was founded to commemorate sportsmanship, skill, character, and contribution to the game of tennis.

First Black Woman to Win at Wimbledon
ALTHEA GIBSON

❦ In 1957, Althea Gibson beat Darlene Hard for the Wimbledon singles title. Before that was possible, however, she had to overcome the disadvantages of a Harlem childhood and break into white tennis. To make that trip, she had the support of the American Tennis Association (formed by blacks in 1917 because they weren't admitted to the U.S. Lawn Tennis Association) and of the growing number of big-name black athletes. The difficulty was that the tournaments leading to Forest Hills, the final destination of American tennis, were by invitation . . . and blacks just weren't invited. Stage by stage, however, the barriers were broken, helped by people like the great Alice Marble, who wrote, "I think it's time we faced a few facts. If tennis is a game of ladies and gentlemen, it's also time we acted a little more like gentle people and less like sanctimonious hypocrites." In 1950, Althea Gibson reached the finals at Forest Hills. Seven years later, two months after her win at Wimbledon, she finally won at Forest Hills against Louise Brough who had defeated her in 1950. Althea Gibson's win at Wimbledon was not matched by a black male player until 1975 when Arthur Ashe beat Jimmy Connors. In November 1975, Althea Gibson was appointed the New Jersey Athletic Commissioner by Governor Brendan Byrne.

Only Woman Regularly to Beat Men in a
Sporting Event
MRS. BERYL BURTON

❦ An amateur British cyclist, in 1960 in Milan Mrs. Burton set a world record time for the twenty kilometer race: 28 minutes 58.4 seconds. Seven years later, in the time trials at which she excelled, she beat the men's record for a twelve hour trial, going a distance of 277.25 miles, more than five miles more than the men's record.

Greatest Hurdle Overcome by
a Champion Woman Runner
WILMA RUDOLPH

❦ A victim of pneumonia and scarlet fever as a child, Wilma Rudolph was left with a crippled and useless left leg. She could not walk until she was eight, and had to wear a special orthopedic shoe until she was eleven. When she finally ran at thirteen, she quickly discovered the joys of high school basketball. A coach at Tennessee State University saw her and started her running in earnest. At sixteen, she participated, unsuccessfully, in her first Olympics at Melbourne, Australia. But four years later, at the 1960 Rome Olympics, three gold medals were hers, as winner of the one-hundred- and two-hundred-meter sprints and as one of the participants in the four-hundred-meter relay, the greatest number of gold medals ever won by an American woman in track and field events.

First Woman to Drive on the
Indianapolis Speedway
PAULA MURPHY

❧ In 1962, Paula Murphy was condescendingly allowed to drive a couple of times around the deserted circuit—with her throttle rigged so she couldn't speed her way into trouble. Indianapolis Speedway had been sacrosanct to men since it was built in 1911.

In April 1972, Mrs. George Wallace, wife of the governor of Alabama, drove the official Indy pace car around the track, more than a month before the actual Indianapolis Speedway 500 race.

In the mid-1970s, when women were breaking down more and more barriers, whether a woman would drive in the famed Memorial Day Indy 500 became a matter of suspense. In 1976, on May 17, Janet Guthrie, a physicist-turned-professional race driver, drove a twenty-lap rookie test watched by judges of the U.S. Auto Club. As Memorial Day neared, however, her car developed problem after problem and it became clear that a woman driver wouldn't run the Indy 500 that year. Another year passed . . . and then another after Janet Guthrie qualified to race but her car failed quite early during the 500. Then, in 1978, the deed was done. Janet Guthrie qualified, drove the entire race, and finished an impressive ninth place . . . all done with a broken wrist.

Only Woman to Own a Championship
Baseball Team
JOAN WHITNEY PAYSON

❧ When the Giants deserted New York for California, leaving New York with only one baseball team, Joan Whitney Payson, heiress to the Whitney fortune, keenly felt the lack of two teams. Having the wherewithal to indulge her preference, she backed a new baseball team, the Mets. Her team, which she had wanted to call the Meadowlarks, was the laughingstock of the baseball world from its beginning in 1962—always at the bottom of the National League—until 1969 when it stunned fans and scoffers alike by winning the World Series.

Lowest Scoring Female Golfer
(Remember, Low Is Good)
MICKEY (MARY KATHRYN) WRIGHT

❦ In November 1964, Mickey Wright shot a low 62 for the 18-hole Hogan Park Course in Midland, Texas, a 6286-yard course. (Several men have achieved 55 on different 18-hole courses.) That same year Ms. Wright won the fourth of her four U.S. Women's Open titles, matching the four previously won by Betsy Earl Rawls. Mickey Wright shot her first 70 at fifteen years old and for four years after 1960 she won the Vare Trophy for the professional woman golfer with the lowest average of strokes per round. She topped off that four-year run by, in 1963, becoming the only woman to win thirteen major tournaments in one year.

Only Woman to Run in the Boston Marathon
before Women Were Admitted
KATHERINE SWITZER

❦ In 1967 Katherine Switzer signed up to run the famed all-male race by registering with only her initial. She gained an entry number for the annual April 19 event and set off, only to have aghast officials try to grab her number off, perhaps hoping they could make her disappear. She finally had to run the race alongside the actual track so that the officials would stop bothering her. The Amateur Athletic Union retaliated by barring all women from competing in the same events as men. But five years later, after innumerable talk-fests, arguments, even court scenes, women were finally permitted to run in the Boston Marathon, though they would not be in direct competition with the men. Katherine Switzer ran again, officially.

Fastest Women Dragsters
DELLA WOODS AND SHIRLEY MULDOWNEY

❦ In 1968, Della Woods became the first woman to exceed 190 mph on a drag strip. Her special car, tended by her brother, could reach 209 mph in less than seven seconds. Even after several years of racing, she told the *New York Times*, she felt that most male drivers thought her place was still "sitting in the parking lot waiting for the after-race party."

In 1975 Shirley Muldowney became the first woman to drive a Top-Fuel dragster, which is as high as you can go in drag racing, and the very next year she won the U.S. Hot Rod Association Spring Nationals. Called "Cha Cha" by the public but not by her friends, she knows she has an advantage over the other Top-Fuel dragster racers, all men, because her less-than-100-pounds weight allows her car to go faster. She also knows there are advantages in being a personality: How many people can name dragsters other than Ms. Muldowney? She told Pat Jordan, writing in

Broken Patterns, "I didn't begin all this 'beating the boys' stuff' until I saw how I could capitalize on it. Now I make a point of it. Oh, they threw tantrums. They beat their helmets on their cars, and some of them swear they'll drive their cars off a cliff if I beat them."

First Juvenile Boxing Competition for Girls
MISSY GOLDEN GLOVES IN DALLAS, TEXAS
❦ The Missy Golden Gloves program of practice and title competition was started by Doyle Weaver, a music teacher, in 1968. He wanted to give girls between the ages of six and sixteen a chance to break the tradition that females and rough sports shouldn't mix. Within a year over three hundred girls were participating but in later years the program ran into problems for lack of a permanent gym. The AAU won't allow official boxing matches for girls, which makes Doyle's "blood boil to hear the absurd arguments of people with personal hang-ups who want to keep women out of boxing. All they see is a set of breasts." In 1975, during a regular Golden Gloves competition, a three-round exhibition bout was held between thirteen-year-old Sheila Cole and twelve-year-old Lily Bera of Missy Golden Gloves. One Golden Gloves executive said quite frankly, "We're going to do everything we can to keep women out. We don't need them in boxing."

Only Royal Princess to Compete in
International Sports
PRINCESS ANNE OF GREAT BRITAIN
❦ Taught to ride horseback by her father, Prince Philip, Princess Anne quickly became known around the palace as "cowgirl Anne." She learned the fine points of dressage—the difficult art of guiding a horse through maneuvers with slight body signals—while a student at Benenden. In 1969, at nineteen, she began winning prizes in jumping and dressage, and two years later trounced five Olympic riders in a grueling three-day event.

In 1976, Princess Anne qualified for the Montreal Olympics as a member of the British equestrienne team; her husband Mark Phillips was an alternate. Because the princess's family attended all the events and royalty-watching became a favorite pastime of TV cameramen and commentators, most of the world saw Anne fall during the long-distance obstacles course in the three-day event. She got back on her horse and completed the day's ride, though with a mediocre score. She later did not remember the ride; doctors found she had suffered a concussion.

Woman with the Shortest Career as a
Baseball Umpire
BERNICE GERA
❦ When some of the minor league New York teams agreed to let

housewife Bernice Gera umpire, the National Association of Baseball Leagues refused to sign her contract because she was too old (thirty-eight), too short (five foot two), and too light (one hundred twenty-nine pounds). Nary a mention that she was also a woman. Thus began a three-year court battle. She won it in 1969 and umpired one game, quitting when not a single soul agreed with an important call she had made during the game.

First Woman to Sail the Pacific Alone
SHARON SITES ADAMS

❦ On May 12, 1969, Sharon Sites Adams of San Diego, California, left Yokohama, Japan, in a thirty-one-foot fiberglass ketch, equipped with an auxiliary engine, a radiotelephone, food and water for one hundred twenty days, and the memory of having said four years before, after a long trip from San Diego to Hawaii, "Never again!" Seventy-four days, seventeen hours, and fifteen minutes later, she found her husband, sailing teacher, and thousands of well-wishers awaiting her at San Diego Harbor.

Most Daring Woman on Earth
KITTY O'NEIL

❦ This title has been appropriately given to stunt woman/race driver Kitty O'Neil, who was:

★ AAU Junior Olympics diving champion

★ Sky diver

★ Speed water skier—she achieved a women's record of 104.85 mph in 1970

★ World speed record competitor on the motorcycle

★ Off-road car and dune buggy racer

★ Fastest woman on Earth when she achieved a land-speed record of 512.706 mph on December 6, 1976 (she is sure she could also have beat the absolute land speed record that day but her commercial sponsor didn't want a woman to do it)

★ Record holder in long-distance falls for women, achieved as a TV "Superstunt"

★ First woman to flip a car over as a stunt

All those feats were accomplished by a woman who's been totally deaf since the age of four months when measles, mumps and chicken pox got together to ravage her hearing.

The Biggest Troubles for Little League
PERSISTENT GIRLS

❦ There may have been girls playing Little League Baseball early when no one complained, but in 1971, Sharon Poole, a twelve-year-old in Haverhill, Massachusetts, was asked by the Little League coach to try out

for the team. She won a position and played in two games. The coach was
dismissed by league officials and the boys had to pay a penalty: the two
games in which Sharon played were declared null.

In 1972, the National Organization of Women brought suit against the
National Little League in behalf of M. Pepe, a girl who was dropped from a
Hoboken, New Jersey, team. And by November the first court decision
was in, saying that girls should be allowed to play. But Little League was
nowhere near ready to acquiesce.

Carolyn King, in Ypsilanti, Michigan, tried to play the next spring.
When the team voted to admit girls, the national headquarters threatened
to lift the team's charter. Carolyn was dropped. Her father filed suit on her
behalf in federal court. In Williamsport, Pennsylvania, at Little League
headquarters, the pressure was building.

Mill Valley, California, added to it by refusing to let Little League teams
use public facilities unless girls were admitted.

Representative Martha W. Griffiths introduced a bill in Congress to
amend the 1964 federal charter of the Little League to make "boy" read
"young people." Across the nation mothers of disgruntled girls marched in
favor of the legislation.

On February 28, 1974, the Appellate Court ordered the Little League to
admit girls. It took Williamsport until June to decide to give in. Headquarters reluctantly agreed to "defer" to the changing social climate. Soon after
that an eleven-year-old named Bunny Taylor pitched the first no-hitter by a
girl. And five months later, after the struggle was over, Congress voted to
amend the Little League charter.

Spring baseball season in 1975 not only brought thousands of girls to
Little League tryouts, but in New Jersey, where the baseball problems
began, a Jersey City high school girl, Ann Cortellino, was chosen to play
varsity baseball for her school.

Gymnast to Do the Most to Popularize
the Sport
OLGA KORBUT

❦ Olga Korbut popularized gymnastics by the simple expedient of being
seventeen, petite, appealing, and talented when she appeared in the 1972
Olympics, not to mention the fact that she was the first person to do a
backward somersault on uneven parallel bars. (The next year the International Gymnastics Federation ruled that move too dangerous.) When Olga
visited the United States in 1973, she drew huge crowds wherever she
went, crowds who for the most part knew nothing of gymnastics before her
arrival in international televised sporting competition. The Soviet press,
however, reprimanded Olga Korbut for seeking attention. She must have
been forgiven, though, because she was named Absolute Champion of the

U.S.S.R. in 1975. By the time of the 1976 Olympics in Montreal, so many
people had become interested in gymnastics because of Olga Korbut that
enthusiasts around the world took it as a personal loss when she was unable
to repeat her performance and her position as center of attention was
usurped by "the little doll" from Rumania, Nadia Comaneci (see page 198).

Only Jockey to Pose Nude for a Magazine
MARY BACON

🐾 A tiny blonde who has been characterized by male acquaintances as a
"tough broad," Mary Bacon learned to ride young, with lessons broken up
by stints in reform school. Posing for *Playboy* was a routine type of work
for Mary Bacon: she had earned the money for steeplechase lessons in
England by jumping topless out of cakes.

First Female Boxing Referee
MRS. CAROL POLIS

🐾 Carol Polis was the first female professional boxing referee. She was
licensed in Pennsylvania at the beginning of 1973. The New York wife of a
former boxer and referee, she judged fifty-five fights in the next eighteen
months. In only one was hers the minority decision. In July 1974, the New
York Boxing Commission followed Pennsylvania's lead and gave Mrs. Polis
a license. A month later, she was among the three judges at a ten-round
bout between Edouardo Santiago and Don Manaco. The fight was declared
a draw. The audience, convinced that Santiago should have won, tore the
arena apart. That was Mrs. Polis's second minority decision: she, too, voted
for Santiago.

Only Person to Be World Champion in Two
Diverse Sports at the Same Time
SHEILA YOUNG

🐾 In January 1973, Sheila Young won the world five-hundred-meter speed
skating championship. Six months later, the skater won the women's world
sprint-cycling race, in the first time an American woman had ever won an
international cycling event. Because her brother was a cyclist, she took up
cycling to keep her powerful legs in shape when skating was out of season.
At the 1976 Winter Olympics, Sheila Young won three medals in speed
skating, the first woman to do so. There are no Olympic women's cycling
events but she did win the world cycling championship again that year.

Most Attention-Getting Tennis Game
BILLIE JEAN KING AND BOBBY RIGGS

🐾 On September 20, 1973, Billie Jean King played Bobby Riggs in a much-
publicized match. The day of the match in Houston, Texas, the betting odds

were twenty-two to ten against the first woman athlete in history to earn more than $100,000 a year in prize money (in 1971). But just four months before, Bobby Riggs had beaten the great Margaret Court in what has been called the "Mother's Day Massacre." Women's libbers and male chauvinists the world round watched the only tennis match on prime-time network TV. They watched as Billie Jean King, Superstar, trounced Bobby Riggs, "male chauvinist pig," taking every set. Grace Lichtenstein in *You've Come a Long Way, Baby*, says, "The consummate female jock, King had picked up feminism the way she picked up tennis as a child; she fiddled around with the basic equipment, juggled the pieces impatiently until they worked for her, then played to the hilt to win."

First Woman Officially Licensed as a
Spanish Bullfighter
ANGELITA

❦ At age twenty-six, after a long court battle, Maria de Los Angelos Hernandez (Angelita) was officially licensed as a bullfighter with the recommendation—at her own request—that she be allowed to fight on foot. She was the first legal woman bullfighter in Spain. On October 7, 1973, she made her bullfighting debut in the southwestern Spanish town of Higuero La Real. But the shattering of tradition was too much for the mayor of the town. Ignoring the official recommendation and sticking to the letter of the law, he decreed that she could fight her bull only from horseback. The legal war began again, but in August 1974, her right to fight was confirmed. This pioneer regards bullfighting as "superbly suited" to women.

Actually, Conchita Cintron, the first great woman bullfighter, started fighting bulls on foot in Mexico at age fifteen and by twenty-one had over four hundred bulls to her credit. But in 1949 in Spain, the mecca for fighters, she dropped off her mount to confront a bull on foot. She was promptly arrested. The crowd-pleasing woman was freed on the demand of the audience. But it proved a decisive incident for the bullfighter and she gave up the ring.

First Female Formula 1 Race Driver
LELLA LOMBARDI

❦ Fascinated with car racing since seeing her first race at eighteen, Lella Lombardi of Italy saved for five years to buy her own car and quickly became the Italian woman champion. At Formula 3 races in Monaco in 1974 she finished twelfth out of eighty-six places (mostly male); that showing entitled her to become the first woman to drive Formula 1 cars, driving for Shell and other companies. Invited to America, the "Tigress of Turin" finished fifth in a fifty-mile heat race for the California Grand Prix. In the Grand Prix itself, she was in the front group of ten cars until the very last mile when her engine died. The male drivers began to watch her with less scorn. As Mario Andretti said in *WomenSports*, "She's a pro. The only difference between her and anyone else out there, as far as I'm concerned, is she doesn't have any balls." In 1975, Ms. Lombardi finished sixth in the Spanish Grand Prix.

Most Determined Woman to Try
to Box Professionally
JACKIE TONAWANDA

❧ In October 1974 Jackie Tonawanda and Marian (Tyger) Trimiar applied for licenses to box professionally in New York, the center of the big-time professional boxing world. The Boxing Commission refused, at first, even to act on the applications, claiming that women would throw "professional boxing into disrepute." Forced by public pressure to take some sort of action, the Commission voted unanimously on January 21, 1975, to reject the applications. Jackie Tonawanda, winner of numerous amateur fights, including three by knockouts, wasn't about to quit. She wanted New York to know what it would be missing. Billing herself as the "female Muhammad Ali," she loudly predicted that in June at the Oriental World of Self-Defense Spectacular at Madison Square Garden she would knock out a one-hundred fifty-five-pound male boxer from Thailand in the second round of a kick-boxing match. The one-hundred-sixty-pound woman did just that . . . but the Commission paid no attention.

Only Woman to Box in
Golden Gloves Competition
MARION BERMUDEZ

❧ Twenty-three-year-old Marion Bermudez, a karate champion and electronic technology student at Arizona State, wanted experience in close-in fighting to augment her karate training. Golden Gloves officials got her to agree not to institute legal proceedings if they didn't admit her and permitted her to participate as a featherweight . . . kind of as a thank-you. With only seven practice rounds under her belt, in March, 1975, she startled everyone by winning her first three-round fight on a split decision. Her second fight, however, was stopped when she received a particularly hard punch from the boy who eventually won the tournament. The next surprise came when the officials who had only tried to avoid a lawsuit found themselves dismissed by the Amateur Athletic Union for letting a woman participate.

Only Woman to Climb Mount Everest
JUNKO TABEI

❧ The thirty-sixth person to conquer the 29,028 feet of the highest mountain on earth, Junko Tabei is a tiny Japanese woman—only ninety-two pounds and mother of a three-year-old daughter. She earned the money for her 1975 attempt by giving piano lessons, and she and the other fourteen women making up the climbing team spent three years preparing for the assault on the mountain. On May 4, 1975, when the team reached 21,000 feet, they were struck by an avalanche and Junko Tabei was injured, but not seriously enough to prevent her going on. Eleven days later, they made the final camp at 27,880 feet. The next morning she and Sherpa guide Ang Tsering made the final climb to the top of the world, reaching the summit at noon, and Junko Tabei became the highest woman on earth.

Oldest Woman to Fly Solo Across the Atlantic
MARION RICE HART

❦ Called "the flying grandmother," Marion Hart hadn't learned to fly until she was in her fifties. In August, 1975, two months before her eighty-fourth birthday, she made her tenth solo flight across the ocean, and became the oldest woman ever to fly alone across the Atlantic.

Most Perfect Scores Achieved by a Gymnast
in Olympic Competition
NADIA COMANECI

❦ In July 1976 at the Montreal Olympics, Nadia Comaneci of Rumania achieved seven perfect scores. The crowd, gathered primarily to see the popular Olga Korbut, was stunned at the tiny, fourteen-year-old's apparent disregard of danger. During her first final, the watchers' hearts stopped time after time as she boldly threw her body around the uneven parallel bars in moves that should have been impossible. Then emotions exploded as the electronic scoreboard revealed a 10.00, a perfect score, though it could not actually read "10.00" because planners had been told that such a score was inconceivable. Nor was that 10.00 the end: before she went home with her dolls and medals, she had repeated the perfect score six more times—three on the bars and three on the balance beam—all leading to three gold, one silver, and one bronze medal. Frank Bare, executive director of the U.S. Gymnastics Federation, told *Time* magazine, "The tiny point spreads she won by don't begin to indicate how much better she is than her nearest rivals. There has never been anyone like her, never been anyone who approaches her."

Almost lost in the Nadia adulation was the fact that soon after she scored her first 10.00, Nelli Kim of the Soviet team also scored 10.00 for her performance in the vault, and then earned another in a flawless floor exercise.

The trouble is that 10.00 is as high as the long-established scoring system goes in gymnastics. Nadia Comaneci, who was cool about her scores because she had already won seventeen other tens in European competition, looked forward to a future in which she could keep on improving. *Newsweek* observed, "To do that she may have to invent a new sport."

Fastest Person to Sail the Globe Alone
NAOMI JAMES

In 1977-78, Naomi James of New Zealand became the first woman to sail alone around the world. She and her fifty-three-foot sailboat *Express Crusader* went from Dartmouth, England, around the Cape of Good Hope, across to Cape Horn (first woman to sail around that nasty spot alone), and back to Dartmouth in 271 days and 19 hours, breaking the record of Sir Francis Chichester by two days. The sailor, whose mother said in amazement, "When she went into Woolworth's as a kid, she always got lost," made the dangerous voyage only two years after learning to sail. She was taught by the man she married, himself a round-the-world sailor and a merchant marine officer. Mrs. James's main fear was of falling overboard, a fear which dissipated after she actually did capsize her boat during a four-week storm and saved both herself and her boat. Her biggest problem was spending months never sleeping more than twenty minutes at a time so that she could keep an eye out for shipping vessels. Her main pleasure: uncounted hours in which to read the hundreds of books she took along. Dame Naomi (she was honored by the Queen in late 1978) wrote at the end of her journey's story, *Alone Around the World*, "In attempting this voyage I risked losing a life that had at last become fulfilling; but in carrying it out I experienced a second life, a life so separate and complete it appeared to have little relation to the old one that went before."

Most Flamboyant Failure in an
Endurance Event
DIANA NYAD

In 1978 marathon swimmer Diana Nyad set out to swim the one hundred and three miles from Cuba to the Florida Keys—for all the money and publicity value she could wring from the venture. For months beforehand, under the guidance of a hype expert, she had been chasing sponsors to pay for it all, chatting up reporters about her plans, giving serious interviews to magazines about her reasons for undertaking the swim. But for Diana, the main reason was to make it as big as possible. A Phi Beta Kappa and doctoral candidate in comparative literature, she had swum across Lake Ontario, around Manhattan through the garbagy waters delineating that island, across Long Island Sound, through the North Sea, along the coast of Argentina. But none of those swims had been big enough to set her up for stardom. She told *New Times*, "This swim fulfills all my fantasies of doing something that no one else could possibly do. I mean, if I get to the Florida coast, that will be one of the most historic moments in sport . . . it is certainly going to be bigger than Gertrude Ederle finishing the English Channel."

The swimmer who had not been able to finish the English Channel in four attempts set out from Cuba on August 13, 1978, backed by a helicopter support service, navigators, trainers, and watched by reporters. But all the hype couldn't help. The six- to eight-foot waves made her nauseated. Warm salt water swelled her lips and made them crack. The hundreds of jellyfish stings couldn't be prevented by her famous shark cage and just added pain upon pain. The wind unexpectedly swept her off course, so much of her motion accomplished nothing. After forty-two hours, about seventy miles of swimming but only fifty miles of actual distance covered, Diana Nyad was forced to give up her dream.

She arrived back to shore to learn that while she had been in the water, so, too, had English swimmer Stella Taylor, on a marathon swim from Bimini to Florida. No publicity, no big sponsors, no TV coverage, just one lone woman (an ex-nun who had swum the English Channel twice) and a couple boats with shark-swatting companions alongside. Stella Taylor made it to within eighteen miles of Florida, but was forced to stop as a current drove her farther and farther north. When she gave up she had been in the water thirty-two hours and had covered an estimated one hundred and forty miles (the great difference in mileage is because Taylor swam *with* the current; Nyad had swum opposite it most of her trip).

What became of Diana Nyad's dream? Well, she had "made a noble effort," proved to herself that she "could have made the swim on a decent day." She wrote a book called *Other Shores*, and looked forward to taking on squash and becoming "the best squash player in the country."

And Stella Taylor? In October 1978, she confronted her personal goal again. This time the quiet swimmer lasted fifty-one hours before having to abandon the one-hundred-and-thirty-mile swim from the Bahamas to Florida.

Index